FRAMES OF EVIL

FRAMES
OF EVIL

THE HOLOCAUST AS HORROR IN AMERICAN FILM

CAROLINE JOAN (KAY) S. PICART
AND DAVID A. FRANK

WITH A FOREWORD BY
DOMINICK LaCAPRA
AND AN INTRODUCTION BY
EDWARD J. INGEBRETSEN

SOUTHERN ILLINOIS UNIVERSITY PRESS / CARBONDALE

Copyright © 2006 by the Board of Trustees,
Southern Illinois University
All rights reserved
Printed in the United States of America

09 08 07 06   4 3 2 1

Library of Congress Cataloging-in-Publication Data
Picart, Caroline Joan, 1966–
  Frames of evil : the Holocaust as horror in American film / Caroline Joan (Kay)
S. Picart and David A. Frank ; with a foreword by Dominick LaCapra and an
introduction by Edward J. Ingebretsen.
      p. cm.
Includes bibliographical references and index.
1. Holocaust, Jewish (1939–1945), in motion pictures. 2. Horror films—United
States—History and criticism. I. Frank, David A. II. Title.
PN1995.9.H53P53 2006
791.43'658—dc22
ISBN-13: 978-0-8093-2723-2 (cloth : alk. paper)
ISBN-10: 0-8093-2723-6 (cloth : alk. paper)
ISBN-13: 978-0-8093-2724-9 (pbk. : alk. paper)
ISBN-10: 0-8093-2724-4 (pbk. : alk. paper)   2006005129

Printed on recycled paper. ♻

The paper used in this publication meets the minimum requirements of American
National Standard for Information Sciences—Permanence of Paper for Printed
Library Materials, ANSI z39.48-1992.∞

Contents

Figures

Foreword
Dominick LaCapra

Trauma in relation to extreme, or limit, events has recently become an important object of study.[1] Now, more than ever, the Holocaust and its aftermath have a particularly important place in the work of those who address the possibilities and limits of representation. In this timely study, Kay Picart and David Frank focus on film in a manner that is theoretically informed and insightful. Taking three important films as case studies—*Schindler's List*, *The Silence of the Lambs*, and *Apt Pupil*—they provide a substantive and formal analysis that is of interest not only for the critical understanding of these films but also for the representation of limit events in film and related media.

Schindler's List appears to be a historical docudrama, but one of the more arresting observations of *Frames of Evil: The Holocaust as Horror in American Film* is that Spielberg's celebrated film employs the visual rhetoric and narrative devices of the Hollywood horror film as its template. In this sense, its seemingly historical veracity is questionable, yet it is close in its assumptions to an important, though highly contested school of historical interpretation—one that found a popular and widely criticized exemplar in Daniel Jonah Goldhagen's *Hitler's Willing Executioners*.

The Silence of the Lambs, undoubtedly the most critically accomplished of the films that are treated extensively in this volume, has no manifest relation to the Holocaust. But Picart and Frank attempt to elucidate its implication in a network of concerns shared by Holocaust films. The authors also provide an analysis that goes beyond the Holocaust frame of reference to bring out the multidimensional interest of the film, including its relation to the controversial complicity of the seeming victim in the fascinating orbit of the perpetrator. *Apt Pupil* may have more symptomatic than critical interest, but it serves in the argument of the book as a good counterpart to *The Silence of the Lambs* in exploring (and often indulging in) disturbing aspects of the victim-perpetrator dynamic and its representation in film.

The book leaves its reader with a number of questions that merit further thought and inquiry. What does it mean for a film to attempt to work through—and not simply repeat in a more or less compulsive manner—the problems it addresses? Can one ever fully escape the tendency to act out or blindly repeat a traumatic past? Even if attempts to transcend fully an implication in trauma and its aftereffects are illusory, are there nonetheless significant differences in the manner in which films (or other artifacts) address problems with greater or lesser degrees of critical acumen? Is one forever complicit in the victim-perpetrator dynamic, and are the affirmation of complicity and the radical blurring of distinctions (such as that between perpetrator and victim) the only alternatives to deceptive binary oppositions between the innocent self and the monstrous "other"? Can one recognize the other in oneself and still acknowledge not only differences between perpetrators and victims but also a variable gray area of complicity between them, indeed an uncanny zone of perpetrator-victims? And can one see working-through in terms of a complex, non-Pollyanna attempt to overcome the victim-perpetrator dynamic in a manner that never cathartically redeems the self or fully heals the wounds of the past but nonetheless provides an ethic of response, even a political incentive, to effectively counteract one's own dubious possibilities along with the posttraumatic effects that differentially affect members of a society or culture? This book may not answer these difficult questions to everyone's satisfaction, and one may take issue with certain of its emphases or conclusions. But it has the distinctive merit of raising these questions in a demanding way and providing a thought-provoking effort to engage them responsibly.

Acknowledgments

We thank the Academy of Motion Picture Arts and Sciences for the camera-ready photographs that appear in this book. We also thank Florida State University, for a creative and research activity planning grant and research leave for Kay Picart to work on this project, and the University of Oregon, for help in acquiring materials for this manuscript. We also thank the assistants who have helped us with various related tasks: Jason McKahan, Peter Reed, Michelle Commander, Laura Pratt, Somara Jacques, and Paul Makaoa. To all those who have critically engaged with our work, we owe a debt of gratitude. In particular, we thank Dominick LaCapra and Edward Ingebretsen for their brilliant commentary and generous and collegial supportiveness. Other people also deserve mention: Julia Lesage, Chuck Kleinhans, Peter Rollins, and Davis Houck, who have read prior sections of the material.

Portions of chapter 3 are reprinted from pages 329–42 of *The Holocaust Film Sourcebook*, edited by Caroline Joan (Kay) Picart (copyright © 2004 by Praeger; reproduced with permission of Greenwood Publishing Group, Inc., Westport, CT); and from Caroline J. S. Picart and David A. Frank, "Horror and the Holocaust: Genre Elements in *Schindler's List* and *Psycho*," in Prince, Stephen, editor, *The Horror Film* (copyright © 2004; first published by Rutgers University Press). Portions of chapter 5 were reprinted, with permission, from Caroline Joan (Kay) S. Picart and Jason Grant McKahan, "*Apt Pupil*'s Misogyny, Homoeroticism and Homophobia: Sadomasochism and the Holocaust Film," *Jump Cut: A*

Review of Contemporary Media 45 (Sept. 2002). The essay, with extensive visual illustration, may be found at the Web site http://www.ejumpcut. org/archive/jc45.2002/picart/index.html.

David in particular thanks Marjorie, Justin, and Michael for persevering when Dad seemed somewhere else.

Introduction
Edward J. Ingebretsen

Kate Ferguson Ellis's commonsense description of the Gothic as "a set of conventions to represent what isn't supposed to exist" could be applied to any of the vast array of plots, persons, perplexities found throughout the genre, whether the "traditional texts" such as *The Castle of Otranto* (1764) and *The Mysteries of Udolpho* (1794) or the countless schlock derivatives that now make up pop-cult subterranean Gothic.[1] Ellis can be glossed to mean that illusion, or nonmimetic instability, is a central feature of the protean Gothic forms. Spectral persons and objects appear and disappear, transmogrify and morph. Indeed, in this genre of the unspeakable and the violated, it is the primary task of spectral objects to come and go.

Understandably, then, some might recoil from the project announced by Professors Picart and Frank—whose scholarship of the Holocaust employs, as its primary tool, an avowedly antimimetic mode of commodity fantasy. What have disappearing spectral objects to do with an event like the Shoah? If anything, the Holocaust must be kept in this *real* world; language about it must be kept *from* disappearing. Further, steps must be taken to ensure that its memory actually *remembers*, rather than fantasizes, the dreadful events of its history. Holocaust scholars, literary critics, and politicians alike would argue that the issue is clear. At risk is the status of a bureaucratic machinery of death whose historicity cannot be questioned but which political, aesthetic, and social pressures are systematically reducing to silence. One can see why, then, that at first glance, Picart and Frank's examination of the representational conventions of Gothic cinema would not please such critics.

The reality of the events of the Holocaust is, however, always under siege. Even with the best of intentions, time, representation, political exigency, and general human shortsightedness transmute, change, sometimes even deny it. In this fact alone, Picart and Frank's taxonomy of Gothic cinematic discourse is quite useful to thinking about the Holocaust, because similar pressures are at work in both. That is, an instability exists at the heart of Gothic texts that is less about appearing and disappearing objects than about the discrediting of language and the evacuation of meaning.

For the Gothic is about the costs exacted by a failure to remember well. In this genre, memory assumes a restless, vampiric life of its own—not unlike representation itself. Although they may seem formulaic and tawdry, the oversize helmets, bleeding statues, and the like that punctuate the Gothic-like exclamation points are objective correlatives, if you will. To someone they bring bad news, usually painful lessons in the cost of forgetting. Even in the twentieth-century fin de siècle variants examined by Picart and Frank, Gothic plots are driven by faulty remembering and by murderous mismemory. Its monsters double, morph, appear as dreadful angels; they are messengers of judgment. Norman Bates and Hannibal Lecter commit grievous transgressions, surely. Nonetheless, by doing so, they call a morally lax community to a pointed accounting. They ask it to remember and reconsider aspects and traits that it denies, represses, or would forget. It is in this primary sense, then, that Gothic discourse provides a way to think through the representational trauma of the Holocaust. Its methodologies of the unspeakable, civil taboo and transgressive memory, can provide insight into the conditions that are required to retrieve the Shoah from the ash heap of that other dark messenger, the angel of history.

Representation has political consequences. Representation—how we imagine—determines beforehand the world to be imagined. That is, what we see and what we do not see, what we read and how we read, are determined to a great extent by the forms, modes, genres, techniques, and grammars that govern the epistemological enterprise. For instance, Ellis's expression—"what isn't supposed to exist"—presumes a metaphysical imperative about what is categorically *permitted* to exist. Memory, likewise, has its politics. Consider the bitter contests over whether, how, and why to remember the Shoah. Battles over the funding and founding of Holocaust memorials demonstrate that the pressure to silence history is at least as great as the pressure to speak it. "Why talk about it?" Indeed, why? It is almost as if systemic cruelty and inhumanity are contagious. Perhaps the Shoah is unspeakable in not only a linguistic or Gothic sense but also a moral sense. That is, perhaps the speaking of witnesses or survivors cannot be detached from the acts of heinousness and cruelty they seek to abjure. Fear of memory's unavoidable taint complicates the politics of remembering that (as the San Francisco memorial reads) ought to ward against the repeating of cruelty.

Similar ambiguities trouble all representations of the Holocaust. In *Imagining the Holocaust*, Daniel R. Schwarz begins by asking a series of pointed questions. The title of his introduction reflects his focus: "The Ethics of Imagining the Holocaust: Representation, Responsibility, and Reading."[2] Throughout this thoughtful essay about imagining "history's nightmare," Schwarz has recourse to language, image, and motif customarily associated with the Gothic: "In our nightmares, we are deported and suffer the horrors of the camps." About the work of memory, for example, he writes, "If ever a past needs a human shape, it is the Holocaust; yet as we shall see, putting a human face upon inhuman behavior challenges our ability to imagine evil and to represent it linguistically."[3]

Language, ungoverned by grammar, moves to its ultimate point of confusion and non-sense. Schwarz's illicit use, as it were, of a Gothic discourse indicates that already Schwarz's text is categorically troubled, as unpoliced—or unpoliceable—language exchanges one grammar for another. Yet one can easily defend his choices. Schwarz, a scholar working in literary modernism, suddenly finds common cause with scholars working in Gothic representation. He cites Herbert Muschamp: "the Holocaust was a crisis of meaning, a calamitous cognitive breakdown" (13). Holocaust narratives, he writes, "unravel mysterious and incomprehensible words and pronounce a verdict on events that have already occurred" (14). Discursive collapse is not unique to this or any single author, of course. Such Gothic markers are everywhere in Holocaust studies; consider Schwarz's aside in which he calls these survivor narratives "buried texts" (14). Readers familiar with the opening pages of *The Castle of Otranto* (1764) know immediately what is to follow: buried texts rarely rest in peace, and their return shatters the world into which they come. Narrative breakdown follows discovery of the buried text, and so in this sense one understands the fierce contesting of memory about the Shoah.

With his inadvertent raids into the Gothic, Schwarz underscores the porousness of the discursive boundaries that exist in Holocaust studies. The Gothic is a discursive mode usually categorized as nonmimetic and often dismissed as fantasy (and so, in western ideology, of no real importance). Yet as we see, under certain conditions it seems to function according to an entirely different set of structural imperatives. Nor, as I noted above, is Schwarz alone. Consider Cynthia Ozick's critique of the commercialization of Holocaust texts. In "Who Owns Anne Frank?" Ozick writes that Frank's "fault—her crime—was having been born a Jew, and as such she was classified among those who had no right to exist."[4] The similarity of Ozick's phrasing to Ellis's description of the Gothic is striking, even if their uses—legal precedent, fantasy discourse—seem resolutely distinct. Similar observations can be made about many texts in Holocaust studies. What can be said about events that are resolutely and historically real but which demand, nonetheless, a wholesale borrowing of Gothic tools and motifs of taboo, violation, transgression, unspeakability? For despite efforts to ground the Shoah in a quotidian world, it persists in spinning away from daily gravity, entering a world of the nonmimetic, the fabulous, and the ideologically unreal.

It can be argued that an epistemology of extremity—of which Holocaust studies are a prime analogue—requires such porousness. Schwarz writes, "Holocaust studies begin and end with the questions, 'How do we remember? How do we interpret?'" The vast enterprise of Holocaust studies is an industry of memory as well as a choral rite of lamentation. Schwarz's questions indicate that all strategies—linguistic, psychoanalytic, social—designed to anchor Holocaust studies in a stable place must fail. How can they not? "Even the original experiences are mediated by hunger, fear, and physical and psychological abuse beyond our imagination."[5] Holocaust texts—witness, polemic, history, even fiction—ape genre coherency even when their contents deny genre intelligibility. One sees why a formulaic language of horror is the last line of defense. For example, Lawrence L. Langer's *Holocaust Testimonies: The Ruins of Memory*, employs Gothic images—ruins and witness—to signal the trauma of intellectual collapse, even while such formulas must fail to contain the "trauma, nightmares, displacement, and guilt."[6] One writer trumps history with its collapse: "the universe of the death camps created a decisive breach in the fabric of the modern world."[7] As these examples show, to "narrate the unspeakable" of the Shoah is to be at once within and outside the bounded comforts of speech, yet compelled by responsibilities to personal witness and collective memory that move beyond mimesis.[8]

There is another, and perhaps prior, sense in which Gothic epistemology is of use to the "unimaginable ordeal" at the center of Holocaust studies.[9] So far I have employed Gothic as it is commercially understood—as a sensationalist genre of transgressive awfulness and commodity fright. And while the Gothic is, as David Punter and others write, "about terror," its terror has a grander lineage than we get at the movies. Its terror derives not from the depths of horror but, as Edmund Burke argues, from the uttermost peak of sublimity. In his *Origins of the Sublime* (published a few years before the "first" Gothic novel) Burke theorizes that terror, rightly understood, expands the soul rather than contracts it; terror of this sort, continues Burke, derives from and is analogous to experiences of the sublime. It is in this sense, for example, that Jonathan Edwards—Burke's contemporary—writes in his "Personal Narrative" of "the Awe-ful majesty of God." Edwards is without exception one of the New World's premier theoreticians of divinity; yet as many of his sermons indicate, he was also a premier Gothicist, cagey in the rich linguistic pyrotechnics by which he worked a congregation up through an experience of God—an experience which by definition, escapes speech, even as it had to be contained within speech.

One sees, then, where Holocaust studies meets the Gothic, even if each discourse seems at first unrecognizable to the other. Listen to Elie Wiesel, who for a moment sounds a bit like Edwards, when he describes God as "All-Powerful and Terrible."[10] The discourses of theology and the Gothic are twinned; each is impoverished to the extent that they are separated. Schwarz writes that Holocaust narratives involve "inextricably related issues of aesthetics, ethics, and politics."[11] Absent from this list is religion, from which discourse, historically, the term *Holocaust* is originally derived. Tracings of a religion-derived master narrative of Chosenness and Diaspora are everywhere in Holocaust studies. The linguistic distance traveled from *Sheol* (Old Testament, "the Pit") to *Shoah* ("Annihilation") may displace the religious cosmology from which *Holocaust* (Greek, "whole burnt offering"; "free will sacrifice") and its ancillary terms take their rhetorical affects, but the distance traveled does not completely erase that cosmology. A similar effacement can be seen in other aspects of Holocaust studies. That is, the polemics, scraps, and survivor diaries of Holocaust literature offer themselves as witness texts. They stake their importance on an a priori moral investment that precedes and, in some senses, transcends their status as literature. Yet the secular gaze remains uneasy about this claim and, as a result, risks cheapening the whole enterprise. A diffidence of this sort was responsible for awarding Elie Wiesel—Holocaust survivor and writer—the Nobel *Peace* Prize rather than the Prize for Literature he presumably should have received. The pretence of the secular gaze, perhaps, is that religious obligation is creedal or social in form and so may be dispensed with by law or custom. To the contrary, the obligation still compels linguistically and thus binds (*religio*) discursively.

Categorical negation ("unspeakable"; "unbelievable") and other apophatic markers signal a collapse of sensible grammars. In mainstream Gothic, such a collapse is marked by taboo and violation; however, even these markers throw us back to a different sort of taboo entirely, even if one doesn't note, or understand, the switch. That is, a discourse of the "unspeakable" and the Awful depends for its effect on a metaphysics of presence that is, in its turn, guaranteed by some ultimate category, God, the Awe-ful. The terms of commodity gothic distill and reproduce the language of the sacred and holy; herein is a major conceptual difficulty with using "Holocaust" as an event-marker description. What are the consequences of using this word, for example, with all of its religious history and its implied meaning of a self-willed sacrifice? Doesn't such usage erase genocide and exculpate its agents? Further, "Holocaust" means human annihilation, but as Wiesel writes in *Night*, it means an annihilation horribly amplified by metaphysical silence. Not even Wiesel can write of these things and stay true to mimesis. The shattering effects of memory reach expression only partly, and then in a language rhetorically marked by excess and non-sense: "Never shall I forget that nocturnal silence which deprived me, for all eternity, of the desire to live. Never shall I forget those moments which murdered my God and my soul and turned my dreams to dust. Never shall I forget these things, even if I am condemned to live as long as God Himself."[12]

By means of their "archeology of . . . film criticism," Professors Picart and Frank "provide deeper insights into how films and their audiences act out and work through the trauma of the Holocaust and horror" (chapter 6, *Frames of Evil*). This statement, of course, vastly simplifies their scholarship for the sake of outline clarity. Nonetheless, some critics would criticize even the more sophisticated form of the argument as still presenting conceptual difficulties. The greatest of these, Holocaust critics might charge, is the implicit psychological reduction of "trauma" that is an aspect of Gothic horror. In "The Alarmed Vision: Social Suffering and Holocaust Atrocity," Lawrence L. Langer observes that "personalization of suffering in a Western mode—as tragic, moving, sentimental, as heroic, as martyr-like—can never do justice to the Holocaust, whose events and systemic death dictate a complete rethinking of trauma in social, rather than personal, terms."[13] In this regard, Picart and Frank undertake a complex task. Commodity horror exploits, even concentrates, mechanisms of psychological terror in the interest of making money. The point is to render fear as exquisitely *personal* as possible. This book carefully argues that cinematic renderings of the Holocaust—silently employing grammars of the horror film—inevitably participates, likewise, in such psychological and economic reductiveness. If this was all they accomplished, however, Picart and Frank would have succeeded in doing little more than preventing the Shoah—in their words, "the most extreme example of Twentieth Century evil" (chapter 6, *Frames of Evil*)—from being reduced to, and re-presented as, one more consumer excitation.

But Picart and Frank do more. Their scholarship explicitly addresses Adorno's somber conclusion that "after Auschwitz to write a poem is barbaric."[14] Gothic representation, they argue, influences aesthetics, the study of film, issues of historical representation, ethics. Finally, as I pointed out earlier, by focusing on Gothic discourses of the negative sublime, they return an examination of religious ritual discourse to its rightful place, central to the study of the Shoah. Professors Picart and Frank argue that, for example, a documentary film about Nazi mechanics of death succeeds *as film* by employing Gothic formulas in its representative technique. At its most basic level, such an approach supplements other genre studies and literary criticism of Holocaust texts. More important, however, Picart and Frank invite a critical reexamination of social evil and trauma within the academy. What do I mean? Grounding liberal notions of the "humanities" is the belief that the examined life—or, at least, the examining of someone else's life—adds a moral dimension to one's own. Such a habit of voyeurism has its problems, especially when offered as *moral* activity and especially when not perceived *as* voyeurism. It is naïve to think that the study of the literary or cinematic text leads invariably, as the humanist might avow, to closer proximity to the good, the true, and the beautiful. But then what does literary study *do*?

Gothic discourse makes explicit its fascination with evil; however, it is not the sole guardian of such moral work. To the contrary, all grammars, every discourse, all structuralist discussions presume—whether articulated or not—that ethics begins with aesthetics. Proper reading, in other words, depends upon appropriate "making." But where to start untying this knot? Picart and Frank argue that aesthetics should be evaluated, not by examining the conditions under which representations are made but by studying the conditions that govern how such films and texts are received. Theories of spectatorship, in other words, take precedence or have at least as much to say as theories of representation.

The Gothic genre may be said to return obsessively to a single point: Evil—inappropriate or unethical human action—causes harm to individuals. More than this, inappropriate human behavior profoundly disrupts all systems, all grammars of thought and belief. Indeed, evil can shatter an entire community of moral consequence. Here again one sees the Gothic's necessary connection to Holocaust studies. Both are vitally concerned with uncovering or recovering memory—the personal and communal structures by which a moral community comes to know itself. Picart and Frank's work in *Frames of Evil* uncovers the self-interested gaze masked by commodity representation. That alone would be a worthy accomplishment, yet the authors carefully argue that representations intend consequences that are not always evident. An economics of fear and fright, of haunt and hurt, frames the viewer's gaze, even when employed in the high-minded task of remembering the Shoah. This fact is to the point not only on the screen but in the events supposedly under examination. That is, representation can erase, distort, and sometimes evacuate the historicity of the Shoah that films are meant to preserve. Evil is reduced to mere formula; words and language, imprecisely used, can miss the meaning they so desperately intend. Such imprecision is an evil of a different order than the death camps, it is true, but no less important for that difference.

It is in resisting such a sideways slip into silence that George Steiner writes, "If silence were to come again to a ruined civilization, it would be a two-fold silence, loud and desperate with the remembrance of the

Word."[15] Steiner, like Wiesel, understands language to be about communal survival. In the ruined land of the death camps, Wiesel's use of the metaphor of *night* asks whether moral thought is even possible any longer. Speech silenced is death, but sometimes speech itself can be a kind of death, and mechanisms of death did not end with Auschwitz. Wiesel remained mute for fifteen years after his experience at Treblinka, as he struggled to clarify how the act of witness, without action, can collude with evil. Picart and Frank demonstrate that the greatest silence and the most pervasive evil are not yet perfectly apprehended; in a culture of media and representation, too often viewers and readers can neither distinguish nor negotiate what W. J. T. Mitchell refers to as the gap between representations and the responsibilities they entail. Given such renderings of the Holocaust as *Schindler's List*—"a primary source for the popular understanding of the Holocaust" (chapter 1), it is imperative to understand how its "sanctioned history" comes, as it were, not only preinterpreted but preinterpret*ing*. Language and human discourse move to death as surely as do individuals, and the means by which they do so are many. Proper remembering of the Shoah implies learning, chiefly the means by which, even against our will and best intentions, we forget.

1

The Horror Frame and
the Holocaust Film

American Holocaust films produced in the twentieth century include *Jacob the Liar, Apt Pupil, American History X, Getting Away with Murder, The Devil's Arithmetic, The Long Way Home, Schindler's List,* and a host of others. Judith Doneson, in *The Holocaust in American Film,* documents the importance of American Holocaust films in the construction of the American understanding of the Holocaust and writes that they have "been the most influential in bringing the event to the attention of an international audience."[1] These American movies are among the more than five hundred that dealt directly with the Holocaust by the close of the century.[2] As Doneson, Insdorf, and Avisar demonstrate, cinematic representations of the Holocaust are at the center of scholarly and popular discussion concerning the history and meaning of the Holocaust.[3] Film has and will play a major role in the re-presentation of the Shoah in the twenty-first century, a topic of concern to several writers.[4]

Some American Holocaust movies are more influential than others. One of the most significant Holocaust movies of the twentieth century is Steven Spielberg's *Schindler's List,* now a primary source for the popular understanding of the Holocaust (or Shoah), having achieved the status of sanctioned history.[5] The movie "has provided millions of Americans with what will surely be their primary imagery and understanding of the Holocaust."[6] Scholars suggest *Schindler's List* placed the Holocaust in the "popular conscience" and that the film has influenced a number of national and international attempts to depict the Holocaust's trauma.[7] Joshua Hirsch rightly notes that *Schindler's List* is the "film most commonly used to teach the Holocaust in several countries, including the United States; and it is one of the first and most influential modernist historical documentaries, especially in its revolutionary use of the image of the present to signify the past."[8] The dominant interpretation offered by critics of *Schindler's List*, one that we support, is that it "mimics" the depiction of "real history" through a fictional framework. As Nichols, Renov, and other scholars have pointed out, all documentaries inevitably attempt a realism that shrouds an underlying ideological agenda.[9] Our goal in this book is to unveil the ideological tenets of the horror frame used in *Schindler's List* and other American Holocaust films. We recognize that documentaries may not be inherently more "truthful" than fiction films; there are, however, important distinctions between the two, and reflecting on their formal cross-pollinations, as well as their distinctions, is a key concern of this book. *Schindler's List* aptly illustrates the problems associated with the use of the term *documentary*, because while its public marketing and commercial success have been based on its appropriation of the documentary, or "factual," look, its narrative content, namely, its construction of "heroes" and "villains," is very much in keeping with the classic Hollywood style and appropriates the more superficial aspects of classic horror films.

Audiences bring with them preconceptions about horror and the monstrous; *Schindler's List* and other Holocaust films receive diverse, sometimes mutually exclusive responses. To account for the audience of film, we have integrated reception theory into our approach to the films we consider. In so doing, we note that Staiger and others suggest that reception theory places film analysis in context of the viewing audience.[10] We do this throughout the book by situating the audiences of the Holocaust, horror films, and Holocaust films. Staiger is clear that she does not want to demote the importance of the author in favor of the reader, as we also conduct close readings of visual and written texts.[11] Reception studies trace "possible dominant and marginal interpretive strategies," an approach we take in this book.[12] We follow Staiger and other reception theorists in identifying dominant patterns of interpretations in the work of film reviewers and scholars.[13]

In this book, we consider the frames used in American Holocaust films. The narrative and visual borders used to demarcate monsters and the monstrous is what we consider a horror frame. Our aspiration is to use the horror frame to illuminate the reciprocal influence of horror and Holocaust imagery in film and how this influence may affect the ways in which questions of evil and genocide are addressed in this century. *Schindler's List* plays a major role in our thinking, for it is set up to be "the ultimate and authoritative Holocaust film that absorbs and replaces all previous Holocaust films."[14] In *Schindler's List* and the other movies we consider, we find evidence that directors and others responsible for the production of the most influential American Holocaust movies default to a frame used in classic horror films to represent the Holocaust. We do not provide a list of criteria by which to judge between "ethically responsible" and "immoral" representations of the Holocaust. Rather, we seek to study how the genres of horror and Holocaust film representations have interacted with each other, resulting in complex narratives and refractory responses that are often left unexamined. Our hope is that through the study of this interaction, one that assumes the historicity of the Holocaust, an ethic of spectatorship might evolve.

To deny the connection between Holocaust and horror films is to render oneself blind to a more complex understanding of how nonwitnesses relate to the Holocaust in the present. And indeed, the notion that the Holocaust actively confronts us with "unimaginable, unspeakable, and unrepresentable horror," repelling all but the bravest among us, does not account for what *attracts* many nonwitnesses to the Holocaust, which is its horror. To pretend nonwitnesses can even attempt to have the privileged access to direct experience a victim has had limits and distorts understanding of how present political and cultural concerns reshape the historical past. For us who were never there and for most people, the only access to this experience is mediated through popular film and culture. As such, the absolute horror of the direct, lived experience is inaccessible; *Schindler's List*, like other movies in the classic Hollywood narrative style (as opposed to a modern avant-garde style), attempts such a direct re-creation, and the results are as stirring as they are problematic. A crucial point the book raises is it is precisely in the absence of such horror that we contemplate and represent the Holocaust, often in an effort to come closer to its elusive reality. And it is important, in this process of attempting to access these limit experiences, to track how these stories are told; how the identificatory systems privilege some characters over others; and how we are rhetorically moved to act ethically in relation to this simulated reproduction of traumatized and traumatic memory.

Central to this tracking are the "frames of remembrance" used to represent the Holocaust in film.[15] These frames are designed to explain the historical trauma of the Holocaust. The most influential theorist on historical traumas is Dominick LaCapra. We draw from his notions of "acting out" (the repetitive rehearsal of a past trauma) and "working through" (an act of analysis that produces interpretations allowing for responsible control) to explain how frames arise and function in Holocaust films. His work provides us with a particularly powerful framework for this study because it allows us to situate Holocaust films as responses to social trauma. We believe many representations of the Holocaust in late-twentieth-century American films "act out" the Holocaust with repetitive cinematic portrayals.

LaCapra draws from the language of psychoanalytic theory to illuminate an explanation of traumatic events. In a series of writings, he calls for an engagement with the Holocaust's trauma.[16] Those who try to make sense of the Holocaust, argues LaCapra, must acknowledge their subject position and the psychological agendas that are "transferred" onto the trauma. Trauma cannot be bracketed, he continues, and studied as an "objective" event that does not reach into the future. Nor is the trauma of the Holocaust something incommunicable, beyond the capacity of language and symbols to convey. Rather, LaCapra believes that those who engage the Holocaust should navigate among the poles of objectivity, subjectivity, and the incommunicability of the Holocaust, resisting the binary oppositions that can produce reductionist reasoning and stereotypic constructions of perpetrators and victims. This requires, according to LaCapra, the employment of critical reason in an attempt to work through and work out the implications of trauma.

In elaborating on the meaning of *working-through*, LaCapra writes, "Working-through implies the possibility of judgment that is not apodictic or *ad hominem* but argumentative, self-questioning, and related in mediated ways to action. In this sense, it is bound up with the role of distinctions that are not purely binary oppositions but marked by varying and contestable degrees of strength or weakness."[17] LaCapra argues frames that produce binaries are less helpful than those that can make contextual distinctions in what Primo Levi calls the "grey zone" of the Holocaust. Accordingly, we join a LaCaprian explanation of social trauma with contemporary film criticism to consider the frames in Holocaust movies. We agree with Oren Stier, Michael Rothberg, and other critics that historians and other scholars of the Holocaust have neglected and continue to neglect the influence of the medium and frame in Holocaust narrations.[18]

As Stier observes, the frame, which includes the narrative structure and the technology used in constructing Holocaust representations, "plays a crucial role in establishing the propriety of memory and in shaping various commitments to Holocaust memory."[19] Our contribution to this line of thought will be to identify a classical frame and a more conflicted (or "postmodern" in the film literature) frame in the cinematic representation of the Holocaust.

By "classic horror frame" we refer to narrative patterns characteristic particularly of Hollywood horror films of the thirties and forties, in which the monster is coded as thoroughly other and is ritualistically staked at the end to restore the normal order. In such filmic narratives, as Pinedo points out, "the boundary between good and evil, normal and abnormal, human and alien is as firmly drawn as the imperative that good must conquer evil, thus producing a secure Manichean worldview in which the threats to the social order are largely external and (hu)man agency prevails, largely in the figure of the masterful male subject."[20] In contrast are conflicted horror frames, wherein these boundaries are violated, with horror residing in the realm of the "normal."[21] The classic horror frame features a transgressive, metaphysically evil monster and a clearly demarcated time and space for horror, all clearly distinct from normalcy. In the classic horror frame, the sane and irrational spheres of "self" and "other" are clearly delineated—an attempt that may obscure what the monstrous shares with the normal. Other frames may create for an audience a sense of ambivalence about the status of the monster or may depict a more diffused sense of evil. Such frames often refract and confront the distinctions assumed in the classic frame.

These distinctions are not absolute, as the films of James Whale and Todd Browning do not easily fit into this classificatory scheme: their monsters or freaks seem both vulnerably human and threateningly superhuman or subhuman. Nevertheless, there is a sense in which, as classic monsters became more common, they lost much of their complex characterization and simply became menacing props to be trotted out at the films' overheated climaxes—only to be burnt or staked or disposed of—and it is this dominant pattern that we address.[22]

Central to our concern is the manner in which the monstrous and monsters are framed and how the frames used in classic horror films were and are absorbed by American Holocaust films. Steffen Hantke highlights not only the use of horror frames in representing the Holocaust but also the persistent imagery of the Third Reich in horror films; he presents, in the following observation, a critical touchstone for our project: "Making a horror film that utilizes the Third Reich as a source of cinematic thrills would appear to many a dubious proposition. This seems paradoxical because horror film is the one cinematic genre devoted primarily to the sensation with which most regard the Holocaust. *But horrors on the screen and horrors in history occur on different ontological levels, a difference that translates into profound ethical differences*" (emphasis added).[23]

The differences between screen and historical horror and the representation of the Holocaust are crucial. Scholars have identified the power of horror as a "sensation" and as a lure to the screen. However, we share Hantke's concern about the conflation of the sense of horror constructed to exploit a sensation with the historical reality of the horror of the Holocaust. In light of this concern, Hantke poses the following questions: "Is there not something frivolous about imagining the tropes of horror film and memories of the Third Reich operating side by side? Are there not moral reservations that go even beyond the realization that there are horrors far worse than those imagined by special effects experts, scriptwriters, and directors? Is not the idea itself, to use the Holocaust as a source of cinematic horror, frivolous and tasteless at best, morally reprehensible at worst?"[24]

We confront these questions in this book, and to address them, we believe it is important to trace the origins and characteristics of the horror frame. Ultimately, the question we struggle with is Plato's age-old question of how aesthetics and ethics intersect. Or as Maya Deren phrased the issue, "For the serious artist the esthetic problem of form is, essentially, and simultaneously a moral problem . . . the form of a work of art is the physical manifestation of its moral structure."[25] And precisely because form and, in this case particularly, frame effectively condition and are shaped by ethical responsiveness and popular appeal, we pay close attention to the ways in which these frames are constructed and what they invisibly advocate.

The Classic Horror Frame

The classic horror frame draws from a preexisting Gothic mode of narration. There are, of course, several expressions of Gothic, but the one that influences how the Holocaust is represented in the films we consider is the supernatural Gothic. This expression of the Gothic features demons, vampires, and other monsters as the source of evil.[26] In a chapter titled "Gothic Returns," Ingebretsen describes the rise of an "American Gothic" best illustrated by an American need to juxtapose normality with supernatural and abnormal monstrosity and evil. The visual image becomes key in American Gothic, as the "spectacular and voyeuristic" are favored.[27] "Horror became a matter of watching," writes Ingebretsen, as monsters "announce, work through, and negotiate social trauma in the very formulaic terms of which they are thought to be unique."[28]

The classic horror frame depicts monsters that "breach the norms of ontological propriety."[29] Stephen Prince, using anthropological concepts of purity and danger derived from the work of Mary Douglas, makes similar arguments concerning the essence of horror, which he says lies in boundary violations that rupture the conventions of normality, safety, and order built into our language and cultural systems.[30] These horrific monsters display evil that is transgressive, beyond the ordinary. The monsters in classic horror films share nothing in common with the audience; they inhabit a different space, which they leave to attack the innocent. Of course, the preceding statement demands some qualification because, as Rhona Berenstein points out, classic horror is "a site of ideological contradiction and negotiation"[31]—and this is particularly true when a monstrous character is first introduced. Yet once the classic monsters have become run-of-the-mill, they essentially become no more than fright props. With Boris Karloff's interpretation, the Frankensteinian monster in the Universal series film productions was portrayed and interpreted as classically horrific. In every way, including sexual orientation,[32] the monsters are portrayed as radically different; despite some crossover into the realm of humanity, at the point at which the narrative demands that they be destroyed, they are essentially and irreducibly other.

The classic horror film also breaches the ontology of normal time. The time sequence of horror is bracketed, as the transgressive monster emerges at a definitive moment and, in classic American Gothic, is eventually conquered. With the monster vanquished, normal time returns. Classic horror films also establish an "ontological topology"; the space of classic horror constitutes the "dark areas of something completely other and unseen."[33]

The horror frame has served political purposes, as Germans, three generations since World War II, have used *Schindler's List* and Goldhagen's *Hitler's Willing Executioners* to create visual and historical wedges between themselves and the Nazis and the period of the Holocaust. With this frame, the Nazis, the time period of the Holocaust, and the space of the concentration camp are dissociated from postwar Germans and from the essential historical and current German identity.[34] The horror frame is also deployed in the testimonies of survivors collected by Spielberg's Survivors of the Shoah Visual History Foundation and Yale University's Fortunoff Collection; these establish a commitment to a particular memory of the Holocaust. Spielberg, having amassed $321 million from *Schindler's List*, created an archive of fifty thousand videotaped testimonies from survivors.[35] Survivors narrate their pre-Holocaust stories in half an hour, devote an hour to what happened to them in the Holocaust, and to complete their narratives, spend the last half hour on their liberation and postwar experiences. These interviews end with the survivor united with his or her family, in symbolic triumph over the Holocaust, in a manner that mimes the ending of *Schindler's List*.[36]

Stier found many of the same patterns in the Holocaust testimonies he reviewed in the Yale archives. He writes,

> Most of the time, survivors' stories begin with some words about their families and lives before the war, often moving soon there-after to accounts of the circumstances under which the Nazi era first affected their own lives. In many accounts, this is followed by descriptions of deportations, of ghetto life, of separating from family members, of entering the camps. After descriptions of experiences in the camps, most tell of liberation, of journeys back to hometowns to try to find family members, of leaving Europe. In almost all the videotapes I viewed at the Yale archive, the survivors close by describing coming to America and, with a quick jump to the present, by reflecting back on life in the United States, their children, and the painful legacy of the past.[37]

Though the frames in both the Survivors of the Shoah Visual History Foundation and Yale's Fortunoff Collection look structurally similar, the methods used by the former in producing these narratives have been criticized. Among these criticisms are time constraints and limited training of mass interviewers; the lack of time to countercheck even basic facts; the informal criterion of whether the interviewee-survivor cries as the measure of the "success" of the interview; and the use of "happy endings" to bring forth a commercially enforced catharsis. The frame of these testimonies begins and ends with normalcy, with an episode of horror sandwiched between.[38] Although the classic horror frame appears dominant in both American cinematic and many historical accounts of the Holocaust, there is a competing frame, one that is conflicted.

The Conflicted Horror Frame

"The monster, as we know it," Judith Halberstam writes, "died in 1963," with Hannah Arendt's publication of *Eichmann in Jerusalem*.[39] Arendt portrays the evil of Nazism, especially that of Adolph Eichmann, as "banal."[40] The banality of Nazi evil was revealed in its commonness as the modernity of Nazi Germany "eliminated the comfort of monsters because we have seen, in Nazi Germany and elsewhere, that evil works often as a system."[41] Halberstam then proceeds, citing Haraway and others, to illuminate what she calls "postmodern horror" through an analysis of Jonathan Demme's *The Silence of the Lambs*.

In contrast to the classic horror movie, which establishes and develops the innately evil monster, some movies weave evil into normality, refusing to recognize an unassailable gap between the two spheres. Hantke, discussing the "construction of social space" in serial killer narratives, describes horror fiction as arising from structural ambiguities that result in the violation of the bounded normal and fantastic.[42] This violation, typical of the conflicted horror frame, does not respect the classical divides of time and space. These boundaries, similar to the ones Spielberg's film erects and ultimately attempts to preserve, define spheres—on the one hand, the domain of the normal, the mundane, the predictable and rational; on the other hand, the irrational, the fantastic, the unpredictable, the other. Horror, according to Hantke, "violates the integrity and separateness of the two spheres," prompting "characters and readers alike" to try to resolve the ambiguities.[43] In Hantke's formulation, horror emerges from the intrusions of the other into "normal" space and, equally, from our own penetration of the province of the other. This penetration of the normal into the other's space, which Hantke identifies as internal to horror but also part of our culture, reverses the threatening gaze.

This more conflicted horror frame offers an alternative to but does not supplant the classic horror frame. As we argue below, a frame that blends the two orientations best captures the historical reality of the Holocaust's horror. In addition, we quarrel with Halberstam's use of the term *postmodern* and the identification of 1963 as the year the classic "monster died" in horror films. Indeed, in appropriating German Expressionism, some of the earliest horror films used conflicted frames to represent evil and the monstrous. To place our discussion in historical context, it is important to appreciate the connections that bind horror, Holocaust representation, and Nazi imagery to the influence of German Expressionism. The history of twentieth-century horror films begins with *The Cabinet of Dr. Caligari* (1919). Siegfried Kracauer's *From Caligari to Hitler; A Psychological History of the German Film* posits the thesis, as early as 1947, that horror films are arguably symptomatic of responses to, and reflections of, societal anxieties. Films like *The Cabinet of Dr. Caligari* reflect a national collective psychology of anxiety and longing for order that ultimately explains how a tyrant like Hitler gained absolute power. In Thomas Elsaesser's words, "*From Caligari to Hitler* boldly suggests that the madmen, machine men, tyrants, supermen and charlatans populating the German screen from the end of the First World War onwards are the prototypes of those madmen, charlatans and tyrants who took Germany, Europe and finally most of the rest of the world, into another disastrous war."[44] Lotte Eisner's *The Haunted Screen: Expressionism in German Cinema and the Influence of Max Reinhardt*, the other landmark text, concentrates on the stylistic continuities of a number of motifs characteristic of literature and the fine arts through more than a hundred years of German sensibility. In brief, Eisner traces the resilient persistence of German Romanticism from the 1820s to the 1920s, with its gravitation toward liminal or ecstatic emotional states and the sublime; ambivalent and divided personalities; and the pull toward grotesque and dark fantasies. The cinema of the 1920s, in her paradigm, is simply the natural offshoot of a deeply rooted aesthetic tradition of the "demonic," which was deepened by the humiliation of the lost war and a national character that seems to turn irrational and manic-depressive during times of crisis.[45] Thus the formal look of German Expressionism in film, which was characteristic of films of the Weimar Republic, became the "genuine" look of horror and eventually became incorporated into classic Hollywood horror films, such as *Frankenstein* and *Son of Frankenstein*.[46] Such a look, in the words of Kracauer, immortalized via a scene from *Caligari*, could be represented in the following type of mise-en-scène:

> The canvases and draperies of Caligari abounded in complexes of jagged, sharp-pointed forms strongly reminiscent of gothic patterns. Products of a style which by then had almost become a mannerism, these complexes suggested houses, walls, landscapes. Except for a few slips or concessions—some backgrounds opposed the pictorial convention in too direct a manner, while others all but preserved them—the settings amounted to a perfect transformation of material objects into emotional ornaments. With its oblique chimneys on pell-mell roofs, its windows in the form of arrows or kites and its treelike arabesques that were threats rather than trees, Holstenwall resembled those visions of unheard-of cities which the painter Lyonel Feininger evoked through his edgy, crystalline compositions.[47]

Eisner makes similar remarks regarding the look of German Expressionism in film and, more important, the emotional response it seeks to elicit.

> In *Expressionismus und Film*, Rudolf Kurtz points out that these curves and slanting lines have a meaning which is decidedly metaphysical. For the psychic reaction caused in the spectator by oblique lines is entirely different from that caused in him by straight lines. Similarly, unexpected curves and sudden ups and downs provoke emotions quite different from those induced by harmonious and gentle gradients. . . . But what matters is to cause states of anxiety and terror. The diversity of planes has only secondary importance.[48]

Mike Budd, commenting on *The Cabinet of Dr. Caligari*, argues that part of the reason this particular film has remained so popular with a variety of audiences, despite the passage of time, is that it straddles two traditions: the popular, commercial storytelling tradition close to the Hollywood "realistic" style that is pleasurable and easy to consume unreflectively and the artistic form of discontinuity, modernism, and active political transformation.[49] Thus, while the film has an "invisible" storytelling style, it adopts three features of German Expressionism: a distorted universe rendered in a theatrical painting style; two characters, Cesare and Dr. Caligari, who belong to this insane world in both costume and demeanor; and a frame tale that eventually reveals its principal narrator to be mad, thus destabilizing the truthfulness of the narrative. We see remnants of this tradition even in the most recently posed "realistic" depictions of the Holocaust: Spielberg's *Schindler's List*, though this time, these traces have become transmuted into Goeth's "stalking" gaze—a feature we discuss in chapter 4 in relation to *The Silence of the Lambs*; and Goeth's gaze is ambivalently reconfigured as a parallel to Schindler's own and as a gaze we inadvertently share in some of the "shower" sequences, as we shall show in chapter 3, in the section on *Schindler's List* and *Psycho*.

This discussion of *The Cabinet of Dr. Caligari* and German Expressionism highlights the narrative and aesthetic ambivalences in the treatment of the monstrous in early-twentieth-century film, suggesting a neat divide between classic and what film critics term postmodern renditions of horror cannot hold. In the next section, we develop an approach to explaining and critiquing the classical and conflicted frames of horror.

Film Criticism of Frames

Contemporary historiography and film studies share a particular problematic: both face the current impasse between realism and aesthetics. We attempt to deal with this impasse by joining the concerns of realism and aesthetics into our critique. The medium of film has unique characteristics that call for more specialized inquiry. Formal film criticism has features that distinguish it from photography, theater, and other media of representation. Unfortunately, even though historians acknowledge the influence of films like *Schindler's List* in the creation of historical accounts, they have yet fully to incorporate film criticism, using a detailed analysis of the frames being shown, into their analysis. Even Stier, who highlights the importance of the medium used in Holocaust testimonies, does not draw from film criticism in his discussion of Holocaust representations. Film analysis requires the tools of textual analysis and close reading, as the various iterations of the film's text must be studied, including the novels and other literary work upon which a film is based. We do not assume novels or the written work that inspire cinematic renditions are superior; movies can surpass in quality the literary materials upon which they are based. For our study, we will need a command of the tools necessary to analyze the formal properties of film, with a particular focus on the horror genre.

We follow the approach used by the first author in *The Cinematic Rebirths of Frankenstein*[50] and further developed in *Remaking the Frankenstein Myth on Film: Between Laughter and Horror*.[51] In these works, film criticism of the horror genre is developed, and our insights about the relationship between horror films and key Holocaust films are an extension of this previous work. Briefly sketched, *The Cinematic Rebirths of Frankenstein* begins with an analysis of the novels on which the films are based in comparison with the evolving cinematic narratives.

Frankenstein films, among the first of the classic horror genre, generally attempt to excise or severely delimit the original novel's embedded critique of the Romantic politics of gender, hiding a politics of masculine domination and narcissism. In place of the novel's complex characterization of the monster, these classic horror films often substitute a grotesque creation doomed to criminality and isolation; in place of the ambivalent relationships that bind Victor to his mother and his bride and surrogate mother, these films eventually obliterate the m/other and set up a more conventional love triangle between male figures, such as Henry Frankenstein and Victor Clerval, who seem monstrously cobbled together from fragments of Shelley's novelistic characterization of them.

Yet this severe repression backfires. At the center of these classic horror films is a retelling of an exaggerated myth of male self-birthing—a myth whose classic analogue may be glimpsed in the story of the birth of Dionysus from the thigh of Zeus. Ironically, this immense narrative strain conjures up something other than a simple victimizer (male)—victim (female) model. Rather, what we occasionally glimpse are the outlines of the feminized or tortured male body, which requires, to sustain the borders of masculinity versus femininity, a radical repression of the powerful female body, negatively re-envisaged as what we call the *third* shadow—either the female monster (as in the female creature in *Bride of Frankenstein*) or the feminine-as-monstrous (for example, the ambitious and seductive Justine in *The Curse of Franken-stein*).[52] Yet this repression, even as it gains an uneasy victory, attests, in the vehemence of its negation, to its dark underside. As Deborah Wilson writes, "Victor never quite makes maternity *exclusively* male; the womb may be displaced, the maternal body reinscribed, but it will not remain subsumed."[53] This strain on the intertwined patriarchal myths of parthenogenesis and of science as an unambiguous guarantor of progress is even more obvious in comedic, science fiction, and horror-comedic film versions of the evolving Frankenstein myth.

Stated differently, these offshoots of the Frankenstein narrative allow a fuller emergence of what Janice Rushing and Thomas Frentz call the dystopian aspects of the Frankensteinian complex.[54] In comparison with their classic horror film counterparts, which strive, even if with some ambivalence, to repress any hint of sexual ambiguity and to create traditionally happy endings, these conflicted or hybrid renditions, which range across comedy and horror, tend to unleash these elements—at least for longer and in a more overt fashion than their classic horror counterparts. Classic horror also ends with the ritualistic staking of the monster, who is, for the most part, othered; conflicted horror cannot end with the apparent exorcism of the monster because monstrosity is an enemy from within, rather than without.

In taking this position, we argue that Rhona Berenstein's position on classic horror (which is especially evident in James Whale's and Todd Browning's films) is actually more apropos for describing conflicted frames. "What I do not argue is that classic horror is transgressive from a larger ideological perspective. . . . [T]o claim that the genre is either politically progressive or conservative oversimplifies one of its most important qualities; namely its function as a site of ideological contradiction and negotiation."[55] Given that the hybrid or conflicted offshoots of the Frankenstein horror myth draw from contradictory and competing meaning systems—as evidenced in the perpetual war between ideologically progressive and conservative forces—we approach these hybrid films from multiple perspectives.

To engage properly the films we consider, we examine the evolving scripts and compare them with the released film versions and, when possible, consider the publicity campaigns, censorship files, and reviews. In thus drawing from diverse approaches, we explore the dynamic and contradictory relationships rooted in social, institutional, economic, and creative discourses and contexts that are reflected in and constitutive of such hybrid or conflicted genres.[56]

We draw from this line of research the following insights: the distinctions between classic horror and conflicted horror in their demarcations of, in particular, power, gender, and monstrosity; the shadow figures that emerge from these narratives; and a pluralistic method that moves across frame and thematic analyses to production history documents and to reviewers' remarks, among other factors. The most significant figure in these studies of the Frankensteinian cinematic myth is the third shadow—a female or feminized entity both terrorized and terrifying, who has the potential of reversing the power relations inherent in the Mulveyan "male gaze."[57]

As we will eventually show, one of the significant findings of this study is that though the third shadow emerges in *Psycho* and its variants, the quintessential template for contemporary horror, it is operative not at all in *Schindler's List* and to only a limited extent in *Apt Pupil* (the novella, not the film)—both instances of contemporary popular cinematic renditions of the Holocaust. That is, while *Psycho* and *The Silence of the Lambs* follow a conflicted horror frame, *Schindler's List* and, to a large extent, *Apt Pupil* employ a classic horror frame.

To this list of observations, we add a fourth: Holocaust films are artistic creations with intentionally fictive elements, but given their role in public memory work, their status as works of art cannot absolve them of a responsibility to history, particularly when they set themselves up as "authentic historical documents." To assess the issues raised by the historical claims made in Holocaust films, we draw from the scholarship of Christopher Browning, Saul Friedlander, and other noted historians of the Holocaust.[58] When Holocaust movies, such as *Schindler's List*, are intentionally constructed or viewed by audiences as historical representations of the Holocaust, they should be judged by historical standards; we do not endorse a collapse of the ontological distinction between screen and historical horror. In maintaining this distinction, we seek to develop what LaCapra calls an "ethic of response" to the frames used to represent the Holocaust. LaCapra argues that an ethical turn in critical theory will require a link between historical inquiry and ethico-political concerns.

An Ethical Response to Frames

Primo Levi may have offered the most humane approach to the issue of judgment and the Holocaust. He sees the Holocaust as a grey zone, rather than one composed in black and white. Accordingly he makes judgments that account for context and degree of complicity, refusing to bow to a "Manichaean tendency, which shuns half-tints and complexities."[59] As we move into this grey zone, we face four obstacles critical theory has erected to prevent a rapprochement with ethics: a separation between thought and action, as well as between ethics and aesthetics; the sense that ethics is a matter of an individual's authenticity; a conflation of ethics with moralizing, which is construed to be an understanding of ethics as a claim to moral superiority; and the sense that all normative values deserve transgression and flouting.

Contemporary critical theory can and often does privilege the aesthetic, thereby displacing history. LaCapra's critique of Shoshana Felman's chapter on Claude Lanzmann's documentary *Shoah* (1985) is a key illustration. Felman's interpretation of *Shoah*, one sanctioned by Lanzmann, emphasizes the limits of representing, understanding, and explaining the Holocaust. Indeed, Felman portrays these limits as absolute, and as LaCapra continues, the trauma of the Holocaust in her account is "so overwhelming that distinctions threaten to collapse and the world emerges as a *univers concentrationnaire*."[60] LaCapra exposes not only Felman's failure to place the Holocaust in historical context but also her pattern of confusing "life with both self-reflexive art and self-dramatizing criticism" (113).

According to LaCapra, a historical challenge of the aesthetic emphasis in contemporary critical theory can produce more sensitive readings of artifacts that account for the historicity and the political implications of representation. Such a turn places a burden of responsibility on those who give voice to or attempt to represent such traumas as the Holocaust to include questions of history and ethics. At the same time, a concern for history and ethico-political concerns does not diminish the importance of the aesthetic and imagination in the creative reconstruction of traumatic events, for they are necessary in any attempt to depict historical events. However, as Schwartz has contended, the memory of the Holocaust victims calls for us to tie the imagination to an ethical mooring.[61]

We agree with LaCapra that critical theory is useful in its focus on the limits of representing, understanding, and explaining historical events like the Holocaust.[62] The alternative is neither the chimera of historical objectivity nor a requirement that events like the Holocaust must be represented as realistic documentaries of "what really happened." Indeed, as William Rothman points out, the issues surrounding truth and representation in a documentary are complex, as his analysis of *Nanook of the North* (1922) shows.

> Nanook claims that its protagonist is a real person, not a fictional character. However, real people too, are characters within fictions (we are creatures of our own imaginations and the imaginations of others). And real people are also actors (we play the characters we, and others, imagine us to be, the characters we are capable of becoming). As opposed to playing a character, Nanook's star appears as himself, or, as it might be more apt to say, plays himself (as opposed to playing a character other than himself). Yet the "self" this man plays and the "self" who plays him do not simply coincide.[63]

Even in the documentary, there are issues of representation.

As such we agree with LaCapra that there be an "interaction among research, theory, and ethicopolitical concerns in the critical attempt to come to terms with specific problems."[64] The ethical turn LaCapra calls for in critical theory would have effects on film studies as well, given the deep influence of critical theory on film theorists. This ethic, in turn, parallels LaCapra's call for an ethic of response to the trauma of the Holocaust and its representation.[65] LaCapra argues that the response made by secondary witnesses to the trauma of the Holocaust is a pressing issue.[66] He observes that the response to the trauma by secondary witnesses may fall into one of two categories. The first is narrative redemption, in which the audience vicariously suffers with the victims to achieve a transcendent affirmation of self or group identity. Such is the case with *Schindler's List* and its Zionist coda. The second is excessive or unqualified objectification, a response that seeks a definitive answer to what happened during the Holocaust. The two responses constitute another Holocaust binary that LaCapra seeks to dissociate.

LaCapra sets forth an ethic of response that navigates between the poles of narrative redemption and excessive objectification. He does not reject the value of narrative redemption or of the search for an objective account of the Holocaust. Instead, he places limits on narrative identification and the search for objectivity, relating the trauma of the Holocaust to Nietzsche's notion of *Schwergewicht*.[67] As LaCapra uses it, *Schwergewicht* is a recognition of the "stressful weight in inquiry, and . . . how history in its own way poses problems of writing or signification which cannot be reduced to writing up the results of research."[68] Here, the excesses of objectivity and identification are mitigated by an understanding that remains open to dialectical tension and the problem of representing a trauma that "cannot be reduced to writing up the results of research" or captured on film. In summary, an ethic of response would call for multiple frames and constant dialectic between those frames and historical discovery. The horror frames used in Holocaust histories and movies significantly influence the aesthetic and historical claims they make, and in a complicating twist, the frames used by historians and directors who share the same or a similar view of evil are remarkably similar.

Frames of History and Film

The fit between Holocaust historical narratives and the horror frame used in film is well illustrated by *Schindler's List* and its academic counterpart, Daniel Goldhagen's *Hitler's Willing Executioners*. As Eley and Grossman observe, "certain themes from *Schindler's List*, both the film itself and the surrounding discussions, have insinuated themselves into Goldhagen's polemic. . . . It is hard to read *Hitler's Willing Executioners* (or about it), with its occasional and perhaps deliberately cinematic registers . . . enjoining us to visualize the horrors of his story . . . without being reminded of [*Schindler's List*] and the discussions it produced."[69] In turn, the horror frame of *Schindler's List* can be paired with the functionalist or conflicted frame of Claude Lanzmann's *Shoah* as a binary, with the latter dealing with the administrative mechanisms and the more "banal" dimensions of the Holocaust.

These two frames are prevalent as well in the two most important scholarly explanations of the Holocaust. The first explanation, "ideological-intentionalist," uses what we call the classic horror frame. The second, the "structural-functionalist," is closely aligned with the conflicted horror frame, represented cinematically with Lanzmann's *Shoah*.[70] There is a deep structure to the narratives used by these schools to explain the Holocaust, with profound precritical assumptions, effectively establishing a preordained blueprint of social trauma.[71]

Ideological intentionalists see the Holocaust as standing outside time and as a nightmare with clear boundaries. This school gives great weight to human agency and purpose, holds that a deeply held anti-Semitism motivated the Germans, views Germany as peculiar and unique in its hatred of Jews, condemns Germans of that time period, casts Jews as the primary targets and victims, and sees the Holocaust as sui generis (unique). The demonic, satanic, anti-Semitic, murderous Nazi becomes the causative agent in this narrative. Structural functionalists, by contrast, put the Holocaust into the flow of Western time, seeing it as a fulfillment of the preexisting patterns of Enlightenment thought and modernity.

Although this school acknowledges anti-Semitism as an influence on the climate and culture of Nazi Germany, it isn't seen as a causative or as a sufficient explanation for the Holocaust. The industrial state and a technological mentality, rather than intentional evil, are seen as the origins of genocide. As Moses notes,

> Structural-functionalists do not conceive of Nazi evil as "demonic," a "negative sublime," or in terms of "satanic greatness," because they deny that the external model of intention applies to the facts of the Holocaust. A new concept of evil is necessary for a radically new type of perpetrator: the so-called desk-perpetrator (*Schreibtischtater*), who systematized the killing procedure without himself being a monstrous personality. Accordingly, they follow Hannah Arendt's controversial proclamation in *Eichmann in Jerusalem* that Nazi evil is "banal," by which they hold not only that Eichmann was a banal man, but that evil can be done by those who do not necessarily believe in what they are doing. Men like Eichmann, so Arendt contended, were not bloodthirsty killers or ideological fanatics, but careerist civil servants, whose faculty of judgment and sense of personal responsibility had been effaced by their imbrication in administrative mechanisms, which removed them from reality and the concrete. Such an evil is the incubus of modern, putatively "normal" societies.[72]

The ideological-intentionalist narrative features anti-Semitism, Nazis, German people, and culture as the agents of evil. The narrative locates Germany as the distinctive milieu of genocide. Finally, this account stresses the "uniqueness" of Jewish suffering and the Holocaust. In contrast, the structural-functionalist narrative emphasizes modernity and bureaucrats as the ubiquitous and transcultural causes of genocide. This narrative stresses the diversity of the Nazi victims and the Holocaust as one of many genocides. Moses concludes, "Most historical scholarship is a blend of both narratives."[73]

As such, we hold that it is best to view the screen horror of the Holocaust through multiple frames; one should not dominate.

A closure to the questions raised by the Holocaust takes place when one frame dominates. *Schindler's List* and other movies that use the classic horror frame vividly depict some of the more Gothic dimensions of the Holocaust. But this frame is not sufficient and should be open to interrogation. Saul Friedlander has called for a resistance to a historical closure of the questions raised by the Holocaust and presses historians and others to use multiple and conflicting narratives to explain the Shoah.[74]

Yet, in the Holocaust films we examine in depth, American filmmakers such as Steven Spielberg and Bryan Singer have fallen back on ideological-intentionalist assumptions that frame key elements of the Holocaust as a subgenre of horror. To gain an understanding of how horror functions in American Holocaust films, it is necessary to consider both the benefits of formal analysis, expressed as the recognition of the unique role played by the medium of film, and criticism that reveals hidden structures of power in relation to representations of gender, race, class and sexuality, among other factors. Because artistic creations penetrate consciousness, create or affect ideology, and can compel action, cinematic representations of the Holocaust are open to criticism for their social worth. A detailed examination of a frame requires an analysis of its formal properties and how well the frame aligns with the most fruitful or thought-inducing social criticism. Frames have histories of their own, often drawn from myth and cultural values.

The deep structures of ideological intentionalism and the classic horror frame are strikingly similar. Both identify evil as a breach with the ordinary, evil as intentional, the space of the monstrous other as dark and the site of the other, the victim in passive relief, and an unproblematic division between ordinary time and the nightmare of suffering and death. The patterns of representing the Shoah in many late-twentieth-century American Holocaust films conflate ideological intentionalism and the horror film genre, consciously or unconsciously framing the genocide as the ultimate horror film.

The peephole and "shower" scenes are recurring images in our analyses of these films (most prominently *Schindler's List*, and *Apt Pupil*). In these movies, the viewer witnesses murder through a peephole, in which the victims, in their nakedness, are utterly vulnerable and sexualized. The audience is separated from murder itself but is able to gaze at the victims. The peephole creates a clear demarcation between the space of murder (the shower stall in the movies) and the position the viewer takes behind the peephole. This demarcation places the agents and site of murder safely outside the ostensible moral province of the audience but keeps the spectacle within their field of vision. As such, the peephole visually yokes ideological intentionalism and horror film conventions by framing the Holocaust as an "ontological breach" with the flow of normality and history. It does so by separating the audience from the agent and space of murder but allowing the audience the "guilty pleasure" of witnessing an evil that is portrayed as radically other and yet alluring or aesthetically fascinating. These visual demarcations are at the core of the classic horror frame.

American Gothic serves as an explanation to "work through" the trauma of the Holocaust and serves as a dominant frame for important American Holocaust films. In chapter 2 we provide the reader with a larger sample of Holocaust and horror films to reveal the significance and continuity of the horror frame in visualizing cinematic narratives of horror and the Holocaust. We then present two films as illustrations of the use of the conventions of the horror-psychological thriller in the representation of the Holocaust, *Schindler's List* and *Apt Pupil* (a 1998 movie adaptation of a Stephen King novel). To bring the patterns of repetition into focus and to demonstrate that crucial examples of the contemporary or conflicted horror genre challenge and undermine the representations of evil characteristic of classic horror films, we highlight for comparative purposes Alfred Hitchcock's *Psycho* and Jonathan Demme's *Silence of the Lambs*, both of which are conflicted rather than classic horror films. In conflicted horror films, where all conventional boundaries are violated, horror resides in the realm of the "normal," and the "efficacious male expert is supplanted by the ordinary victim who is subjected to high levels of explicit, sexualized violence, especially if female."[75] Ultimately, beyond the intent of describing the horror frame, we draw from LaCapra to develop an ethic of response to frames of remembrance.

In the next chapters, we juxtapose crucial examples of the American Holocaust film alongside contemporary and American iconic horror-psychological thrillers to show how these fictional Holocaust films constitute an attempt to work through the trauma of the Shoah. Our goal is to illuminate the recurring use of the classic horror frame in the American Holocaust film's depiction of genocide. We devote chapter 2 to a consideration of a large sample of Holocaust and horror films to show the significance and prevalence of the classic horror frame, as well as its evolution to a postmodern frame, which does not displace but coexists beside the classic horror frame. This chapter serves as a backdrop for our close readings of *Schindler's List* (as well as *The Silence of the Lambs* and *Apt Pupil*). In chapter 3 we identify the persistence of the classic horror frame in Spielberg's *Schindler's List*. Chapter 4 is devoted to an analysis of the frame used in *Silence of the Lambs*, which has been billed as the "new *Psycho*" and displays a postmodern or conflicted horror frame. In chapter 5, we reveal how *Apt Pupil*, which has generally been decried as a "poor" version of *Schindler's List*, actually has strikingly formal and narrative similarities to that film, such as its emphasis on shower scenes; however, much of the ambivalent misogyny-glorification of the Jewess in *Schindler's List* has been replaced with an equally ambivalent homoerotic-homophobic depiction of the relationship between Todd (the young American boy-man) and Dussander (the aging Nazi in hiding). We believe viewers of *Schindler's List* and *Apt Pupil* may learn more about Spielberg's and Singer's attempts to work through representations of the Holocaust, using the traditional conventions of Hollywood film technique, than about the tragedy itself. The last chapter expands themes introduced in this introductory chapter and examines the ethical implications that follow from the increasingly pervasive consumption of the film iconography of framing the Holocaust as a horror narrative.

Horror in Holocaust Films and
the Holocaust in Horror Films

A large sample of horror and Holocaust films is necessary to illustrate the patterns identified in the succeeding chapters. Such films show that a relationship between Holocaust and horror films is traceable to eras before the 1990s and that Holocaust imagery is used in many horror films. These two points form the backdrop of close readings of particular scenes, suggesting that while the films we select for sustained analysis are representative of a larger pattern, they are more influential and serve as representative anecdotes.

Both the frame used to represent the Nazi metaphor and the host of tropes associated with the Nazi symbol infiltrated the American consciousness through cinema and television. According to a Roper poll conducted in 1994, 58 percent of the American adults surveyed cited television as a source of their knowledge concerning the Holocaust. Thirty-three percent of those who took part in the survey identified the movies as the source of their information about the event. Until 1980, these films tended to portray neo-Nazis as a recalcitrant (and delusional) remnant of German National Socialists who were forming clandestine networks outside the United States to establish the Fourth Reich. As Lawrence Baron claims,[1] among the twenty-one English-language feature films released between 1945 and 1979 that deal with neo-Nazi movements, only five situate their stories in the United States. Instead, they typically depict neo-Nazi activities either as a spillover of World War II in distant Europe or as the sinister machinations of Nazi war criminals hiding in exotic South America. The latent message of these films was that Nazism is utterly alien to American politics.

The location of Nazism outside the fold of ordinary American life is at the center of American Gothic and the use of the horror frame in representing the Holocaust in American-made movies. Among the first Holocaust images American audiences encountered was Wanda Jakubowska's *The Last Stage*, released in the United States in the late 1940s. *Nazi Concentration Camps* was the first American-made film to deal explicitly with the Holocaust atrocities (though not necessarily the first American Holocaust film). Certainly, the history of film in relation to Holocaust representation is complex. Even newsreels and photojournalistic accounts depicted atrocities, and many of the first documentaries themselves were shown only to military audiences long before the public saw them. Meanwhile, a number of Hollywood films made during the war addressed the Holocaust, as mentioned earlier. There is legitimate debate over when to date the Holocaust, but certainly by 1943, well after Nazis had landed on the final solution, Hollywood was making anti-Nazi films that alluded to atrocities. See for example, Fritz Lang's *Hangmen Also Die* (United Artists, 1943), which depicts the massacre at Lidice, or Andre De Toth's *None Shall Escape* (MGM, 1944). De Toth, like Lang, was a refugee himself. Incidentally, De Toth directed one of the most famous horror films of all time, the 3-D *House of Wax* (Warner Bros., 1953).[2] Yet, until 1959, "American motion pictures [addressed the Holocaust and anti-Semitism] through abstraction, omission, and allegory," writes Steven Carr in his *Hollywood and Anti-Semitism*.[3]

Nevertheless, *Nazi Concentration Camps* remains a critically important film, although it complemented photojournalism and radio commentary in awakening the American public to the Holocaust. The film was based on the Nuremberg Trials, which lasted from November 21, 1945, to October 1, 1946.[4] As preparations to screen *Nazi Concentration Camps* were under way at the court, James Donovan, an assistant trial counsel, declared, "These motion pictures . . . speak for themselves in evidencing life and death in Nazi concentration camps."[5] Janet Flanner, who reported on the trial with Rebecca West for the *New Yorker*, remarked that the use of the film provided "the irrelevant diversion of horror movies."[6] The use of graphic footage of atrocities as proof of criminal wrongdoing was unprecedented and served not only juridical purposes but also didactic and pedagogical purposes. As Zelizer points out, the use of photographs in the immediate aftermath of the Holocaust was intended to "simply document what the Nazis had done" and to facilitate "the act of bearing witness to Nazi brutality."[7] Without question, these images were sympathetic to the victims, but "groups of German perpe-trators . . . were almost always portrayed at harsh angles to the camera and in rigid, upright postures. These individuals looked angry and cruel, almost maniacal."[8] In the wake of the war, *Nazi Concentration Camps* and newspaper photographs framed the horror of the Holocaust like that of the horror mov-ies, helping the American audience to make sense of the atrocity.

We do not suggest that *Nazi Concentration Camps* created a uniform un-derstanding of the Holocaust. As Jonathan Culler points out, a nuanced reading of how audiences have responded to a text entails "an attempt to understand their changing intelligibility by identifying the codes and in-terpretative assumptions that give them meaning for different audiences at different periods."[9] Thus, as we noted in chapter 1, our study acknowledges Janet Staiger's emphasis on the reception historian's concern with events of interpretation and affective experience, while moving between production history and milieu, text and context.[10] Despite the eventual use of *Nazi Con-centration Camps* as a pedagogical tool, American audiences had already been primed through initial newsreels (culled mostly from European sources), docudramatic Hollywood depictions before 1945, photojournalist accounts in magazines and newspapers, and on-the-spot radio descriptions of the atrocities by journalists such as Edward R. Murrow.[11] There were public screenings of films of the Nazi concentration camps as early as April and July 1945. These screenings showed many of the same scenes that would be incorporated into *Nazi Concentration Camps*; the footage was shot by British and U.S. soldiers and may also be seen in *Death Mills*.[12]

The reaction to *Nazi Concentration Camps* is available in several accounts. Douglas compared four such sources, including a *New York Times* article; a diary entry from G. M. Gilbert, a prison psychologist; a memoir entry from Airey Neave, an Oxford lawyer who assisted the British prosecutorial staff; and an excerpt from Telford Taylor's *The Anatomy of the Nuremberg Trials* (1992) that covers the screening of *Nazi Concentration Camps* at the Nurem-berg Trials. Despite their differences, all four accounts shared one rhetorical feature: they do not mention what the film shows but focus on the reactions of the defendants. "They ask us to see the film voyeuristically through the eyes of not just any viewers but of those allegedly responsible for the very atrocities captured on film."[13] It is also interesting that the Army's decision to shoot the Holocaust documentaries in monochrome was based purely on economic reasons rather than on some kind of aesthetic or ideological commitment. The Technicolor process involved the use of three strips of film in cameras, which were bulky and not conducive to on-location documentary filmmaking. By the end of the war, single-strip color processes had been developed, so most likely the reason for shooting in black and white was simply an economic one. Processing and developing raw film stock was expensive, and color film still being relatively new, the costs of using it may have been prohibitive. Also, the Army had its own labs to process the negatives, and since they were set up to process black-and-white footage, processing color negatives at the time may also have been too cumbersome. Hence, black-and-white images such as those conveyed in figure 2.1 emerged as the dominant template for the Holocaust.[14] This decision shaped the evolution of the conventional "authentic look" of the Holocaust as unfolding in black and white—a visual marker Spielberg himself consciously appropriates, as we shall show in chapter 3. What began as a didactic, voyeuristic attempt to attest to the guilt of perpetrators by looking through their eyes at a documentary during the Nuremberg Trials evolves, in Spielberg's *Schindler's List*, into an apparently value-neutral "documentary" gaze in a film packaged as a historical document. In Singer's *Apt Pupil*, this gaze simply becomes the hallmark of the Nazi/homosexual-as-monster, partaking of the ambivalent visual pleasures that the filmic Gothic provides the audience. Of course, other points of view—those of the witness, of the victim, and of the liberator—coexist with that of the perpetrator in Holocaust and Hollywood films, but they do not form the fulcrum that the perpetrators' points of view occupy in Holocaust and horror films—as both didactic mechanisms and spectacles of Gothic monstrosity.

Filmmakers adopted the Nazi-infiltrator as a monster as early as Orson Welles's *The Stranger* in 1946. Such 1950s films as *Devil Makes Three* (1952), *Foreign Intrigue* (1956), and *Verboten* (1959) deal with neo-Nazi paranoia. In the 1960s and 1970s, the threat of a political revival of neo-Nazism in West Germany was visualized for American audiences through British espionage movies. For example, in the internationally produced *The Odessa File*, journalist Peter Miller obtains the diary of a deceased Holocaust survivor. Its grisly descriptions of the slaughter of German Jews deported to Riga are visualized in black-and-white flashbacks that resemble documentary footage. Miller discovers that Riga's SS commandant has returned to Germany with the covert assistance of the SS fugitive organization ODESSA. The Mossad (an Israeli intelligence agency) then recruits Peter to ferret out ODESSA's membership list; this operation is necessary to prevent German companies from

Fig. 2.1. The monochromal Holocaust. Still from *Schindler's List* courtesy of the Academy of Motion Pictures Arts and Sciences. Amblin/Universal, 1993.

manufacturing a guidance system that the nefarious ODESSA plans to sell to Egypt to target missiles against Israel. Miller infiltrates the ODESSA, kills the Riga commandant in self-defense, and coincidentally discovers that the commandant had executed Peter's father for refusing to obey an order.

More overt in showing the link between Gothic representations of violence and the Holocaust, 1960s and 1970s American movies often exploited the infamy of the Third Reich as grist for horror and science fiction movies. By then, because the Soviet Union had replaced Germany as the principal enemy of the United States, the directors of these movies portrayed neo-Nazi conspiracies as the schemes of demented fanatics hiding in the tropics. Thus, once again, such films tended to locate the dis-ease of neo-Nazism squarely outside the borders of American society. Movies such as *They Saved Hitler's Brain*, *The Frozen Dead*, *Flesh Feast*, *Shock Waves*, and *The Lucifer Complex* stereotyped their neo-Nazi characters as deranged scientists who were reviving or cloning dead Nazi leaders and soldiers to resume the war they had lost on the battlefield. These exploitation films were created on shoestring budgets, and their hackneyed dialogue, poor acting, and unbelievable plots made their

Nazi villains seem more ridiculous than menacing. For instance, in *They Saved Hitler's Brain*, Nazi loyalists on a South American island kidnap an American woman as bait to trap her father, a famous professor who has invented an antidote to nerve gas. A CIA agent charged with finding the missing girl discovers that Hitler's head has been kept alive on the island. In an escape attempt, the Nazis spirit the head away in a car, and it is hardly surprising that the heroic agent saves the day by lobbing a hand grenade at Hitler's limousine and literally blowing the former fuehrer's brains out. In addition, the practice of using concentration camp inmates as specimens for medical experiments prompted filmmakers to transform the stock figure of the manic doctor in science fiction movies into the deranged Nazi scientist.

Despite the mythologized growth in sophistication of Nazi technology, the equally mythic atavistic Nazi obsession with racial purity and total power remained constant, as evidenced in plots that ranged from the resurrection of the corpses of high-ranking Nazis in *The Frozen Dead* or dead *Wehrmacht* soldiers in *Shock Waves* to the cloning of ninety-four baby Hitlers in *The Boys from Brazil* or exact replicas of world leaders in *The Lucifer Complex*. All too often, both in popular culture and in film, as Robert Leventhal notes, "The Nazi scientist is depicted as a deranged, marginal figure operating on the periphery of society and the state."[15] This stereotype is certainly true of many popular narratives about Mengele; the pathological rendering of the Nazi dentist in *Marathon Man* is another such example.

Clearly, there was a time in the 1960s and 1970s when Nazis usurped the stock racial villain roles once the main province of "devious Orientals" in the 1920s and the dreaded Communists in the 1950s and 1960s. Following is the barest of outlines of this long association between the Holocaust and horror in film: Nazis became the standard villains in such thrillers as *The Quiller Memorandum* (1967), *The Night Porter* (1974), *Marathon Man* (1976), *Voyage of the Damned* (1976), *Bear Island* (1979), and *The Formula* (1980), not to mention *Raiders of the Lost Ark* (1981). But Nazi notoriety has been best exploited by low-budget horror films such as *She Demons* (1958), *The Frozen Dead* (1966), *Flesh Feast* (1970), *Shock Waves* (1975), *Death Ship* (1980), *Night of the Zombies* (1983), and the already mentioned Z-movie classic *They Saved Hitler's Brain* (1964), as well as the pornographic and sadomasochistic Ilsa movies, beginning with *Ilsa, She Wolf of the S.S.* (1974) and continuing with *Commando Mengele* (1986), whose thinly plotted script, typical of Jesus Franco, hinges on the repeated capture and release of a stripper whose body is targeted for artificial insemination by the relentless Mengele.

Despite the variety of genres in which Holocaust and horror themes merge, the face of the monstrous after World War II, particularly for American audiences, is the face of the Nazi. Yet what is strikingly discernible, particularly in some 1990s American films that mesh Holocaust and horror themes, is that Evil is no longer Out There, which is a primary characteristic of the classic horror frame, but within the heartland, imperceptibly imbricated within the intimate structures of the domestic, thereby recasting the horror frame to include normalcy. In the next section, we describe the rise of this more conflicted horror frame.

Psycho and Its Spawn as the New American Gothic

The Americanization of the Gothic in film, with its conflicted frame, may be traced to *Psycho* (1960) and its variants. *Psycho*'s villain, Norman Bates, is based on the serial murderer Ed Gein. Harold Schechter, the author of *Deviant: The Shocking True Story of the Original 'Psycho,'* a biography of Ed Gein, claims, "The really significant thing about Gein is . . . the Americanized horror. Before Gein and the films that sprang from the obsession with this case, the monsters that populated horror films were always foreign in some way. They either came from Transylvania, or Egypt, or from outer space. With Gein you really get the beginning of a very specifically American kind of horror."[16] Norman Bates's infamous Gothic legacy of the "woman suit" (with its affinities to the Nazi use of dried human skin for various purposes) becomes hyperbolized into a house of death in *Texas Chain Saw Massacre* (1974, reissued 1999). In this film, the realms of fact and fiction, characteristic of docudramas and, in particular, Holocaust cinematic narratives, are not distinct. According to the film's director, Tobe Hooper, "My relatives that lived in a town close to Ed Gein told me these terrible stories . . . these tales of human skin lampshades and furniture. I grew up with that like a horror story you tell around a camp-fire. I didn't even know about Ed Gein, I just knew about something that happened that was horrendous. But the image really stuck."[17]

The Silence of the Lambs (1991) and *Hannibal* (2001) reflect the conflation of vampirism and cannibalism in contemporary horror (with its fixation on the use of human beings reduced to cattle, as sources of meat and leather—a Holocaust-derived Gothic artifact) but restore to the serial killer–cannibal the vampire's aristocratism, combined with a supernatural intelligence and the ever-present threat of his barely contained physical power, which "rationally" explain Hannibal's ability to terrorize and feed on others' terror.[18]

In *The Silence of the Lambs*, Clarice Starling (Jodie Foster), a student at the FBI academy, probes Hannibal Lecter (Anthony Hopkins) for clues to identify and apprehend a serial killer nicknamed Buffalo Bill (Ted Levine). Lecter, who feeds Clarice tidbits of information in return for details of her personal history, becomes one of the film's ambivalent figures of monstrosity: intriguing and horrifying at the same time—not unlike the characterization of Nazis as cultured monsters. Alongside his apparent elegance is Lecter's monstrosity, which the film figures in terms of his ability to return the gaze—to echo, even in confinement, the voyeurism of Norman Bates. In *The Silence*, Ed Gein's cannibalism was split apart from his gender uncertainties and fetishistic obsession with obese women's flesh. Cannibalism, conjoined with vampirism's ability to hypnotize and seduce, becomes a feature of the powerfully heterosexual, upper-class, and brilliant Dr. Lecter; and the desire to be transformed into a woman, conjoined with vampirism's gender uncertainties, becomes a feature of the gender-disturbed, blue-collar, and not-so-brilliant Jame Gumb. Nevertheless, both characters are offshoots of not only the "real" Ed Gein but also *Psycho*'s quintessentially American Norman Bates, in whose figure the Nazi propensity for the fetishistic appropriation of human body parts becomes crystallized.

Resurrecting and Remaking Norman Bates in *Ed Gein*

Ed Gein (2000), also known as *In the Light of the Moon*, begins (and ends) with bleak documentary footage of the well-known killer's arrest in his hometown of Plainfield, Wisconsin.[19] The audience is primed to see why and how Ed Gein became the cannibalistic necrophiliac who created a "woman suit" and whose crimes provided the inspiration for Norman Bates in *Psycho*, Leatherface in *The Texas Chainsaw Massacre*, and Hannibal Lecter in *The Silence of the Lambs* and *Hannibal*. There is a forensic look to this film, which bears a certain resemblance to the look of "upmarket TV dramas, especially *Prime Suspect* whose first ever episode . . . dealt with a serial killer of prostitutes."[20]

Yet there are clear problems with taking *Ed Gein*'s claim of authenticity at face value. To explain the actions of Ed (Steve Railsback, who played Charles Manson in an earlier film, *Helter Skelter*), the movie resorts to creating the monster-behind-the-monster, popularized by Hitchcock's Psycho. Ed's mother, Augusta (Carrie Snodgress), with her misdirected and excessive religious zealotry, physical abuse, sexual repression, and "bedtime" stories of the more lurid sections of the book of Revelation from the Bible, emerges as the reason for Ed's psychopathology. There is evidence to support the view that many of Ed's complexes arose from his tangled relationship with his mother, but the film, in deflecting the responsibility of monstrosity from the abused son to the abusive mother, simply falls back on stock representations of the mother-as-devouring-and-poisonous-figure, yet another standard Gothic fixture. In one scene, Ed prays at his mother's grave, asking that she be returned to him; a raven suddenly hovers overhead in circles, breaking the stillness with its cries. Later, as Ed sets out to claim his first victim, Mary Hogan (Sally Champlin), a quick close-up of the raven implies that his mother's "ghost" (whether as a subjective delusion or an objective fact is immaterial in this characteristic blend of horror and psychological thriller) is present and urging him on to commit the crime. Unfortunately, this way of framing the story can be traced to the all too familiar Hitchcockian rendition of Robert Bloch's novelistic depiction of Gein's life, in which the "monstrous mother," a product of pop psychology and Gothic cinematic representations, constitutes the compulsive urge in Gein to commit the heinous acts that have granted him a certain mythic status.

Repeatedly, the movie alludes to Hitchcock's *Psycho*. When Ed reenters the general store to murder Collette Marshall (Carol Mansell), the camera is at an extreme high angle, pointing down at the dwarfed characters as if from the point of view of a bird of prey; this is a signature Hitchcockian move. The resemblance of Gein to Anthony Perkins's Norman Bates has been noted by film reviewers. For example, Carl Cortez remarked in 2001, "Steve Railsback stars as Gein and plays him as a maniacal little simpleton. In fact, Railsback seems to be resurrecting the ghost of Anthony Perkins (via Norman Bates) in this performance, but missing the humanity Perkins brought to his famous *Psycho* role."[21] Later, when Ed has been arrested and is committed to an asylum, the Hitchcockian flourishes are all over the place: the camera zooms into a close-up, with the shadows of the outline of a window in low-key lighting at Ed's back, often signifying entrapment in the Hitchcockian universe. Like Hitchcock's Norman, Ed is revealed through his monologues, shot in close-up or medium close-up, as a character steeped in self-delusion and madness, in contrast with his quiet and self-effacing veneer. The ending inserts the same documentary footage of Ed being arrested but this time zooms into the interior of the car where Ed sits, a diminutive figure who tries to cover his face with his gloved hands. The juxtaposition of the documentary footage once again is supposed to bolster the authenticity of the look we have at Ed Gein—but the style of the montage sequences built around the embedded documentary bear such a striking resemblance to *Psycho* that it is difficult not to collapse Hitchcock's Norman into Chuck Parello's Ed.

As the closing credits begin, Ed utters a prayer while he lights a match and asks that "this evil spirit [be stopped] from invading [his] body"; subsequently, he is shown from a high angle shot in low-key lighting, exhuming his mother's body. In close-up, he fiercely enunciates his mother's views concerning whores; then placidly he calls the mental institution that houses him a "good place" where people treat him "nice"[ly]—only to grin and say that one drawback to the place is that there are some people who are "really screwed up." The closing sequence ends with a black background and the matter-of-fact statement that Ed Gein died at the asylum and was eventually buried beside his mother and brother. Yet the last image we see is of Ed, tearfully and vehemently proclaiming his mother "a saint"; this portrait is not altogether different from Hitchcock's wild-eyed and tight-lipped Norman, whose thoughts, revealed through a voice-over, are those of his "mother" deciding to be "silent" just in case anyone is watching. Gein's mother, as played by Snodgress, is a tall and thin woman with a low, husky voice who repeatedly calls Ed "boy"—once again a derivation from *Psycho* rather than from "real life," because Gein's mother was obese (which explains why the women Ed killed were large—a fact that *The Silence of the Lambs* more accurately details in its graphic depiction of "Buffalo Bill"'s skinned victims).

The second feature film that *Ed Gein* references repeatedly in its gothically styled "true" rendition of Gein's portrait is Jonathan Demme's *The Silence of the Lambs*. When Brian Hillman (Frank Worden) descends into the darkness of Ed's basement to find Collette Marshall's nude body hanging upside down from the ceiling (once again, reminiscent of Nazi torture), gutted like a deer, the scene is shot like Clarice Starling's penetration of Jame Gumb's (Ted Levine) basement. In both, the subjective point of view is used, and the camera pans over the details of contents of the underground, bringing to light its obscene contents. Later, as Sheriff Jim Stilwell (Pat Skipper) sits, dumbfounded at the discovery that the quiet man who used to babysit his young boys finds lurid descriptions of Nazi war crimes entertainment, the scene is shot in a manner reminiscent of the ending of *The Silence of the Lambs*. A fast-paced montage, transitioning in keeping with the flashing of cameras taking shots (similar to the ending of *The Silence*, after Clarice has shot Gumb and the contents of his basement are being documented), reveals the numerous items in Ed's house of horror: a heart steeped in blood in a skillet on the stove, various body parts floating in a bottled solution, the "woman suit" and the belt of human nipples resting on a mannequin. The purportedly real portrait is obscured by prior renditions, resulting in the "real" Ed emerging as a caricature. The result, as one critic notes, is that "the original cannibal now seems like a pale imitation."[22]

Vampirism and Nazism in *The Addiction* (1995)

The cross-fertilization between Holocaust and horror themes (imbricated with vampirism and serial killing) is also vividly illustrated in Abel Ferrara's *The Addiction*. The gist of the plot is easily summarized: Kathleen Conklin (Lili Taylor), an NYU philosophy doctoral candidate, is the epitome of normality. While Conklin walks home one night, she is accosted, dragged off the street, and bitten by a strange woman. Kathleen soon finds herself subject to some new appetites: Her need for blood is like an addict's need for drugs, as she is vividly shown in one scene shooting up blood with a syringe. Yet the ultimate addiction is revealed to be humankind's propensity for violence.

The part of the movie that was most controversial and which garnered the most consistent critical objections is a beginning sequence in which the film employs the motif of the round-the-clock slide show featured by the Holocaust Museum in New York City to associate the face of contemporary radical evil (Nazism) with vampirism. At the outset, the movie's opening images show us horrific pictures of the massacres at My Lai and the Nazi death camps from Kathleen's point of view. The philosophy student then walks away, debating the effectiveness of convicting political leaders of war crimes that arguably are crimes of mass guilt, not of individual responsibility.

The film touts quotations from Sartre and Kierkegaard and debates about determinism and redemption through guilt. Ferrara regular Christopher Walken makes an appearance as a vampire who views himself as an avatar of Nietzschean metamorality. The film reinvents classical vampire mythology: thus vampires cannot bear to look at themselves in a mirror because their reflections expose the raw face of evil à la *The Picture of Dorian Gray*. They are undead precisely because evil cannot die and they are the incarnations of evil. The complexity of the conceptual framework sits uneasily alongside the film's attempt at a simultaneously gritty and elegant look with the use of black-and-white film (a technique also characteristic of *Schindler's List*). In the background we hear funky rap music and witness the all too familiar street action of Greenwich Village.

Despite the praise heaped on Taylor's performance, the film's "Holocaust as horror" theme was generally panned. Dennis Schwartz bewails the comparison: "the film's credibility suffers from such an unjust comparison. In case Ferrara forgot, vampires are not real but the Holocaust was only too real."[23] Walter Addiego of *The Examiner* writes, "Ferrara and writer Nicholas St. John try to draw an analogy between vampirism and what they call mankind's ultimate addiction to evil (we're shown photographs of Dachau). The vampire's high is to dominate a victim completely. But these grim reflections don't mesh too well with the narrative."[24] Hal Hinson praises Ferrara's serious and passionate critique of contemporary evil but criticizes the insertion of a scene: "However, when [Ferrara] flashes images of historic atrocities of both the distant and recent past—Nazi death camps, the war dead in Bosnia—his ideas come across as shallow and banal. Also, the insertion of scenes of real-life horror into what is essentially a glorified genre exercise may strike some as the essence of bad taste."[25]

Nevertheless, the film is haunted by the same tensions or fluctuations between humor and horror characteristic of some representations of the Holocaust. As Desson Howe of the *Washington Post* notes, when Conklin, newly reborn as a vampire, visits her philosophy professor (Paul Calderon), "there's an unmistakable chuckle to be had—as in: Guess what I changed into!" During dinner, she spouts foreboding opinions; declaring the restaurant music depressing, the teacher confesses, "It hasn't been the most enjoyable evening, you know?" Despite the artistic spottiness of this film, it does render overt the cross-fertilization between Holocaust and horror themes and formal properties, particularly in its adoption of black-and-white footage.

Neo-Nazism and Shower Scenes in *American History X*

At an initial reading, the inclusion of *American History X* (1998) among American films of the 1990s relevant to the conjunction between horror and the Holocaust seems absurd. The topic is now neo-Nazism rather than its German World War II variety; and no overt horror techniques are used. Yet the movie drives home a crucial point: that neo-Nazism, an offspring of the Holocaust, is alive and well in America. The reincarnation of World War II's monster, once thought staked safely to death, bears the visage of white America's angry youth, embodied in Derek Vineyard (Edward Norton), a former high school English honors student, whose conversion to neo-Nazism is catalyzed by personal tragedy and the hypnotic influence of neo-Nazi guru

Cameron Alexander (Stacy Keach). The film, scripted by David McKenna and directed by Tony Kaye, in another docudramatic maneuver, uses black and white to uncover or document the events of the recent past and color to show the twenty-four-hour period after Derek is released from prison. Ebert, despite reservations, praises the gritty cinematography of the film, which grounds the setting of the narrative squarely in contemporary America: "In the immediacy of its moments, in the photography (by Kaye) that makes Venice look like a training ground for the apocalypse, and in the strength of the performances, 'American History X' is a well made film."[26]

Nevertheless, Janet Maslin's summary of salient points in the marketing of *American History X* strike at the essential core of the appeal of this film: "Advertisements for the controversy magnet that is 'American History X' seem to be selling Edward Norton's buff physique, savage scowl and swastika tattoo in equal measure. So they reflect the film's bold but reckless synthesis of visual enticement and rhetorical fever."[27] Despite the rhetorical attempt to establish Norton's heterosexual masculinity, as evidenced in the drawn-out sexual tryst with Fairuza Balk, who plays his racist sweetie, it is clear that Norton's rippling body is the sexual object; the prison sequences, with their displays of rivaling and raced masculinities, brim with homoerotic tensions. Such themes are relevant to the popular conjunction of Nazism with sexual perversions—a theme also explored in another film we later examine in greater detail, *Apt Pupil*. Most relevant is Derek's renunciation of his neo-Nazi convictions, a result of a brutal rape by white supremacist prison inmates. The scene bears the hallmarks of the equation of shower scenes with sexualized violence, arguably a testimony to the enduring cultural trauma evoked by *Psycho's* shower scene. This scene, shot in black and white, is depicted in graphic slow motion and formally parallels, with its tight close-ups, an earlier scene that results in Derek's prison stint: his violent unmanning and murder of two African American youths who try to steal his car.

This survey sketches the relationship between Holocaust films and horror films. The results demonstrate patterns of representation in which the trauma of the Holocaust is depicted through the frames of horror. The classic horror frame, in which evil is located outside the borders of the United States and normalcy, identified the Nazi as the premier archetype and precipitator of horror. This frame is contested by one that is conflicted, which moves the monstrous and the horrific, along with Holocaust imagery, inside the fold of the normal. These frames of horror have been present since the middle of the twentieth century and remain with us in the twenty-first.

In the films we have discussed, the status of the Holocaust as a historical event was less important than its ability to yield frames and tropes of evil. The Holocaust as historical object moved from the periphery to the center of American consciousness and underwent a particularly American interpretation in the 1970s.[28] The screening of NBC's television drama *Holocaust* in 1978 prompted a much greater awareness of the genocide as a historical reality.[29] However, it was the last decade of the twentieth century in which the World War II genocide emerged as a cultural anchor in the United States. The Holocaust became a key issue in 1993, what some call the "Year of the Holocaust," with the opening of the Holocaust Museum in Washington, DC, and the debut of *Schindler's List*.[30] As a symptom of the increasing visibility of the Holocaust, Boyd Farrow hailed 1999 as "The Year of the Nazi," citing as many as thirty films being created, in both Europe and the United States, that intersect with a Second World War setting or a contemporary scene that has Nazi themes.[31]

In this late-twentieth-century return to the Holocaust in America, the Holocaust Museum and many American films attempted to achieve authenticity in representing the Holocaust. The contemporary cinematic template for the American representation of the Holocaust was and is *Schindler's List*, a movie that has provided many with the dominant history of the Shoah. As Gourevitch observed in a 1994 review, "*Schindler's List* has been treated less as a Hollywood movie than as a work of documentary history that will instruct audiences on the nature of good and evil."[32] To convey this instruction, *Schindler's List* drew from a preexisting tradition of narration that "explained" evil: the horror film. The instruction, based on the conventions established by makers of American horror films, favored one historical explanation of the Holocaust. We reexamine *Schindler's List* in the next chapter with the goal of demonstrating the genealogy and power of its classic horror frame.

Classic Horror in
Schindler's List

Schindler's List has simultaneously been praised as forging "a searingly illuminating portrait of the human heart, mankind at its most depraved and most noble"[1] and of being "a cartoon in which an Aryan superhero outwits the forces of evil while stereotyped Jews provide the local color."[2] David Denby gives it the accolade of being an epic "made in a style of austere realism—flat, angry and hardheaded—that is utterly unlike anything Spielberg has attempted before,"[3] while Leon Wieseltier lambastes it as "hale and self-regarding," robustly trumpeting a "complete absence of humility before its subject matter."[4] Of more serious import are claims, made by the Jerusalem correspondent of the *Times* of London, that survivors found the portrayal of Oscar Schindler "unrecognizable" and its story "nothing like what really occurred" and that not a single survivor was consulted in making the film.[5] Those who praise the movie do make legitimate points about its impact, and the movie's critics rightly point to its limitations.

We believe the movie's strengths and limitations are due to the frame Spielberg uses—one that requires critical scrutiny. Rothberg, in his book *Traumatic Realism*, suggests that "an understanding of the *Schindler's List* phenomenon necessitates the crossing of boundaries between media, genres, and disciplines" and that "the film also deserves a more textual analysis."[6] The boundaries we cross in search of a deeper textual analysis allow us to delve into the deep structure of *Schindler's List* as arguably one of the most influential popular cultural representations of the Holocaust. Our addition to the critical commentary about *Schindler's List* is to reveal how the movie assumes the principles of ideological intentionalism and uses the classic horror frame.

We believe Spielberg's choice to frame the story of *Schindler's List* with elements from horror films—specifically the subgenre of the psychological thriller—is a function of what LaCapra calls acting out "transference," or the "projection of various psychological agendas onto other texts."[7] These agendas involve the tendency to "repeat in one's own discourse or practice" processes active in traumatic historical events.[8] Critics can detect indicators of transference in the rhetorical artifacts of those who act out—or obsessively repeat, using a simplistic narrative of victimizers and victims—the trauma of the Holocaust. The most important implication of casting *Schindler's List* as a film that uses a classic horror frame in key scenes is that this approach unveils how *Schindler's List* enacts the ideological intentionalist Holocaust narrative, thereby embedding it deeply in the public consciousness.

In addition, there is a sense that the separation between Spielberg, the man, and *Schindler's List*, the film, is a porous one. Spielberg is, after all, the director-producer-screenwriter whose imagination has cast a visual vocabulary so distinctly "Spielbergian" such that "we understand what we're being told about a soda can when it arrives in a Spielberg spaceship; we get the joke when an approaching basketball star shakes the earth like a Spielberg dinosaur."[9] Spielberg, a producer-director of more than one-third of the thirty highest-grossing films of all time, also closely tied *Schindler's List* to his maturation and to the reclaiming of his Jewish identity.[10]

Indeed, many biographers tie Spielberg's growing awareness of his Jewish identity to teenage experiences of racist ostracism, such as the repeated incidents of his being pelted with pennies during study hall periods[11]; another repeated story involves the young Spielberg learning his numbers from a former Auschwitz prisoner, who used his identification tattoo to illustrate the "magic trick" of how a 6 could become a 9 by crooking his elbow.[12] In an interview, Spielberg deliberately framed his coming-of-age as a filmmaker with his creation of *Schindler's List*: "I had to grow into that. . . . It took me years before I was really ready to make *Schindler's List*."[13] Douglas Brode astutely notes how Schindler is essentially a continuation of Spielberg's autobiographical self-portraiture: "Like Spielberg, Schindler early on is interested only in escapism; like him, he learns to appease sharks in order to survive; like him, he views the Holocaust (Schindler firsthand; Spielberg as a visitor to the historical setting) and knows he must do something about it."[14]

In filming *Schindler's List*, Spielberg used the traditional conventions of the classic Hollywood horror film, turning to an intimately familiar narrative of good and evil, one in which he was well practiced. Film scholars have grouped Steven Spielberg with Brian De Palma, Wes Craven, Tobe Hooper, John McTiernan, and other directors of horror films.[15] Indeed, Spielberg's embrace of the horror genre began at an early age, when he cast one of his sisters in a science-fiction-horror film called *Firelight*.[16] In many ways, the narrative of *Schindler's List* functions like that of a classic horror film, particularly given its portrayal of the Nazi perpetrator and Jewish victim, its representation of suffering borrowed from sadomasochistic horror conventions.[17] This use of traditional horror techniques helps aestheticize the visual enjoyment of vulnerable and tortured female bodies and renders German Nazis as unproblematically and monstrously (understood in the etymological senses of *monere*, "to warn," and *monstrare*, "to demonstrate") other.[18]

The perpetrator-victim binary established in the movie is problematic: the status of the Nazis as perpetrators and the Jews as victims is not in question; rather, the issue hinges on the binary as a simplistic rendering of both the perpetrators and the victims. Key moments that illustrate this dynamic in Spielberg's movie are the shower scene at Auschwitz and the seduction-turned-torture of Helen Hirsch (Embeth Davidtz) by Amon Goeth (Ralph Fiennes).

Of course, other scenes illustrate the problems with Spielberg's use of Hollywood conventions in depicting events of the Holocaust. For example, the use of color to differentiate the movements of four-year-old Genia (Olivia Dąbrowska) from the chaos going on around her during the liquidation of the Kraków ghetto illustrates Spielberg's hallmark use of children as symbols of innocence and absolute good within the modes of fantasy and melodrama, as in his top-grossing *E.T.* The scene is shot subjectively—that is, from Schindler's and his mistress's point of view, as they look down from a hilltop. "Schindler thought that if a child such as she perished he would be the only witness to the crime, and he decided to assume the role [of witness] and also to save as many Jews as he could for the future."[19] Though Mila Page, one of the Schindler Jews, attests that the girl in the red coat did exist,[20] there is no evidence that Schindler's turning point occurred particularly during this period or that the murder of the little girl was what pushed him into accepting his role as the protector of "his" Jews.

Another scene in the film conflates two different events into one to enhance the dramatic action.[21] This scene, in which Schindler is presented with a birthday cake by his Jewish employees and their families, as represented by a child and a young woman, combines two historical incidents: the presentation by Niusia Karakulska (played by Agnieszka Makuszewska) of the birthday cake to Schindler when she was a child; and Schindler's passionate kissing of a young Jewish woman (played by Magdalena Dondurian) in celebration of the opening of his factory in Kraków. Schindler actually did spend a few days in the Gestapo prison at Pomorska Street as a result of the second incident, for having violated the prohibitions of the law of racial purity.[22] What is important is less the conflation of the two events (which is in itself problematic in a film that claims to be a historical document) than the reasoning behind the changes: "[Spielberg] needs a passionate kiss to enhance the dramatic action, but an actor should not kiss an underage girl on the mouth because the audience may perceive it as an act of molesting, which has complicated the reception of more than one American film."[23] Dramatic impact (correlated with sexual titillation) and audience appeal trump historical accuracy within a film that markets itself as a historical document. Thus, while several scenes are symptomatic of the issues we raise, the two we focus on—the Auschwitz-Birkenau shower scene and Goeth's seduction-torture of the sweating Helen, who has the "shower victim" look—best illustrate the formal properties of the horror–psychological thriller conventions we illuminate to problematize the politics of spectatorship that is naturalized as a "documentary look." Both scenes emphasize the imagery of the peephole and the shower as principal motifs of the Gothicizing of the Holocaust as horror.

These two scenes were not part of Steven Zaillian's original screenplay[24] and therefore must have been due to Steven Spielberg's reworking or, at least, endorsement. The scenes are at the narrative center of the film and have earned much critical attention.[25] Before we consider them, we review Spielberg's stated goal of capturing an authentic depiction of the Shoah and return to the narrative techniques set up by *Psycho*.

There is a significant convergence, in both the use of film technique and the hinting at thematic elements, between the famous shower scene in Alfred Hitchcock's psychological thriller *Psycho* and the above-mentioned scenes in *Schindler's List*. An analysis of these scenes allows us to reflect on how "visualizing the unvisualizable" eventually falls back on a recall of familiar images cemented in public memory by the force of popular culture and conventions of classic Hollywood cinema. Some do argue that Hitchcock directly influenced Spielberg.[26]

To fill in the imaginative blanks for creating these scenes, Spielberg did not replicate exactly the techniques Hitchcock used in *Psycho*. What occurs is a rough recall or pseudomiming of *Psycho*'s cinematic techniques. *Schindler's List* reverses *Psycho*'s blurring of the lines that separate the sane from the mad, the safe from the dangerous, the same from the other or the monstrous. The Amon Goeth character becomes the synecdoche of Nazism and evil (fig. 3.1). He is a monster, breaching in his behavior "the norms of ontological propriety."[27] The portrayal of his evil as innate leaves viewers with a deep sense of revulsion. When the Amon Goeth character is paired with the shower scene, we see that *Schindler's List* draws significant elements from the horror film tradition, one of which ends up both miming and reversing the cinematic patterns in *Psycho* and thus reverts to the classic rather than the conflicted frame of horror.

Fig. 3.1. Amon Goeth, the synecdoche of Nazism. Still from *Schindler's List* courtesy of the Academy of Motion Picture Arts and Sciences. Amblin/Universal, 1993.

As we saw in chapter 2, Hitchcock's *Psycho* established key cinematic patterns of depicting contemporary horror, effectively establishing a template that located evil in the real and ordinary—a representation mimicked in *Schindler's List*. In attempting to work through the Holocaust, Spielberg and his crew made it clear that authenticity, and not simply verisimilitude, was the goal. Spielberg declared to his cast that "we're not making a film, we're making a document."[28] It is a document that Spielberg intended to scare the audience. Spielberg's own remarks, as he staged the scene in which German soldiers used stethoscopes to hunt down Jews hiding in crevices, reveal this conscious manipulation: "The composition comes together quickly, and it's characteristically beautiful: One guy is up on a ladder and two others stand below him, making a dark pyramid framed by shadows and backlit by streetlights shining through lace curtains. Never mind that it's a gorgeous composition of Nazis about to murder Jews. 'Ooh, nice,' Spielberg says. 'That's scary. That's scary.'"[29] The choices Spielberg and others made in rendering the film "authentic" are revealed in its color, costumes, and depiction of mass murder—choices that echo those made by directors of horror films.

The bulk of the film was shot in black and white, the "colors of reality" for Spielberg.[30] As Lisa Grunwald notes, the actual lens Spielberg chose for *Schindler's List* was attached to a camera that shot black-and-white film.[31] According to Spielberg, "Shooting in black-and-white gives everything a sloppy urgency . . . which is what real life is."[32] Anna Sheppard, who was in charge of preparing seventeen thousand costumes, was able to rent one thousand striped prisoners' uniforms in Poland, but she had to dye them gray to make them credibly filthy. She explains: "I ruined what I rented, but it was unavoidable. . . . Spielberg wants his film to have as close to a documentary look as possible."[33] (Nevertheless, in an interesting and contradictory aside, one production history tale recounts how Spielberg lost his temper with the "costume woman" because he had wanted a "Darth Vader effect" for the *Aktion*, the slaughter that cleaned out the last refugees hiding in attics and closets of the ghetto; she had bought "dull, pea-soup green coats" when he had wanted "thick, splatter-proof silver gray coats."[34])

In addition to color and costume, the conventions of the horror genre influenced the choices made in depicting genocide in the concentration camps. The "peephole" and the famous shower scenes in *Schindler's List* illuminate the ideological intentionalist assumptions of *Schindler's List* as they are visualized through these conventions. The movie is at least three times removed from traditional documentaries: first, the film is based on a book that the author labeled a fictionalized account; second, Spielberg took liberties in moving the book into film; and third, some of the scenes in the movie are not found in the book. Regardless, the manipulation of the audience's gaze and their experience of terror is best illustrated by the shower scenes in both *Schindler's List* and *Psycho*.

The Gaze and Terror in Shower Scenes

Both *Psycho* and *Schindler's List* use peepholes as prisms through which the audience witnesses murder. In *Psycho* the peephole is porous; Hitchcock's camera includes shots of the viewer-voyeur (who is himself a victim; fig. 3.2) and the victim (who had earlier preyed on an unsuspecting but loathfully boastful man, Cassidy [fig. 3.3], the "overgrown child who has not mastered—or cared to master—the rules of middle-class social intercourse"[35]).

In contrast, the camera in *Schindler's List* does not consider the role of the viewer-voyeur or the complexities of the victim-victimizer relationship. Instead, it enters the gas chambers through the peephole, using soft-core pornographic effects to visualize the terror of naked women. That the peepholes in both movies are used in such different manners reveals much about their directors' views of how evil is best represented. Hitchcock's camera captures the literal gaze of Norman Bates as his eyeball fills the screen. The peephole refracts the vision to conflate the audience and Bates. In *Schindler's List*, the audience is separated from the women by the peephole and is not acknowledged as a direct participant; it masquerades as a "neutral" or documentary gaze.

Hitchcock himself actively dissected the politics of the gaze in *Psycho*. At the beginning of Truffaut's interview about that film, Hitchcock commented that the long zoom opening into a dark window, which establishes the locale as "Phoenix, 2:43 PM," penetrates that dark space, to reveal Marion (Janet Leigh) and Sam (John Gavin) as erotically involved and thus allows the viewer to become a "Peeping Tom."[36] Later, with Norman Bates, Hitchcock explicitly implicates the viewer in voyeuristic gaze and murder. Robin Wood notes, "Much of the film's visual significance is summed up in a single visual metaphor . . . making use again of the eyes. . . . It is as if we have emerged from the depths behind the eye, the round hole of the drain leading down into an apparently bottomless darkness, the potentialities for horror that lie in the depths of us all."[37] *Psycho's* visual metaphor of the eye captures the complexity of its view of evil and horror; the movie invites a study of the viewer as well as the victim. In contrast, as we shall show, there is no such reflexiveness in *Schindler's List*.

Fig. 3.2. Norman Bates as voyeur and victim. Still from *Psycho* courtesy of the Academy of Motion Picture Arts and Sciences. Shamley Productions, 1960.

Fig. 3.3. Marion as victim-predator tempted by Cassidy, the loathfully boastful man. Still from *Psycho* courtesy of the Academy of Motion Picture Arts and Sciences. Shamley Productions, 1960.

Janet Leigh renders clear the narrative significance of the shower scene in the archetype of contemporary horror that proved to be the progenitor of many later slasher films. "Hitch was very clear about what he wanted from me. . . . The shower was a baptism, a taking away of the torment from [the character's] mind. Marion became a virgin again. He wanted the audience to feel her peacefulness, her kind of rebirth, so the moment of intrusion is even more shocking."[38] This moment of intrusion culminates in Marion's death, which is startling in juxtaposition with the shower scene in *Schindler's List*. Spielberg, while employing similar cinematic tactics, reverses the narrative, indulging in the murderous propensities of the voyeuristic gaze and yet withdrawing from it at the last moment, replacing a moment of confrontation with one of survival and ultimate redemption, as the women, unlike Marion, do not die in the showers.

Psycho's shower scene was viewed by Hitchcock and his associates as pivotal, and elaborate preparations were made to use black-and-white film to imbue the scene with a sense of realism and immediacy while simultaneously using extreme backlighting to conceal the killer's face (fig. 3.4). The choice of the victim and the use of camera angles to narrate the story were also critical to the composition of the movie. An inside look behind the scenes of *Psycho* reveals the ever-pervasive and relentless presence of the camera. "The storyboards detailed all the angles," Leigh remembers, "so that I knew the camera would be there, then there. The camera was at different places all the time."[39] Strikingly, one production history anecdote eerily prefigures the gendered aesthetics of the shower victim replicated in *Schindler's List*, which similarly features a smorgasbord of naked young, thin, and attractive female bodies.

> When [Janet Leigh (Marion Crane in *Psycho*)] confronted Joseph Stefano, the author of the film's screenplay, with a statement published in an earlier book to the effect that Hitchcock had wanted a "much bigger" actress for the part . . . , Mr. Stefano told Ms. Leigh that he and Hitchcock had been discussing "body size, not name value." Mr. Stefano continued: "I believed if Marion was a large person, we would lose her vulnerability; she *wouldn't be as effective as a victim* [italics ours]. You do have to watch how you phrase your remarks, don't you."[40]

Hitchcock and Stefano understood that the use of diminutive and attractive victims is essential in maintaining an audience's gaze through a peephole.

Fig. 3.4. Murder in black and white. Still from *Psycho* courtesy of the Academy of Motion Picture Arts and Sciences.
Shamley Productions, 1960.

Embeth Davidtz, who played Helen Hirsch, an attractive Jewish woman
who is the object of Amon Goeth's desire and cruelty in *Schindler's List*, reflected on a parallel experience of nudity before the camera. Nude, her head
shaved, she was in one of the scenes in which naked bodies teem, reduced to
livestock. "It's not like a love scene where you disrobe and there's something
in the moment. Here I'm standing there like a plucked chicken, nothing but
skin and bone. That is to say, stripped of human dignity."[41] While there are
some differences in the contextual construction of the two scenes (Leigh
refused to do the scene nude, and so a moleskin suit was sculpted to cover her
breasts and the essentials),[42] Kevin Gough-Yates brilliantly points out that
the aesthetic of *Psycho*'s shower scene evokes images of the prototypical victim
of the Holocaust gas chamber. "When [Marion] is savagely murdered in the
shower, her hair has become flattened by the water and she looks as though
her head has been shaved. The shower sequence relates to the whole social
guilt of mass murder and the propensity to pretend it does not exist."[43]

Robin Wood, along a parallel track, argues that *Psycho's* ability to shock derives from its groundedness in an awareness of sex shaped by the discoveries of Freudian psychoanalysis and the horror of the Nazi death camps. In addition, he notes that Hitchcock himself accepted a commission to create a compilation film of captured Nazi materials from such camps.[44] In 1945, camera crews went with the American, Russian, and British armies into the Nazis' death camps and filmed the horrors they discovered. A group of directors, including Alfred Hitchcock, developed a script for a movie, initially titled *F3080*. Forty-eight years later, after myriad holdups and bureaucratic delays, the footage was released from the vault of the Imperial War Museum in London under the title *Memory of the Camps*.[45] It makes no attempt to censor the events that took place in the camps. The narration also makes clear that the German officers at the camps knew what their actions led to and that they should be held accountable. Although the film was not completed in the 1940s, the edited footage was bought by PBS's *Frontline* in 1985. Trevor Howard read the original transcript for the narration. The film first aired May 7, 1985, to mark the fortieth anniversary of the liberation of the Nazi death camps. Some of the camps featured in the film include Dachau, Auschwitz, and Buchenwald.[46] Thus Hitchcock was not unfamiliar with the "look" of the Holocaust victim and was all too aware of the atrocities of the Holocaust.[47] His experience with that project may have influenced the shower scene aesthetic of the victim in *Psycho*.

One of the mythic stories about the production of *Psycho's* shower scene involves the construction of a low-angle shot of a showerhead spurting water. Rebello provides the essential narrative details.

> [Hitchcock] insisted upon a shot showing water pulsing out of the shower head straight toward the camera. Schlom recalls that everyone involved wondered the same thing: "If we shoot right at it, how are we going to keep the lens dry?" Hitchcock came up with a solution: "Use a long lens," he said, "and block off the inner holes on the shower head so they won't spout water." The long lens allowed the cameraman to stand farther back from the showerhead. Though the water appeared to hit the lens, it actually sprayed past it. "The guys on the sides [of the set] got a little soaked," says Schlom, "but we got the shot."[48]

A breakdown of the formal properties of this part of *Psycho's* famous shower scene could be cataloged as follows: (1) In a low-angle shot, the showerhead sprays toward the camera in close-up. (2) Water sprays on Marion's head as she lathers soap onto her face in a frontal medium close-up. (3) Marion lathers her arms and turns around in a profile medium close-up shot. (4) There is a match cut on Marion, as she lathers her neck and shoulders in a frontal medium close-up while she turns. (5) In a profile medium close-up shot, the showerhead sprays toward the right side of the frame. (6) Marion tilts back her head as water saturates her in another profile medium close-up shot. Like *Schindler's List*'s shower scene, *Psycho*'s shower scene appears to teem with frenetic activity when very little action actually occurs. As Rebello recounts, "'After all,' says graphic designer Bass, 'all that happens was that a woman takes a shower, gets hits and slowly slides down the tub. Instead, [we filmed] a repetitive series of motions: She's taking-a-shower, taking-a-shower, taking-a-shower. She's hit-hit-hit-hit-hit. She slides-slides-slides. She's hit-hit-hit-hit. She slides-slides-slides. The movement was very narrow and the amount of activity to get you there was very intense.'"[49]

The formal dynamics of the violent and erotic killing of Marion may be detailed, in a slightly truncated way, in the following manner: (1) In a profile medium close-up shot, the showerhead sprays toward the right side of the frame. (2) Another profile medium close-up shows Marion tilting her head back as water saturates her. (3) A medium close-up shot from the opposite side of Marion within the shower, with the curtain and tile in the background, signals the entrance of an intruder. (4) The camera is now on the other side of the 180-degree line, signifying another viewpoint. Marion is in the foreground, frame right. We glimpse, through the opaque curtain in the background, the bathroom wall and door. We see the door open from a privileged position, but the sound of the shower conceals the noise of the door from the unsuspecting Marion. The figure enters slowly from the left side of the frame. The camera zooms and pans in on the left portion of the frame, leaving only the mysterious figure in frame left. This figure approaches the shower and pulls the curtain open to frame right. The figure holds the knife high. (5) At a frontal medium close-up angle, a reaction shot shows Marion as she turns, sees the figure, and begins to scream. (6) In a tighter close-up shot, which enhances the feeling of her entrapment, Marion continues to scream. (7) An extreme close-up creates an even tighter choke shot of Marion's mouth. (8) There occurs a medium close-up shot from a low angle on the killer from within the shower. In the foreground, water sprays across the frame. In mid ground, the back lighting reveals only the silhouette of the killer as "she" lifts up the knife. (9) There is a continuity cut on the stabbing knife. In a medium close-up, Marion is shown in mid ground; the knife enters the frame from the right top section and leaves the frame from the bottom middle. (10) In a reverse medium close-up, the killer draws back a knife and again stabs (always backlit). (11) Marion's face is shot in a close-up as she screams and turns to the left, out of the frame. (12) There is a high-angle shot of Marion on the right side of the frame, in medium close-up. The knife stabs in the left side of the frame, and she grasps at the killer's arm. (13) An extreme close-up shows Marion's anguished face in profile. (14) A frontal medium close-up shot of Marion's waist shows her abdomen; the knife enters the top right of the frame in profile and moves downward, nearly touching Marion's abdomen (fig. 3.5). (15) Marion's head is framed diagonally, in a frontal close-up. (16) There is a low-angle shot of the shower sprinkle in the foreground and the corner of the ceiling in the background. The killer's arm, with the hand holding the knife, enters at the top right of the frame and moves downward in a close-up. (17) A medium close-up shows Marion in profile from the waist to the shoulders as the knife enters the frame. (18) In a frontal close-up, Marion's head turns to the left and her arm reaches up, out of the frame. (19) There is a high-angle shot of Marion's feet and the floor of the shower. Blood drips on the floor and runs toward the drain. (20) Marion's head fills the bottom right portion of the frame, and her hand fills the bottom left in medium close-up. She leans against the wall with her back turned to the camera but with her head in profile. She turns to be in a frontal medium close-up. The camera tilts on her as she slinks down the tile wall and stops frozen at the bottom of the tiled wall and the top of the tub. Her hand rises into the bottom middle of the frame and reaches nearly to the camera as the camera recoils, dollying back. (21) There is a continuity cut on Marion's hand, shot in close-up, as she grabs at the shower curtain at frame left. (22) An extreme high-angle shot on the curtain rod (composed diagonally across the frame) shows Marion in the top left of the frame, grabbing at the curtain. (23) In a close-up shot of the shower rod, its curtain rings break, one by one, under Marion's weight. (24) A low-angle shot at floor level, with the toilet in the background, shows Marion's hand descending into the frame and hanging toward the floor; her head falls to the floor. (25) There is a low-angle shot on the showerhead as it sprays toward the camera in a frontal close-up. (26) A medium close-up shows Marion's feet and lower legs within the shower; the blood runs under her legs. The camera pulls out and pans the shower floor to reveal blood running in a vortex down the drain; the camera zooms in on the drain. (27) A match dissolve on Marion's eye is shot in extreme close-up. The camera pulls back and turns slowly. The rotation stops as the camera continues to pull out, revealing Marion's face on the floor, shot in close-up. (28) In a close-up, the shower head is shown in profile.

The detailed description of *Psycho's* shower scene, which is shot in black and white and thus participates in the "look of the real," enables us to catalog and confront the formal construction of this gaze. The discomfort that the cataloging produces not only could constitute a rupture with the naturalizing function that narrative cinematic conventions cement but also could further a rupture in an examination of ethical questions about depictions of eroticized violence, which appear to be symptomatic of fictional filmic depictions of the Holocaust.

Sara Horowitz remarks that the aesthetics of *Schindler's List's* shower scene simulates the camera technique used and the mood conveyed in the shower scene at a Nazi brothel in Zybneck Brynuch's *The Fifth Horseman Is Fear*.

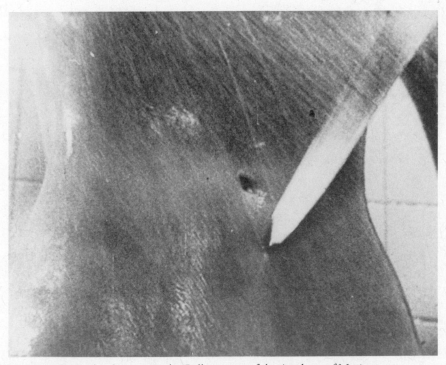

Fig. 3.5. Eroticized violence in *Psycho*. Still courtesy of the Academy of Motion Picture Arts and Sciences. Shamley Productions, 1960.

In Brynuch's shower scene, a group of Jewish women prepare themselves to "service" soldiers in a Nazi brothel where the film's male protagonist comes to find his sister. The camera lingers on the faces and bodies of the women. Slow, fluid, and softly lit, the scene is markedly different from the rest of the film in mood, tone and lighting. Moreover, its depiction is superfluous to the development of the film's plot. Indeed, after the film's completion, the shower scene was inserted at the insistence of the producer Carlo Ponti, in hopes of making the film more marketable.[50]

Thus both the contents of the scene and the circumstances of its production reveal it as yet another instance of the eroticization of the female Holocaust victim.

Gary Weissman echoes similar observations regarding the alternation of scenes of violence with portrayals of women as beautiful objects. In relation to the shower scene just described, he writes,

> This sequence treats the viewers' uncertainty as to whether or not these women will be gassed as part of an extended drama involving two kinds of voyeurism, or pleasure taken in illicit seeing. One concerns sex, the other atrocity; both raise the question of how much will be shown. Helen provides the answer to one of these questions in a shot which shows the women in the undressing room at Auschwitz-Birkenau. Centered on screen and dramatically lit, she stands out while the other women frame her. Whereas these other women, half-hidden in shadow, slowly remove their dresses and long undergarments, Helen pulls her dress and slip over her head in one smooth, continuous motion, revealing a three-quarter view of her naked body. The erotic image is so inconsistent with the narrative that viewers may disregard what they see. Why is this image in the film?[51]

In *Schindler's List*'s shower scene, the freneticism characteristic of the latter part of *Psycho*'s shower scene is conveyed by the camera's rapid cuts and tracking shots as it follows the women into the showers' darkened interior; yet as they stare at the showerheads, the camera pace appears to slow down and the mood intensifies, heightening an atmosphere of tense anticipation (fig. 3.6).

Reminiscent of *Psycho*, the Auschwitz-Birkenau shower scene in *Schindler's List* details the shaving, disrobing, and frightened huddling together of mostly

Fig. 3.6. The Schindler women staring at the showerheads in fearful anticipation. Still from *Schindler's List* courtesy of the Academy of Motion Picture Arts and Sciences. Amblin/Universal, 1993.

young women, seen through a round glass opening that resembles a peephole. These shots, which culminate in scenes of water pouring out of the shower heads, resemble the frames characteristic of Hitchcock's *Psycho*, in which Norman Bates, whose gaze alternates with that of the audience's, voyeuristically enjoys the sight of his victim's undressing and nude indulgence in the pleasures of a shower.

In the creation of some of his images, Spielberg may have been influenced by several sources, which Ian Freer catalogs: *The Diary of Anne Frank* (1959); *Judgment at Nuremberg* (1961); *The Pawnbroker* (1965); *Sophie's Choice* (1982); and *Shoah* (1985).[52] Publicly, Spielberg and Janusz Kaminski, his cinematographer, have acknowledged three cinematic influences on *Schindler's List* and one photographic one: Stanley Kubrick's *Dr. Strangelove*, which featured handheld camerawork during the shoot-out at the Burpelson Air Force Base; Greg Toland's photography in John Ford's *Grapes of Wrath*, which Kaminski studied extensively; the Polish film *The Passenger*, which Kaminski screened before they left for Poland; and most important, Roman Vishniak's photography of East European Jewish settlements between 1920 and 1939, which became Kaminski's "bible."[53] Nowhere is "Hitchcock" even whispered in any of Spielberg's or Kaminski's public pronouncements. Yet the signature Hitchcockian shower scene aesthetic, with its expectations of violence and vulnerability, is writ large in *Schindler's List*'s shower scene. As Brode remarks, "Spielberg effectively employs his *Psycho*-inspired manipulation of the audience's ongoing fear of showers, acceptable enough in the middle of an escapist film, perhaps less so when the material is of such a highly serious nature."[54]

Noting a similar pattern in *Schindler's List*, Omer Bartov writes, "It seems that Spielberg, possibly unconsciously, catered to Hollywood's tradition of providing sexual distraction to the viewers. Most troubling of all, of course, is the shower scene, since that mass of attractive, frightened, naked women, finally relieved from their anxiety by jets of water rather than gas, would be more appropriate to a soft-porn sadomasochistic film than its context."[55] The shower scenes in both *Psycho* and *Schindler's List* provide sexual distraction for an audience expecting to witness a murder.

Stephen Pizzello recounts in detail how Spielberg and his associates, cinematographer Kaminski and production designer Allan Starski, conceived of the sequence in which the Schindler women workers are led through the showers at Auschwitz as "one of the most important moments in the film."[56]

> In lighting the scene, Kaminski and Spielberg heightened the terror by using techniques that would make a viewer a *participant* [italics ours] in the scene. "When I read the scene in the script, I wanted to make it gritty and realistic; I didn't mind if I got some grain or some flares in the lens," says Kaminski. "Once we were in the set, I decided to put a bunch of practical lights inside the room and not introduce any other light. Steven really liked the idea, but he added a suggestion. He thought we should rig the lights on dimmers. That way, once the women entered the room, we could turn the lights off. There would be darkness for a few seconds, and then we would introduce a very strong spotlight, aimed directly at the camera, that would outline the women. It was a very stylized idea, but when we rehearsed it, we realized that it was an extremely intimidating, horrifying way of telling the audience that these people might die."[57]

This moment, captured in figure 3.7, asks us whose point of view the camera invites us to share and what type of spectatorial participation is being encouraged, particularly during the long sequence in which the women, huddling, weeping, and utterly vulnerable in their nakedness, are followed into the inner recesses of the shower interior. An analysis of the formal elements of this scene yields the following details: (1) Guards stand in the anteroom and close the shower doors in a long shot. Side lighting from the left partially illuminates the scene. (2) The sound of slamming doors motivates a cut, but its abruptness is smoothed out by a graphic match on the shutting doors in a medium close-up. (3) Then a guard fills the left frame as the camera dollies into the peephole on one of the shower doors and peers through it at the prisoners inside the shower. (4) A medium long shot from a high angle looks down on the prisoners in the shower. The row of ceiling lights goes out as prisoners scream. (5) A fade-in via spotlights in the background reveals a handheld close-up shot of a woman who is petrified; side lighting comes from the left. (6) There is another close-up handheld shot of a young girl crying in the middle of the frame; a woman on the left has her hands on the girl's face. Side lighting again persists from the left. (7) Another close-up handheld shot shows women holding one another; side lighting from the

Fig. 3.7. Stylizing genocide. Still from *Schindler's List* courtesy of the Academy of Motion Picture Arts and Sciences. Amblin/Universal, 1993.

left persists. A pan reveals a frightened woman with her hand to her mouth. (8) There is a handheld medium shot of a group of women in mid ground; heavy back lighting from two spotlights creates silhouette composition.[58] The camera takes no shot–reverse shots, which would have allowed a potential equalization of perspectives. The choice to avoid shot–reverse shots renders relatively invisible that the only point of view is through the eyes of an SS officer while seemingly presenting a purely objective account.[59] The women in the gas chamber are framed, through the use of a peephole, in an oval structure reminiscent of Jacques-Louis David's Romantic paintings of nude odalisques, whose exposed flesh is heightened in their whiteness as objects of forbidden desire. *Schindler's List* privileges the documentary-style gaze of the camera to the position of apparently neutral witness (over the perspective of the hysterical female victims).

Spielberg, in *Schindler's List*, assembles this series of shots in a manner that appears to reverse the order of the shower scene shots in *Psycho* rather than directly replicate that sequence. Nevertheless, even this time, the camera hovers at the side, rather than directly below, the showerhead, still maintaining the position of the voyeur. An analysis of the relevant formal properties of this parallel scene from *Schindler's List* could be cataloged as follows: (1) There is a handheld shot of a group of four women standing in the foreground, who look up at showerheads in medium close-up. (2) Two women are better lit: one holds her hands over her mouth and looks down; the other woman holds her hand over her mouth and looks up. (3) A low-angle shot of the ceiling shows the tops of women's heads filling the bottom of the frame in a long shot. There is use of back lighting and silhouette. (4) The camera tilts up to show ambiguous outlines of fixtures and conduit. (5) Then the camera tilts back down to show the reaction of the women looking up in a close-up shot. (6) The camera then pans to reveal more women looking up; side lighting is used to illuminate the faces. (7) As in *Psycho*, there is a high-angle shot: women are in the middle bottom of the frame, while the showerheads fill the top of the frame. The shot is backlit by spotlights. (8) The showers sequentially begin to sprinkle water, which intermingles with the backlighting. (9) There is a shot of a woman being sprayed with water from above; in a close-up, she holds up her hands to feel the water as though in disbelief; side lighting comes from the left. (10) In a high-angle medium close-up shot, women in another area are still in disbelief; side lighting persists from the left. (11) A medium close-up shot reveals another group being sprinkled by water; side lighting persists from the left. (12) A medium close-up shot shows hands receiving water from the top left of the frame. A woman in the center looks up to her hands; again, there is side lighting from the left. (13) Two medium close-up shots of women are juxtaposed. The woman in the left portion of the frame is sprayed with water and looks down at the floor, crying. The woman at the right side of the frame looks up, not yet having been sprayed; side lighting from the left persists. (14) In a close-up the first woman cries and uses her fingers to lift the dripping water to her mouth. Lighting comes from the top left. (15) A close-up shot from a high angle looks down on a showered woman looking up, then turning her head down, crying as she lifts her hands to her face. Lighting comes from the top left. The camera tilts as she reaches toward the shower. In a manner reminiscent of *Psycho*, the camera continues to tilt, revealing the showerhead. Ultimately, the scene ends with the women weeping and sighing with relief, underlining how the sequence is a reverse-*Psycho*, culminating in relief, pleasure, and life (fig. 3.8) rather than shock, terror, and death.

There are two additional ways in which *Schindler's List* reverses *Psycho*: First, *Psycho* makes vivid the fractured personality that drives Bates's psychopathology; he is both a dutiful son and a homicidal mother. Second, the

Fig. 3.8. *Schindler's List*'s reverse-*Psycho*. Still courtesy of the Academy of Motion Picture Arts and Sciences. Amblin/Universal, 1993.

Vera Miles character, who boldly enters the basement of the Bates house, is portrayed as valiant, unlike the compliant Helen Hirsch. The encounter between Goeth and Helen is suggestive of *Psycho*'s climax, when the viewer sees the mother in the severe light of a bulb in the basement. *Schindler's List* does not explain Goeth's sadism; the spectacle of the Holocaust trumps any attempt to understand his psychopathology. Hitchcock in *Psycho* challenges the innocence of the viewer, threatening the safe divide between the sane and the insane.[60]

In summary, Hitchcock and Spielberg use similar images to depict murder but diverge in the meaning they derive from their representations. Reflecting the tenets of ideological intentionalism, Spielberg seeks to separate the viewer from genocide, where Hitchcock makes the relationship between the viewer and murder transparent. In the next section, we see that a similar nonreflexive impulse guides Spielberg's portrayal of the stereotypic Nazi monster and Jewish seductress.

The Seductress and the Monster

David Mamet argues that *Schindler's List* transmogrifies Jewish suffering into "emotional pornography."[61] We believe that the film exploits suffering not only within the sphere of the emotional but also within a politics of representation in which documentary techniques hide visual cues that naturalize the pornographic delectation in human suffering and exonerate viewers from the guilt of the pornographic gaze by creating the image of the Nazi as monstrous. As Arthur and Joan Kleinmann remind us, "Watching and reading about suffering, especially suffering that exists somewhere else, has . . . become a form of entertainment. Images of trauma are part of our political economy. Papers are sold, television programs gain audience share, careers are advanced, jobs are created, and prizes are awarded through the appropriation of images of suffering."[62] The consumption of Helen Hirsch's erotically charged masochistic relationship with Amon Goeth is visually naturalized as inevitable by playing on two stereotypes: the German man as irrational, demented killing machine and the Jewish woman as irresistible, tabooed, and therefore even more intriguing seductress. Just as the Jewish woman is hyperfeminized as a vulnerable body (visualized in Helen Hirsch's wet nipples heaving against her clinging and semitransparent shirt), the German man is hypermasculinized as mad, unconstrained fleshly desire (Goeth's corpulence around his waist and his appetite for killing, eating, and sex), as illustrated in figure 3.9.

Fig. 3.9. The hypermasculinized monstrous German male. Still from *Schindler's List* courtesy of the Academy of Motion Picture Arts and Sciences. Amblin/Universal, 1993.

These characterizations render Helen and Amon illustrations of what Janice Rushing and Thomas Frentz would call "shadows of our cultural imaginations"—sites of primordial ambivalence to which we are drawn and from which we are repulsed because they represent parts of ourselves we would prefer to excise and disavow. Rushing and Frentz characterize the first type of shadow as the "inferior" or feminized one, represented by women, minorities, the body, and anything that deviates from rational ego consciousness.[63] This portrait fits the stereotype of the hyperfeminized victim profile of the Jewess. This stereotype is particularly heightened in the portrait Spielberg draws of Helen Hirsch, in yet another shower se-quence—which again did not appear in the original screenplay.[64] Rushing and Frentz also characterize the second shadow, which they call "hyper-masculinized," "technological" and "overextended," as monstrous,[65] harking back to Mary Shelley's iconic image of Frankenstein's creature as a demonic "fallen Adam."

Despite Fiennes's masterly performance, it becomes increasingly clear that Amon Goeth, unlike Norman Bates, is psychologically two-dimensional at best. Ultimately, Spielberg's portrait of Goeth renders him inscrutably, perhaps even congenitally or genetically, evil and therefore thoroughly and monstrously other. As Quentin Curtis remarks, "Though Fiennes gives a compellingly detailed psychological portrait, Spielberg hints that Goeth's evil may be *innate*" [italics ours].[66] Goeth, who appears to be obsessed with guns and is similarly addicted to alcohol and sex, emerges as a powerful instantiation of this second shadow. Sara Horowitz perceptively excavates how the film links Goeth's passions for guns, violence, and sex in its visual construction of masculinity.

> The film pursues this connection in the sequence where Goeth stands bare-chested on his balcony, randomly firing at Jews with his rifle. The camera cuts from the commandant to the naked woman lying in his bed, to Goeth shooting, to the Jews below, to his mistress. Finally Goeth struts into the bedroom, aims the rifle at the woman, then urinates into a toilet. The series of images links killing to masculinity. Goeth aims his rifle at his mistress, making the weapon the equivalent of a penis. Instead of discharging from his rifle and shooting her, he moves past her and urinates. The sequence equalizes the acts of shooting, fornication, and urination. . . . Atrocity is enacted with semen, urine, or gunshot.[67]

Like Anthony Perkins, Ralph Fiennes, despite his gaining weight to play the part of the debauched hedonist, displays a boyish attractiveness and has been described by Hoberman as "the sadistic SS commander Amon Goeth (Ralph Fiennes), a dead-eyed, baby-faced Caligula."[68] Yet unlike Perkins's Bates, whom the audience learns not only to care about but also to identify with, at least until the revelation of the killer's identity, the humanity of Fiennes's Goeth is displayed mainly through his excesses, which render him a fascinating figure, though one difficult to identify with, much like Anthony Hopkins's Hannibal Lecter in *Silence of the Lambs*. In fact, Spielberg himself seemed aware of the possible parallelism, which he tried to obscure: "[Spielberg] had Fiennes play many of his scenes 'behind dull, drink-shrouded eyes, because I don't want him to become the Hannibal Lecter of the Holocaust genre.'"[69]

The resonances that bind Goeth to the compellingly repulsive figure of the cult psychopath have not gone unnoticed by critics. Ken Jacobs, in a collective interview conducted by J. Hoberman, remarks, "What's bothering some of us is that this is a trendy movie—it's sexy psychopath season—about a kind of Jekyll and Hyde character split between two major male characters."[70] The seduction-turned-torture scene features Goeth's clumsy attempt to confess his feelings to a silent and immobilized Helen and culminates in his brutal beating of her. Once again, the catharsis of violence substitutes for repressed sexual desire and establishes his active hypermasculinity against her passive hyperfemininity, though it is clear that Goeth is depicted as reactive. Philip Koplin notes that the depiction of Helen reifies the all-too-common view that Jewish women "possess a passive sex magic that beguiles and imperils Aryan virtue,"[71] as illustrated in figure 3.10.

The narrative space Helen Hirsch occupies converges with the dangerous and endangered space Marion Crane occupies in *Psycho*. Her sexually charged and imperiled body becomes the backdrop against which the story of Goeth's insanity is told. As David Thomson observes of *Psycho*, "When you see the film now, you realize that [Janet Leigh's] character, Marion Crane, was a new kind of figure on the screen. She was somewhere between a flagrant stooge and a seductive distraction, a sly means of triggering that spooky story of the Bates house, up there in northern California, only 15 or so miles short of Fairvale."[72] One of the production history anecdotes backs

Fig. 3.10. Helen's "passive sex magic" luring the hovering Goeth. Still from *Schindler's List* courtesy of the Academy of Motion Picture Arts and Sciences. Amblin/Universal, 1993.

up this conceptualization of Marion as someone who exudes fatal sexual allure. In an interview with John Gavin, Janet Leigh claimed that Hitchcock had given Gavin no direction at all for their love scenes. "I was the one Hitch had used," she writes, to make the lovemaking more passionate, an image captured in figure 3.11. Hitchcock also convinced her that she was central to the story. It was not until she saw the first screening that she began to understand how early in the story her character had been killed off.[73] Marion's narrative significance, like Helen's, is simply that of being a catalyst through whom the madness of the monstrous figures, such as Bates and Goeth, may be indulged in but eventually punished.

Fig. 3.11. The fatally beautiful victim in *Psycho*. Still courtesy of the Academy of Motion Picture Arts and Sciences. Shamley Productions, 1960.

As in the earlier scene, in which Goeth substitutes shooting off his mistress's head with urinating (yet another scene that is not in Zaillian's original screenplay),[74] the seduction-turned-torture scene does not, ironically, destabilize Goeth's hypermasculinized depiction of masculinity (set against his hyperfeminized other, Helen) but simply replicates it. The position of the camera throughout the entire scene tells us plainly whose point of view is privileged: it hovers above her, circling predatorily, calling forth a mood charged with suspense reminiscent, to some extent, of the high overhead or high angle shots in Hitchcock's *Psycho*, signaling the imminent imperilment of one of the characters. As Gertrud Koch remarks, "When it comes to a highly emotional film like, let's say, a horror film, it's often shot from the sadistic—the killer's—point of view."[75]

That Helen wears skimpy white underclothing, which reveals, rather than hides, her figure, is no less significant than that Goeth, long before this scene, has been established as an irrational and pathological cipher (fig. 3.12). Helen's physical and emotional vulnerability are heightened through shots that show her wet body glistening through the sheer fabric, whose whiteness against the dark backdrop is emphasized. It is not clear why her body is wet—it could be that she was taking a shower when Goeth surprised her, because her hair is also damp and clings to her face (once again producing the look of the shower victim); but it could also be that fear has caused her to perspire excessively. Yet if it is perspiration, it is depicted not as an animal secretion but as an aphrodisiac-like sweat that simulates the exertions of sexual excitement; her heavy breathing as her breast heaves with fear does little to dispel the eroticized atmosphere of this strange amalgam of courtship and stalking. Ken Jacobs is devastating in his critique of this segment of the film: "For instance, the Jewish girl that Goeth takes in as his housemaid. Out of nowhere, for no reason—who needs it—we have this scene where he circles around her; we circle around her, her wet nipple against the cloth. We are drawn into this thing, into the sadistic scene, circling for what? I mean, these are kicks, these are psychopathic kicks . . . the film is offering to people."[76] Sara Horowitz concurs with these observations on the not too subtle politics of the gaze in this particular scene. "As Goeth catches sight of her and she fills the camera's gaze, Helen is clothed in an inexplicably wet shift which clings to her breasts. The audience thus anticipates in Goeth's erotic gaze. Like Goeth, the viewer is meant to desire Helen's body, visually sexualized by the wet clothing. As Goeth's desire resolves in a physical beating, the audience participates in a voyeurism which encompasses both sex and brutality, with the victimized Jewish woman as its object."[77]

Weissman provides some important production history material that backs up the claims of this chapter even more vividly. He asserts that Keneally's novel is perhaps more notable for its omissions, which are magnified in the film, than for its exaggerations. Helena Sternlicht was Goeth's housemaid at his villa by the Plaszow camp; she shared a room in the basement with another house servant, named Helena Hirsch. Keneally consulted with Hirsch, but Sternlicht, because she was approached at the time she was mourning her husband's death, declined to be interviewed. Consequently, Sternlicht was effaced from the novel as well as the film, whereas "Helen" Hirsch figures prominently in both.[78] "Spielberg's film goes further than the novel in depicting Hirsch as Goeth's solitary maid, creating a special relationship between the commandant and the Jewess. . . . The film . . . fabricates an overtly sexual relationship between Goeth and Helen, eroticizing his violent treatment of her. . . . As Horowitz points out, this scene, having no basis in the historical record, is beholden to a tradition of depicting eroticized

Fig. 3.12. The fatally beautiful victim in *Schindler's List*. Still courtesy of the Academy of Motion Picture Arts and Sciences. Amblin/Universal, 1993.

female victims in films and novels about the Holocaust, such as *Night Porter* and *Sophie's Choice*."[79] An analysis of the formal properties of this series of shots can be detailed in the following way: (1) Cut to Goeth's cellar, which is cast in low-key lighting. In a medium long shot, Goeth comes down the staircase in the background left of the frame. He stops at the bottom of the stairs. (2) The camera pans to reveal Helen, in a thin nightgown, standing on the other side of the room in a medium shot. (3) From there, a reverse shot behind Helen in medium close-up focuses on Helen's back in mid ground. (4) The camera then follows Goeth in pan as he paces in the background. (5) Goeth then begins to circle Helen (which may be an ironic allusion to the bride circling the groom under the huppah, since this scene crosscuts with a Jewish wedding scene).[80] (6) Goeth's face passes through shadows until he is in the foreground, looking at Helen's back (his back to the camera). He pauses. (7) Then he continues to circle into the background again. (8) There is a low-angle shot reverse on Helen. (9) Goeth fills the left of the frame, while Helen stands trembling in the right side. (10) In the background space between them is a dimly lit brick wall. A ray of light shines down on the right side of Helen's face, while the left side is in shadows. (11) Goeth approaches her again and, while passing, stares at her—a gaze the camera shares. (12) There is a low-angle reverse shot of Goeth in medium close-up; he begins to circle Helen again, and the camera follows, panning. (13) Another reverse medium close-up shot on Helen occurs. She stands silently looking at the floor while Goeth circles her again; he comes around to her side and pauses again. Goeth walks out of the frame as Helen remains frozen.

In a manner reminiscent of *Psycho's* repeated shots, *Schindler's List* repeats shots that emphasize Helen's vulnerability to Goeth's roving and penetrating gaze. The rest of the scene may be detailed in the following way: (14) In a reverse medium shot of Goeth, the camera pans as he steps forward again, pauses, and continues toward Helen. He stops again and turns away. (15) A medium close-up of Goeth, shot from a low angle, shows him in the foreground center, emphasizing his centrality and dominance; Helen's face is in background right of the frame. (16) A reverse shot lurks behind Helen. She is in the right side of the frame, while Goeth stands in the background, at the left side. He paces again, and the pan follows his motion in a medium shot. He pauses. Then he turns and paces, dictating the movement of the camera, as the panning continues on him. He stops in front of her. He pauses and begins to circle around her again as the pan continues to follow him. (17) Another reverse shot of Helen in medium close-up occurs. Goeth stops behind her, talking into her ear. He circles around to her front. The camera stays on Helen and this time does not pan with Goeth. (18) A shot juxtaposes Goeth and Helen in close-up. Goeth occupies the left side of the frame; Helen is on the right side. Shadows cling to their faces from the backlighting, simulating an effect between noir and horror. In a gesture that strangely simulates *The Silence of the Lambs*, as we shall show in chapter 4, Goeth raises his hand and touches Helen's hair.

It is hardly surprising that Helen remains silent as Goeth indulges in his monologue, which begins as an apparent attempt to reach out to the young woman and ends in his cruel verbal and physical abuse of her as subhuman vermin. Any sympathy that might have been elicited by Goeth's clumsy attempt to come to terms with his forbidden desire is instantly shredded. He again emerges as the prototypic German Nazi male: inhumanly exploitive, devoid of genuine compassion, incapable of apprehending moral issues.

Through such narrative techniques of erotization and distance, the audience is allowed to share Goeth's sadistic and pornographic gaze and yet may deny this affinity because Goeth is depicted as monstrous. *Schindler's List* thus invites the viewer to take on a "murderous gaze" of violent and eroticized images under the guise of a merely documentary look.[81] Spielberg's film ends up as a reverse-*Psycho* in at least one other way. Hitchcock's *Psycho*, with its extensive use of doublings (Vera Miles, as Lila Crane, being made to resemble her sister, Marion [Janet Leigh] by wearing a wig; Anthony Perkins, as Norman Bates, bearing a striking physical similarity to Sam Loomis [John Gavin], Marion's lover [fig. 3.13]), forces us to confront the fact that this monstrous other, Norman Bates, lurks within each of us, with our voyeuristic and violent impulses and our vulnerabilities.

Wood also notes the striking resemblance and physical doubling of the characters and remarks, "The characters of *Psycho* are one character, and that character, thanks to the identifications the film evokes, is us."[82] (Figure 3.13 is a publicity still, rather than a film still from the movie; nevertheless, it illustrates the point that we, alongside the other critics, are making.) Similarly, Thomson astutely captures the complexities of the gaze in *Psycho*: "Even as the picture ended—with the whole thing made clear; too clear, perhaps—there was another face gazing back at us, grinning or enduring. A face that knew we were watching, with a mind sensitive or cunning enough to know that maybe the whole thing had been about watching."[83] Whereas *Psycho*, as a postmodern or contemporary horror film, potentially allows what Rushing and Frentz would term a reconciliation or at least confrontation between

Fig. 3.13. Evil and vulnerability within: doubling in *Psycho*. Still courtesy of the Academy of Motion Picture Arts and Sciences. Shamley Productions, 1960.

the ego and its alienated shadows, *Schindler's List*, like a classic horror film (in which the monsters remain irredeemably other and are reassuringly killed off at the end), continues the rupture, enabling the audience to maintain the safety of its boundaries between sameness and otherness.

Comparing Frames in *Judgment at Nuremberg* and *Psycho*

The film *Judgment at Nuremberg* (1961), which is certainly not a horror film but a fictional docudrama, uses atrocity footage to relate the story of the Holocaust as a Gothic narrative while appearing to have the look of a documentary, much like *Schindler's List*. Historically, at the same time *Nazi Concentration Camps* (in modified form—now spliced with images from Birkenau and documentation of the activities of the *Einstazgruppen* [traveling extermination units])[84] was used as evidence at the Eichmann trial, it also made its Hollywood debut as a film within a film in Stanley Kramer's *Judgment at*

Nuremberg. The film featured Spencer Tracey and Burt Lancaster and is a loose dramatization of only the *Alstoetter* case, one of the twelve Nuremberg proceedings tried by the American courts, after its indictment of the major war criminals. The film hinges on the stories of defendants in the Reich's Ministry of Justice and of other legal officials; this particular trial was used, in Kramer's film, to examine the way in which the very members of a legal apparatus, in this case, esteemed judges, can themselves become the instruments of legal perversion. The film finally achieves its climax by displaying evidence of the inhuman atrocities effected by the Nazis; and the witness called to the stand to testify is the film *Nazi Concentration Camps*. What is particularly striking about Kramer's filming is that he mimes precisely the way in which the four accounts described in chapter 2 attest to the guilt of its Nazi criminals: he cuts from the shocking footage to the reactions of key players, displaying the overt shock and revulsion of the American prosecutor (Richard Widmark) and a quiet, prominent German jurist (Burt Lancaster). In a later remake of the film, which features Alec Baldwin as Justice Jackson, *Nazi Concentration Camps* occupies the same starring role: once again, it is a film within a film, the omniscient witness who provides the climax to the movie. Yet as Lawrence Douglas points out, the history of this particular documentary, in relation to the court trials that followed the Holocaust, is not a straightforward one, and "ironically . . . *Nazi Concentration Camps* has been used as irrefutable proof of an event the film did not originally see itself as documenting."[85] Relevant to our critique is that *Judgment at Nuremberg* is an uncritical acceptance of the "facts," just as *Schindler's List* is, given its marketing trappings (rather than its actual production history) and visual mimicry of the documentary form. To gaze at the film's black-and-white account is, metaphorically and literally, to grasp "the facts"—which, as we have shown, is problematic.

The problem is that *Judgment at Nuremberg*, much like other Hollywood productions of narratives of the Holocaust, such as *The Diary of Anne Frank*, depends on clearly recognizable Hollywood qualities: a confined theatrical setting, superfluous dialogue, star turns, classical editing (mainly with close-ups), and musical scores whose violins swell at dramatic moments. The use of black-and-white formats, which give the productions an austere look, is undercut by its lush, melodramatic musical scores; the result is predictable. As Annette Insdorf notes, "These studio productions essentially fit the bristling new material of the Holocaust into an old narrative form, thus allowing the viewer to leave the theater feeling complacent instead of concerned or disturbed."[86]

One could conjecture that Stanley Kramer thought he was making the film less theatrical by panning 360 degrees around a speaker like General Lawson or by zooming into a tight close-up for emphasis; nevertheless, both of these techniques seem gratuitous and manipulative. For instance, when Lawson takes the stand as commander of the American troops who liberated the camps, he shows harrowing archival footage of the camps and inmates, including children tattooed for extermination. The material is already in itself emotionally stirring enough to provoke a strong reaction, but rather than let the images imprint themselves on us, Lawson and Kramer effectively hammer them in: Lawson's voice-over is an emotionally heavy-handed harangue, and Kramer intercuts reaction shots that essentially force audiences to identify with the surrogates in the courtroom rather than to see them as individuals with unique responses. Although we are forced to look at the footage, we are not helped by the film to really see it, particularly given its histrionic verbal accompaniment. The footage is used in a sensational way to shock us into acknowledging the moral enormity of the crimes, but we are not asked to probe deeply into their nature and origins or to inquire about the identity of the victims, whose bodies form an undifferentiated mass. Nor are we given a rubric within which to locate what we are watching. "The films themselves are the core of [the prosecutor's] argument," observed Ronald Steel.[87] And as Alan Mintz points out, "in the absence of a true argument, our attention does not linger after the initial shock, and our outrage is available to be enlisted on behalf of the highest principles."[88]

A film such as *Psycho* reverses the spectatorial politics characteristic of *Schindler's List* and *Judgment at Nuremberg* (which are not devoid of merit but certainly leave themselves open to the types of issues we raise). Like *Silence of the Lambs* in the way it involves multiple intrusions and reversals of power relations, *Psycho* places visual emphases on curtains, drapes, and blinds—which are porous boundary demarcations—but especially windows. Windows are significant for establishing frames of viewing, because one may peep through them as a voyeur (if the window is transparent), see one's image reflected back (if the window is opaque, effectively converting it into a mirror), or see some combination thereof, as if glimpsing through a mirror darkly. Windows, as transparent surfaces that both divide and connect spatial and visual areas, are crucial to understanding the relationships binding us to Norman, Norman to other characters, and Norman to his own private universe. David Sterritt notes a startling observation regarding the much-studied shower scene whose spectatorial dynamics we examined earlier: "In a pivotal scene, Norman makes a window out of the wall between his office and Marion's cabin. Mirror imagery also comes into play here: As he gazes through his peephole, the camera moves so close to Norman's eye that we see it (albeit from a profile view) as closely as *he* would see it were he gazing not through a hole at Marion, but into a mirror at himself."[89] It is significant that the "mirror" in *Psycho*'s crucial voyeuristic scene is replaced by a "peephole" in *Schindler's List*'s principal documentary-style descent into the shower and possible gas chamber.

Yet the Gothic aestheticization of atrocity footage from the Holocaust is complex and rooted in the primary evidentiary footage taken by the Allied Signal Corps troops as they invaded Axis enemy camps.[90] A brief look at some of the footage, which eventually formed the basis of *Nazi Concentration Camps*, among many other films,[91] reveals the following sequence: One pair of shots shows a dead prisoner in a striped uniform lying in the corner of a freight car. The first shot of the pair is a long shot. The floor of the freight car is covered with thick snow, which even lies on the man, as the body no longer has heat to melt it. The second shot moves into a medium close-up, again showing the victim's face as if to stimulate the viewer's self-identification. The victim fills the frame diagonally from bottom left to top right of the frame. We see that not only his body but also his face is covered with snow. One cannot help noticing that the hideousness of the helpless victim is always marked by canted framing, in which the victim's face fills the frame at a diagonal angle. At times, the canted shots of victims verge on overly aestheticizing the subjects, which seems in this context both stylized and tactless.[92] It is thus, in some ways, hardly surprising that *Schindler's List* continues the same narrative and formal tradition.

Spielberg, in attempting to work through the Holocaust in *Schindler's List*, falls back on a reification of familiar techniques and themes characteristic of classical Hollywood conventions (especially the psychological thriller), with its masculine gaze masked as neutral. Far from creating a new discourse about the Holocaust, as Loshitzky claims, *Schindler's List* attempts to convince us of its veracity by telling a familiar story using well-known classic horror storytelling techniques while camouflaging itself as documentary material.[93] We believe the film should be seen as one that effectively draws significant elements from the horror–psychological thriller genre rather than as a strictly historical document to be used uncritically for pedagogical and legal ends. By reifying the familiar techniques and themes characteristic of classical Hollywood horror and psychological thriller films, *Schindler's List* locates the genesis of action and inaction in the demonic motives of the monster Nazis and the eroticized but passive Jewish victims.

Simplistic attempts to use Spielberg's work as a historical document or as a didactic text are problematic. However, a more dialectical approach, such as the one we use, which engages in LaCapra's characterization of the problematics of the Nietzschean *Schwergewicht* or his differentiation between "acting out" and "working through," would be more fruitful in tracing the complex interplay that binds aesthetics, ethicopolitical aims, and historical claims of authenticity. Such approaches actively interrogate the social peepholes through which we view evil and horror, inviting the possibility of an ethical response challenging binary thinking. As we have shown, *Schindler's List*, by casting the Holocaust as the mise-en-scène for a story whose mode of representation is more in keeping with horror-psychological conventions, embraces the ideological intentionalist position on what produced the Holocaust and uses a classic horror frame in its representation.[94] According to this position, a preexisting anti-Semitism is given unquestioned causal significance in the movement toward the Holocaust; the Nazis are viewed as planning and carrying out the genocide of the Jews because of a deep and passionate hatred. As represented by Goeth in *Schindler's List*, the Nazis are depicted simply and congenitally as depraved monsters, innately evil, seeking to inflict pain on Jews. The time and space of the Holocaust are clearly separated from us and our territory. The classic horror frame captures one dimension of the horrific. The conflicted horror frame, which is the subject of the next chapter, discovers the monstrous within, refusing to place horror beyond our time and space.

The Monstrous Gaze:
The Silence of the Lambs
as the New *Psycho*

Judith Halberstam identifies the relationship between the Holocaust and the horror in *Silence of the Lambs*.[1] "Modernity," she writes "has eliminated the comfort of monsters because we have seen, in Nazi Germany and elsewhere, that evil works often as a system, it works through institutions and it works as a banal . . . mechanism."[2] She sees systemic evil and monstrosity on display in *Silence of the Lambs*. Although we foreground Holocaust films in this book, we believe an understanding of the trajectories of the horror genre helps us to comprehend the deployment of preexisting frames of horror and the monstrous in narratives of the Holocaust. Holocaust narratives and tropes have affected the horror genre as well, often subtly. In this chapter, we highlight the development and evolution of the horror genre to account for the complexity of the monstrous, particularly that which is conflicted, by conflating and defying the classic boundaries of evil.

The narrative of evil and horror is constrained in *Schindler's List* to the superficial aspects characteristic of a classic horror movie, like the early *Frankenstein* and *Dracula* films; in such caricatures, the monster is depicted as the unproblematic embodiment of evil. In contrast to this narrative dynamic are films, such as *Psycho* and *The Silence of the Lambs*, in which evil is not so easy to demarcate or to exorcise. The horror frame in these movies is conflicted. Perfect symmetry between horror films, like *Psycho* and *The Silence of the Lambs*, and Holocaust films, like *Schindler's List* and *Apt Pupil*, does not exist; neither does a universalized intermediate gray zone that lumps together perpetrators and victims. Rather, we compare in this chapter the politics of spectatorship in these two horror-psychological thrillers with the politics of spectatorship encouraged by the two fictional renditions of the Holocaust.

The focus is not on likening Clarice Starling, the protagonist of *The Silence of the Lambs*, to Holocaust victims or Hannibal Lecter to Hitler. One could argue that Starling's innocence and Lecter's magnetic gaze, hypnotic voice, and charismatic personality, which resemble George Steiner's provocative description of Hitler in *The Portage to San Cristobal of A.H.*,[3] suggest such analogies.

Our focus, however, is on the formal representational properties these two genres of movies share but that nonetheless result in different spectatorial relationships. The "peephole gaze" and shower mise-en-scène that form such an integral part of *Schindler's List* and *Apt Pupil* are also symptomatic of horror films such as *Psycho* and *The Silence of the Lambs*. However, a different spectatorial relationship emerges when one views *Psycho* and *The Silence of the Lambs* and then *Schindler's List* and *Apt Pupil*. *Schindler's List* contains the monstrous as other, using documentary "objectivity" to disavow any complicity in the horror. This "historical document" of binaries becomes possible precisely because *Schindler's List*, despite its hinting of a kinship between Schindler and Goeth, ultimately upholds a clear separation between the point of view of the "good" German (with which we, the audience, identify) and that of the "bad" German (which we repulse as monstrous in the more simplistic sense of the word, because Spielberg's narrative tends to appropriate the more superficial aspects of monstrosity and to forgo the pathos more complex monsters evoke; fig. 4.1). *Schindler's List* has framed the way in which many explain not only the Holocaust but also the nature of good and evil. The gaze it constructs for the viewing of murder is one drawn from the horror genre but lacking the nuance and complexity of the horror films considered in this chapter. *Schindler's List* acts out a response to trauma with a simplistic set of binaries; some cinematic productions, such as *Psycho* and *The Silence of the Lambs*, however, resist binaries or at least set forth comparatively more complicated visions of human motivation and action.

In *Psycho* and *The Silence of the Lambs*, the efforts of the characters (and finally of the audience itself) to resist permeability between binary dichotomies of the normal (good) and abnormal (evil) are defeated. *Psycho* signifies

Fig. 4.1. "Good German" versus "bad German" in *Schindler's List*. Still courtesy of the Academy of Motion Picture Arts and Sciences. Amblin/Universal, 1993.

this failure of demarcation through the voice in Norman's head at the end, which reveals this "entity" has been watching, recycling the audience's gaze, blurring the boundaries between normal and other. Both films have defined and redefined the hallmark gazes or "looks" of the horror films,[4] and *The Silence of the Lambs*, in particular, has been compared many times to *Psycho*, even dubbed "the new *Psycho*" by its own marketers.

The Silence of the Lambs extends *Psycho*'s conclusion, revealing the permeable boundaries between self and other in the triumphant voice of Hannibal Lecter (Anthony Hopkins) on the telephone at the end of the film. His subsequent disappearance into the anonymity of public space—the sphere of the normal, the visible, the known—also blurs the two domains. The film also implicates its heroine, Clarice (Jodie Foster), and the audience in the same, often brutal penetrations into private space committed by the monstrous others (Buffalo Bill and Hannibal the Cannibal) in the film. Hantke observes that the fantasy of horror narratives involves the audience separating itself from the killer, a disavowal that in effect narrows the gap. "The more we fantasize about him without acknowledging that we are separated by nothing but genre conventions, the more we close the gap between him and ourselves."[5] Jonathan Demme's film, in contrast, chronicles the collapse of the distinction between these spheres, exposing the "artifice that public and private space [and, by extension, the penetration and violation of these spaces] ultimately depend upon."[6]

In contrast to these two films, *Schindler's List* (even as it visualizes the Holocaust in a manner reminiscent of *Psycho*'s or *The Silence of the Lambs*' storytelling techniques) reinforces the separation of these spheres, drawing the audience into its guilty pleasures without acknowledging them, enacting the dynamic of fantasizing explained by Hantke. Its use of visual cues from horror films attempts to contain the intrusions of the other, marking the monster and his victims. In so doing, the penetrations and intrusions of fantasies of horror inevitably and duplicitously draw the audience in, re-enacting the same violations of boundaries performed by the monstrous. Nevertheless, the claimed objectivity of Spielberg's film allows it to deny its investment in techniques of horror film and prevent any acknowledgment of multiple and shared complicity in the atrocities of the Holocaust.

Horror and Monstrosity in *Psycho* and *Schindler's List*

Spielberg's horror techniques, which establish a narrative space populated by monsters and their victims, follow Hitchcock's lead in locating monstrosity not in external appearances but rather in the penetrations of the other's gaze into the "normal" space of the victim. As *Schindler's List* depicts the Holocaust, the monsters it creates are not the outwardly horrific, the startling, or the ugly. In keeping with the film's claims to documentary truth, the perpetrators of the Nazi horrors do not appear fantastically other; the demands of historical accuracy ensure that monstrosity has a human face (and even a glamorous one, in the figure of Ralph Fiennes's depiction of Goeth), though not necessarily a human soul. *Schindler's List* renders characters like the Nazi concentration camp commandant Amon Goeth superficially realistic, only to reveal an essential and hideous otherness camouflaged beneath the mundane.

Ultimately, *Schindler's List* adopts Norman's version of monstrosity, identifying the monstrous with the penetrating gaze; however, the film falls short of both *Psycho* and *The Silence of the Lambs* in acknowledging that the "normal" viewer shares that gaze as well. That is, unlike *Psycho* and *The Silence of the Lambs*, which make us, the spectators, aware of our looking through the peephole like Norman or Gumb, *Schindler's List* does not problematize the peephole mode of viewership its narrative mode encourages.

Shower Scenes and Voyeurism in *Psycho*

Psycho's shower scene, with its emphasis on voyeuristic intrusions, provides a model for the way that *Schindler's List* visualizes Nazi monstrosity and female victimhood. However, a sustained focus on the shower scene in *Psycho* illustrates that Hitchcock works through the murder scene by rendering porous the boundaries that separate the audience and the protagonist.

As Norman surreptitiously watches Marion in the moments before her murder, the film foregrounds the firm link between his voyeurism and his homicidal attack. Cutting between shots of Norman and those of the view through the peephole, the viewer participates in Norman's voyeurism, in effect taking turns at peering through the hole. The camera's subsequent presence in the bathroom with Marion again points to our participation as voyeurs, deliberately identifying the audience's gaze with that of the monstrous killer. *Psycho's* shower scene draws the viewer into Norman's voyeurism, reminding the audience that it has been participating all along.

While the narrative has not yet revealed the identity of the killer, it explicitly locates monstrosity in Norman's invasion (via the gaze) of Marion's private space. Immediately before this scene, he examines the hotel's guest book, directing his gaze at Marion's signed alias and, one may suppose, detecting the ruse of her assumed identity. Likewise, it seems significant that the final shot of the murdered Marion, her face pressed against the floor, is an extreme close-up of her unseeing eye: the image could serve as a reminder of Norman's wide-eyed gaze. The camera then pans outwardly and cuts to a subjective shot that tilts and pans hesitantly, suggesting the furtive point-of-view of an intruder in her hotel room. By the end of the sequence, Marion's private space, not only her room but also the shower, has been thoroughly violated. The audience, extending Norman's peeping, has followed Marion into the shower (before Norman himself does) and identifies with the killer's point of view after the stabbing.

Schindler's List frames its shower–gas chamber scene in a way that permits the audience to view the victims just as Norman watches Marion. (This is the scene in which the Schindler women are accidentally routed to Auschwitz-Birkenau and are stripped, shaved, and led to a shower room, not knowing whether it may in fact be a gas chamber.) However, in contrast to *Psycho*, which renders porous the boundary between Norman's monstrosity and normality by drawing the audience into his voyeurism, Spielberg's film reveals no such self-reflexivity. The camera uses no shot–reverse shots, which would have allowed a potential equalization of perspectives, nor does it reveal the audience as the voyeuristic co-conspirators that they, by default, must be, since they watch through the peephole in the way that Norman watched Marion.

Furthermore, within the framing of the voyeuristic intrusion, *Psycho*'s shower scene visualizes the victim and the scene of the penetration of her private space in a manner that proves central to the presentation of the shower scene in *Schindler's List*, as we have shown in detail in chapter 3. Just as Marion's appearance evokes the Holocaust victim, the film techniques of *Psycho*'s shower scene provide a visual template for imagining the victim of the penetrating gaze, a composition that emphasizes the sexualizing of horrifying violence and which Spielberg would rework in his own version of the potential murder in the shower.

The female victim, portrayed beneath the purifying waters of the shower, embodies the essence of vulnerability; Marion, like the Jewish Holocaust victims, personifies hyperfeminized victimhood. The camera's subsequent shift to the other side of the 180-degree line and into the shower with Marion subtly signals the approach of the killer. Marion, in the right foreground of the frame, is unaware of the ominous development, but the privileged position of the camera allows us to see the door open. This reversal of perspective, identifying us with Marion, puts the audience in the viewpoint of a potential victim but one that simultaneously possesses the power of foreknowledge.

Under formal analysis, *Schindler's List* appears to manipulate *Psycho*'s sequence of shots in reverse order of Marion's last shower rather than directly replicate that sequence. Nevertheless, the camera hovers from the side instead of directly below the showerhead, still maintaining the position of the voyeur. While *Schindler's List* uses similar techniques of backlighting and voyeuristic hovering, the camera never switches perspectives. Unlike *Psycho*, *Schindler's List* never openly acknowledges the body behind the gaze, concealing that the only way the audience can see this particular scene is if they were in the position of the Nazi guards. The voyeurism of the shower scene in *Schindler's List*, hinted at but never openly acknowledged, returns later in the depiction of Goeth's attempted seduction and torture of Helen Hirsch, whose formal properties were detailed in chapter 3.

Despite the audience's sharing of Goeth's subject position, the film never develops his character; he is clearly unsympathetic in this scene, because any attempts at depicting his humanity are lost in his explosion of brutality. His invasion of Helen's private space (defined by her meager attempts to domesticate it with curtains and the like) then becomes monstrous, other, and Goeth himself becomes the prototypical male Nazi, devoid of any traces of humanity. The scene also clearly eroticizes the encounter between the monster and his victim, extending his sadistic voyeurism to the audience, as we saw in chapter 2.

Monstrosity and the Self-Reflexive Gaze in *The Silence of the Lambs*

The Silence of the Lambs, by elaborating on Norman's (and the audience's) problematic voyeurism in *Psycho*, allows for a more complex rendering of monstrosity than that found in *Schindler's List*. Adding to this complexity, the film's two overt monsters provide very different styles of monstrosity. The heroine, Clarice Starling, enacts the audience's problematic response to horror as she responds to both monsters with simultaneous attraction and revulsion.[7] Monstrosity in *The Silence of the Lambs* initially appears in the person of Hannibal Lecter, a brilliant but institutionalized psychiatrist known as "Hannibal the Cannibal." Clarice, a student at the FBI academy, probes Lecter for clues in an attempt to identify and apprehend a serial killer nicknamed Buffalo Bill (Ted Levine). Lecter, who feeds Clarice tidbits of information in return for details of her personal history, becomes one of the film's ambivalent figures of monstrosity: intriguing and horrifying at the same time.

Clarice's role as an agent of the gaze permeates the narrative, further complicating the film's presentation of monstrosity. In a 1991 interview with Jonathan Demme, the director of *The Silence of the Lambs*, Gavin Smith identifies the central device of the film as the "voyeuristic-subjective camera."[8] In a genre that Smith describes as "essentially cinematic," Demme's film complicates the relationship between monstrosity and normality—in the process problematizing the status and meaning of the gaze and the audience's role.[9] The voyeuristic camera technique figures prominently from the opening scenes of the film, in which Clarice negotiates an FBI obstacle course peppered with the signs of traditional masculinity—including the oft-remarked-on placards reading "Hurt," "Agony," "Pain," and "Love It."[10] The camera shadows Clarice as she runs, climbs, and tumbles her way through a punishing training course, self-consciously referencing the stalking sequences of numerous slasher films. This sequence, which sets Clarice up as a potential victim, did not appear in the novel. That work simply has Clarice waiting for Crawford in his office, though it gives hints of the training she had been undergoing earlier: "She had grass in her hair and grass stains on her FBI Academy windbreaker from diving to the ground under fire in an arrest problem on the range."[11]

Similarly, the script does not necessarily lend itself to the allusions to visual stalking that the produced film does:

> EXT.—FBI OBSTACLE COURSE—YELLOW BRICK ROAD—DAY
> Clarice runs on the obstacle course, she climbs up the hill with a rope and
>   continues on.
> Clarice runs through the course, vaulting a log.
> Clarice continues running the course.
> Clarice runs up to the net climb and climbs over. She hears her name.[12]

Like the shower sequence and the seduction-brutalization of Helen Hirsch, which were either minor events or nonexistent in the original novel by Keneally, the visual stalking of Clarice in the opening sequences of the film version of *The Silence of the Lambs* reveals the importance of this type of camera dynamic in terms of its genre recognizability and its attendant pleasures, made clear in figure 4.2.

Fig. 4.2. Visual stalking in *The Silence of the Lambs*. Still courtesy of the Academy of Motion Picture Arts and Sciences. Orion Pictures Corporation, 1991.

With its menacing soundtrack and subjective camera angles, *The Silence of the Lambs* places the audience in the point of view of Clarice's potential stalker, only to later reveal, as Gavin Smith points out, that the film "precisely inverts the psycho-chases-girl format."[13] After this initial scene, the camera assumes Clarice's point of view, taking the audience along as she probes the back of a corpse's throat, the bedroom of one of Buffalo Bill's victims, and eventually the killer's basement itself. The heroine's role ironically mirrors that of the serial killer, as she also pursues a quarry, probing into the private spaces of victims and killers alike. The audience's participation in the gaze as it undergoes these shifts signals its cinematic implication in a probing desire to watch, which is exhibited not only by Clarice but also by the more clearly marked monsters of the film. Like *Psycho* (but in contrast to *Schindler's List*), Demme's film openly portrays monstrosity as an ambivalent trait that extends beyond the screen and to the audience itself.

To enhance this contrast, the stalking scene at the end of *The Silence of the Lambs*—one that could be interpreted structurally as a counterpart to Goeth's penetration of Helen's private space in *Schindler's List*—reveals the monstrosity and ambivalence of the film's voyeurism. After Clarice follows Jame Gumb (the killer's true identity having by this time been revealed) into his labyrinthine basement, the tables are again turned and the serial killer begins hunting her (fig. 4.3). Finding herself caught in complete darkness, she becomes the unknowing prey of Gumb, who with his night-vision goggles circles her in a way that recalls Goeth's voyeuristic domination. The scene (the only one, after the opening sequence, in which the camera does not take Clarice's point of view) merited special attention in the production process. Demme remembers that he relished "the idea that we'll be predominantly in the shoes of the protagonist throughout, and then when she's deprived of her sight, we'll be in the shoes of the killer."[14] When the lights go out, the view through Gumb's goggles reveals a trembling Starling, unsteadily pointing her drawn weapon in the direction of the slightest sound. Like Goeth, Gumb stalks his victim from only inches away. Gumb's hand, as it reaches out to stroke Clarice's hair, visually renders his monstrous desire, ironically picturing the serial killer as invasive in his own private space. Again, an examination of the transformation of the monstrous gaze from novel to film reveals the same trend of prolongation and hyperbole of what seems a heartbeat in the pacing of the novel. Though Gumb's desire to possess Clarice's hair is evident (he having remembered her hair from their brief conversation in his kitchen and then fantasizing putting her "glorious" hair on himself), he does not reach out and toy with her for what seems like an interminable period. "It was fun to watch her trying to sneak along. She had her hip against the sinks now, creeping toward the screams with her gun stuck out. It would have been fun to hunt her for a long time . . . No time for that. Pity."[15]

Fig. 4.3. Turning the tables in *The Silence of the Lambs*. Still courtesy of the Academy of Motion Picture Arts and Sciences. Orion Pictures Corporation, 1991.

The shooting script, however, already reveals how this scene is to be drawn out in the final product.

> CUT TO:
> INT. MR. GUMB'S WORKROOM—DAY (GREEN LIGHT)
> Clarice emerges from the bathroom in a half-crouch, arms out, both hands on the gun, extended just below the level of her unseeing eyes. She stops, listens. In her raw-nerved darkness, every SOUND is unnaturally magnified—the HUM of the refrigerator . . . the TRICKLE of water . . . her own terrified BREATHING, and Catherine's faraway, echoing SOBS . . . Moths smack against her face and arms. She eases forward, then stops again, listens . . . She eases forward again, following her gun, and creeps directly in front of, and then past—

MR. GUMB

Who has flattened himself against a wall, arms spread like a high priest, Colt in one hand. He wears his goggles, and over his bare chest—draping down over his naked arms, like some hideous mantle—his terrifying, half-completed suit of human skins. This is an exquisite moment for him—a ritual of supreme exhaltation [sic]. She moves beyond him, pauses again.

PAST CLARICE'S FACE—

We watch as he steps out behind her, in utter silence. His free hand reaches slowly out, covetously, as if to stroke her skin—his fingers floating delicately through the air, just an inch or so away from the side of her face. And then, as he steps back and slowly, almost reluctantly takes his gun in both hands, raising it—then, in that excruciatingly suspended instant—she senses his presence. He's *here*, in this room—but *where?*[16]

Like that of Norman or Goeth, Gumb's monstrosity depends on the penetration of the gaze. Also akin to Spielberg's filmmaking, Demme's technique invites the audience to view the scene through the eyes of the monster (fig. 4.4).

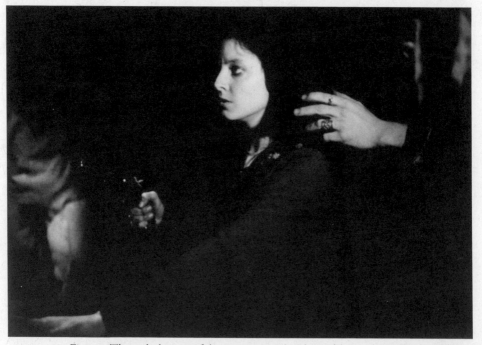

Fig. 4.4. Through the eyes of the monster in *The Silence of the Lambs*. Still courtesy of the Academy of Motion Picture Arts and Sciences. Orion Pictures Corporation, 1991.

At the most critical part of this dynamic, the film positions the audience firmly in the same perspective as the killer, watching Clarice through Gumb's point of view. The lights abruptly go out, and after a moment of suspenseful confusion, the camera reveals the image of Clarice filtered through Gumb's night-vision technology. The audience, seeing Clarice as much more helpless than at any other time in the film, views her through the killer's eyes (as the nearly helpless potential victim) and must participate, albeit unwillingly, in his cat-and-mouse hunting activities.

Despite the resemblances between *The Silence of the Lambs* and *Schindler's List*, the female victims receive very different cinematic treatments. Gumb's stalking of Clarice does not render us clandestine participants in guilty pleasures. Instead, Demme observes, the switch to Gumb's point of view was intended to "make the situation even more distressing on a certain dialectic level," intensifying his monstrosity.[17] Clarice, unlike Helen, remains clothed; the full frontal glare of Gumb's light-intensification technology contrasts with the backlighting in Goeth's basement. In addition, the dynamics of space in this scene differ from those in *Schindler's List*. Whereas Goeth invades the powerless Helen's private space, Clarice's encounter consists of two intrusions, one nestled within the other. Clarice first penetrates the private space of the serial killer, and Gumb in turn encroaches on Clarice's space, albeit the much more intimate space of her immediate bodily environs. The scene, with Clarice's intrusions mirroring the serial killer's, acknowledges Hantke's claim that horror narratives reveal the interpenetration of the "separate" spheres; the acts of the normal mirror those of the monstrous in their violent, visually enabled forays into each other's space (figs. 4.5, 4.6).

Even before he stalks Clarice, Buffalo Bill further complicates the boundaries between monstrous and normal, enacting complex versions of the voyeurism and fetishism of *Psycho*'s shower scene and Goeth's attack on Helen. The camera fetishizes Buffalo Bill from his first appearance, foreshadowing his later feminization as the object of the gaze. When the film first pictures him, the serial killer appears in extreme close-up shots that objectify him, denying a full view of his person. His hands, parts of his bare torso, and his eyes are all the audience can glimpse of him.

Buffalo Bill's monstrosity, like Norman's as well as Goeth's, resides in his ability to see and to control with the gaze. His use of night-vision goggles to track one of his victims, Catherine Martin (Brooke Smith), whom he intends to murder and skin, reveals him as not simply voyeuristic but unnaturally so; he possesses, albeit via technology, superhuman powers of observation.

Fig. 4.5. Multiple intrusions in *The Silence of the Lambs*. Clarice draws her gun in an infringement on Gumb's private space. Still courtesy of the Academy of Motion Pictures Arts and Sciences. Orion Pictures Corporation, 1991.

Fig. 4.6. Clarice drawing her gun in defense of the private space of her body. Still courtesy of the Academy of Motion Pictures Arts and Sciences. Orion Pictures Corporation, 1991.

Diane Negra observes that the serial killer's monstrosity is equated with a gender crisis—one that Dr. Lecter characterizes as "coveting the feminine."[18] Buffalo Bill's gender deviancy, however, even stems from the gaze. The film makes this connection explicit, as Lecter reveals that the killer covets the familiar, that which he sees every day. The serial killer's monstrous behavior, like that of Hannibal Lecter, emerges as his gaze penetrates and violates his victims' worlds.

Complicating this characterization of the monstrous is that Buffalo Bill also provides one of the film's most marked moments of voyeuristic fetishism, another version of *Psycho*'s shower scene or, in structural analogy, Goeth's circling of Helen in *Schindler's List*.[19] The camera takes us into Gumb's basement, where he carefully makes himself up with lipstick, a wig made from the scalp of one of his victims, and a gauzy scarf (fig. 4.7). Almost completely naked, he then dances in front of a video camera, genitals tucked between his legs. The mise-en-scène figures Gumb's recreational activities as deviant, cluttered as it is with the products of his murderous activities, including a half-completed suit of female human skin.

At the same time, however, the very presence of the camera mirrors Gumb's voyeurism; the acts of monstrosity become the acts of the viewer. The audience sees this scene through a sequence of extreme close-ups of Gumb's lips, eyes, tattooed torso, and pierced nipple, panning out to a medium long shot as the serial killer performs his dance. As he writhes, the audience watches from the perspective of a video camera Gumb has set up to tape himself; the visual framing of the scene compels the audience to participate, however uncomfortably, in Gumb's self-directed voyeurism. Once again the film embellishes the novel by adding its self-reflexive dimension. In the novel, though Gumb preens in front of a mirror, he does not use a camera to record himself. He does sing but does not dance in front of the mirror. He is naked, devoid of the rainbow-colored cloth that drapes the neck of his more effeminate-looking cinematic counterpart. "Gumb toweled himself pink and applied a good skin emollient. His full-length mirror had a shower curtain on a bar in front of it. Gumb used the dish mop to tuck his penis and testicles back between his legs. He whipped the shower curtain aside and stood before the mirror, hitting a hipshot pose despite the grinding it caused in his private parts."[20] In comparison, the shooting script is somewhere in the middle: carrying on the narcissistic themes characteristic of both the final film and the novel but devoid of the self-reflexive dimensions of the final product. Unlike the released film, which places us squarely within the visual frame of the

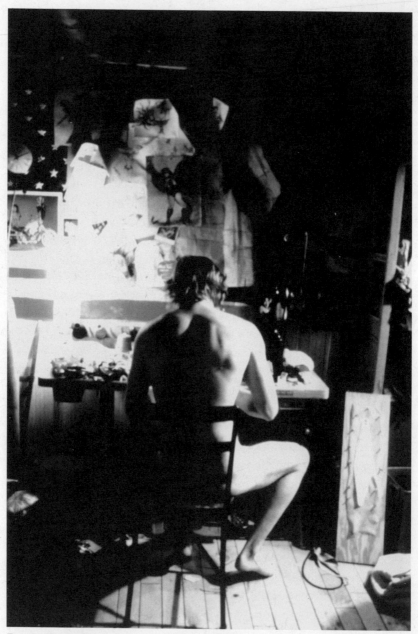

Fig. 4.7. Constructing monstrosity through gender deviance in *The Silence of the Lambs*. Still courtesy of the Academy of Motion Pictures Arts and Sciences. Orion Pictures Corporation, 1991.

monster gazing upon himself narcissistically, we remain voyeurs, peeping in as Gumb displays himself in front of the mirror.

> INT. MR. GUMB'S MIRROR ROOM—DAY
> Mr. Gumb, in his full-length mirror. Make-up completed, wig in place, just so. He reaches down . . . hunching his shoulders to make a final, somewhat painful adjustment below the waist.
> MOVING ANGLE—
> The CAMERA REVOLVING around him, as Mr. Gumb slowly spreads out his arms, opening his Kimono, revealing his naked, utterly hairless body, his rouged nipples, his genitals tucked out of sight between his thighs. As he stares at himself, trembling with awe at his own terrible and mysterious beauty, the ARIA soars triumphantly.[21]

Unlike *Psycho*, with its voyeuristic shower scene, and *Schindler's List*, with its eroticization of the female victim, *The Silence of the Lambs* presents the object of our voyeurism not as a hyperfeminized victim but as a monstrously feminized serial killer.[22] By scrutinizing a perverse, monstrous version of the female victim's body, the camera creates a new form of the sexual distraction offered in *Psycho* and *Schindler's List*.[23] Reversing the conventional scene, Gumb's dance (it being not the killer's victim who undresses and performs before the voyeuristic camera but rather the perpetrator) suggests a chain of victims and voyeurs, each one becoming the other in turn. (After Gumb is gunned down—effectively exorcised by Clarice [fig. 4.8]—the camera shows glimpses of Vietnam veteran paraphernalia—a hinted explanation of how Gumb became the monster that he is. In addition, some excised footage has Hannibal, bathed in dramatic low-key red lighting, creating a psychological profile that implies Gumb's troubled childhood and internal hell.) Ultimately, it seems that Gumb directs the murderous gaze of the audience at himself in an ironic, monstrous version of both his own stalking and Clarice's pursuit.

In comparison, the film's other monster, Hannibal Lecter, also collapses the distinction between monster and victim; he is both viewer and viewed, and Hannibal can fulfill his desire to extend his gaze only with the permission of the FBI, another supervising and controlling entity. Like *Schindler's List*'s Helen or *Psycho*'s Marion, Lecter is confined within systems of observation and control, but unlike the female victims, Lecter manages to return the gaze, remain essentially impenetrable, and eventually escape.

Fig. 4.8. Clarice's exorcism in *The Silence of the Lambs*. Still courtesy of the Academy of Motion Pictures Arts and Sciences. Orion Pictures Corporation, 1991.

Early in the narrative, the film provides clues to the nature of Lecter's monstrosity. Dr. Chilton (Anthony Heald), the administrator of the asylum where Lector is being held, describes the prisoner as "a monster. A pure psychopath."[24] Chilton, while briefing Clarice on her way to visit Lecter for the first time, shows her a snapshot that proves that the madman is capable of extreme physical violence. Lecter, however, menaces not simply by assaulting but by possessing a terrifying ability to insinuate himself into the minds of his patients-victims. The other characters in the film recognize this subtle threat. "Believe me," FBI section chief Jack Crawford (Scott Glenn) warns Starling, "You don't want Hannibal Lecter inside your head." Craig McKay, the film's editor, describes Lecter as "leaning back, drinking it all in, vampirically" as he elicits personal information from Clarice.[25] One of the guards echoes this sentiment when he asks Clarice whether Lecter is "some kind of vampire." Traditional concepts of monstrosity clearly inform the film's portrayal of Lecter; nevertheless, he is tellingly characterized in terms of an attractive and fascinating monster—a suave Count Dracula (rather than a clumsy and inarticulate Frankensteinian creature) who achieves penetration not so much by force as by the allure of his otherness.

The film figures, alongside Lecter's apparent elegance, his monstrosity in his ability to return the gaze—to echo, even in confinement, the voyeurism of Norman or Goeth (fig. 4.9). The exchanges between Clarice and Lecter in the psychiatric ward reveal the complex interpenetrations of the monstrous gaze. His first appearance was carefully staged: Clarice finds the doctor, awaiting her approach, standing in the middle of his well-lit, glassed-in cell and staring out at her. Lecter's monstrous gaze, uncontained by his cell, penetrates, threatens, and controls the scene. The novel more vividly depicts this: "Dr. Lecter's eyes are maroon and they reflect the light in pinpoints of red. Sometimes the points of light seem to fly like sparks to his center. His eyes held Starling whole."[26] The shooting script makes use of contemporary vampiric allusions (which seem to have some resonance with Anne Rice's vampire chronicles) to strengthen the powerful unnaturalness of Lecter's gaze: "A face so long out of the sun, it seems almost leached—except for the glittering eyes, and the wet red mouth. He rises smoothly, crossing to stand before her: the gracious host. His voice is cultured, soft [unlike the novel, where it is raspy and metallic from disuse]."[27] The marble whiteness of skin; the red mouth dripping with blood; the soft, cultured voice; and the wealth, taste, and aristocratic manners are all hallmarks of Rice's vampires, with their hypnotic and seductive gazes.[28]

Fig. 4.9. Return of the monstrous gaze in *The Silence of the Lambs*. Still courtesy of the Academy of Motion Picture Arts and Sciences. Orion Pictures Corporation, 1991.

In the film, the cell was carefully designed to promote this effect. Demme recalls in an interview that "Kristi Zea—the production designer—and I spent a tremendous amount of time trying to deal with the bars on Lecter's cage," eventually opting to dispose of the offending obstructions altogether.[29] Demme was concerned with showing each character's face clearly, transmitting an unobstructed gaze between Lecter and Clarice, his protégé and analysand.[30] Later, Lecter's wardens fit him with a mask, which, although it obscures his face almost entirely, leaves his eyes expressively visible (fig. 4.10). The specially constructed and eminently recognizable prop reveals the significance of his monstrous gaze.

Fig. 4.10. Highlighting the monstrous gaze in *The Silence of the Lambs*. Still courtesy of the Academy of Motion Picture Arts and Sciences. Orion Pictures Corporation, 1991.

Lecter's confinement in a glass-fronted cell functions ironically as well; it clearly indicates that he has been denied private space and must endure exposure to the gaze of administrators and authorities. His monstrosity is in a sense on display, observed on closed-circuit television. Significantly, the production documentary "Into the Labyrinth" reveals that set designers based Lecter's cell on depictions of the prisoners' accommodations at the Nuremberg war crimes trials.[31] Thus Lecter's association with the monstrosities of the Holocaust reveals the crossovers of visualizations of monstrosity. Demme imagines Lecter as a fascinating, attractive (yet still horrifying) monster like the bureaucratic perpetrators of the Holocaust, suggesting an antecedent to the use of horror techniques in the portrayal of the SS officers of *Schindler's List*. On the surface, the monster of the psychological thriller becomes the Nazi, and the Nazi becomes a monstrous other, but Lecter, as the object of fascination to Clarice (and the audience), takes the concept a step farther, acknowledging the other's origins in the self and the self's complicity in the monstrous. We do not claim that victims and victimizers are equally complicit in the performance of atrocities but that the spectatorial relation in *Schindler's List* differs radically from that set up in *The Silence of the Lambs*, despite their sharing many similar formal properties.

As reviewers of the film and observers of pop culture have noted, Lecter became a wildly popular figure, audiences enacting on a larger scale the dynamic of Clarice and her strange attraction to the "therapist." Novelist A. L. Kennedy observes, "The nice folks in my cinema just cheered" at the triumphant ending, where Hannibal Lecter announces his intentions for yet another cannibalistic dinner date.[32] Anthony Hopkins, celebrated for his performance of the character, explains that he wanted to defy the expectations of the audience when it came to the horror of Hannibal Lecter. "The thing is not to act in a frightening way," he explains. "I meant to play Lecter very friendly and very charming, very silky and seductive."[33] David Sundelson describes Lecter's ambivalence with the oxymoronic phrase "flashes of highbrow savagery."[34] As Hopkins implies, his character's monstrous power emerges not despite but precisely because of his genteel, cultured dignity.

While Lecter's propensity to create gourmet meals from his victims does indeed horrify, he stands in clear contrast to the simply offensive "Multiple" Miggs and the other inmates of his ward. Maintaining a calm, commanding presence in his cell, Lecter never physically threatens Clarice; instead, he plays an almost gallant role. Hopkins himself describes Lecter as the "prime dark angel" of the film's fairy-tale structure, emphasizing the grotesque attractiveness or elegant savagery of his character. He acknowledges that the story is "all very erotic."[35] Critics have observed the intimacy and implied attraction of Lecter's relationship with Clarice, and the film itself does nothing to dispel the notion. For example, upon Clarice's arrival in Memphis, Lecter remarks that since she had taken the trouble to interrogate him again, "People will think we're in love." His caress of Clarice's hand, shot in close-up at the conclusion of this scene, emphasizes that Clarice's interests on some level involve more than simple questioning. The allure of Lecter's monstrosity, the film reveals, brings Clarice back time and again. This is one scene that the film transfers faithfully from the novel, with its numerous ambivalences, though in the book, it is Clarice who touches Lecter, perhaps inadvertently, rather than Lecter who deliberately caresses Clarice's finger with his own, in the film and the shooting script.

> For an instant the tip of her forefinger touched Dr. Lecter's. The touch crackled in his eyes. . . .
> And that is how he remained in Starling's mind. Caught in the instant when he did not mock. Standing in his white cell,

arched like a dancer, his hands clasped in front of him and his head slightly to the side.[36]

Driving home the charisma, rather than the repulsiveness, of Lecter's monstrosity, the editing process cut out the most overt representations of his violence from the final version of the film. Chilton, for example, shows Clarice a photograph that documents Lecter's assault on a nurse, but the film does not treat the audience to the same view. The most violent scenes (Lecter's escape from the Shelby County courthouse) emphasize his power and brutality but at the same time deny the graphic details. At the conclusion of the attack, the camera switches from a low-angle shot to a high-angle view of the madman calmly surveying the domesticated cell, a phonograph, his drawings, and (ironically) a copy of *Bon Appetit* accessorizing the scene.[37] Ted Tally's detailing of the editing process reveals that shots of Lecter's escape elaborating on the madman's brutal violence were cut, ostensibly in the interest of pacing.[38] The resulting rendering, however, not only moved the plot along but also produced the image of Lecter as a brilliant, refined, and dangerously sympathetic character.

Watcher and Watched, Monster and Victim

Correspondingly crucial are Clarice's interviews of Lecter, which extend *Psycho*'s theme of voyeurism while complicating any clear distinctions between watcher and watched, monster and victim. In *The Silence of the Lambs*, Clarice is the authority figure (sent by the FBI) and Lecter the confined, perhaps feminized male in his cultured elegance and confinement. Clarice circles his cage in the Shelby County courthouse; it ironic that she, who is outside the cage, paces restlessly as though it were she who is entrapped. At the same time, however, Lecter himself wields monstrous power based on his ability to return the gaze, to penetrate visually, and like a vampire, to drink in the pain of the objects of his gaze. The film makes it clear that at the same time that Clarice examines and circles him, the doctor possesses the knowledge and power she desires for herself. As he analyzes the personal anecdotes she must trade for clues, Lecter calmly returns her scrutiny, blurring the lines between the observer and the observed (fig. 4.11).

The camera techniques that represent Lecter demonstrate this deliberate complication of the monstrous gaze. Production interviews stress the importance of the subtle dynamics of the gaze in the asylum scenes; the camera work, which initially uses oblique angles to picture the shot–reverse-shot views of Lecter and Clarice, shifts to direct frontal views of their faces, emphasiz-

Fig. 4.11. Blurring distinctions of voyeurism, gender, and power in *The Silence of the Lambs*. Publicity still courtesy of the Academy of Motion Picture Arts and Sciences. Orion Pictures Corporation, 1991.

ing the eyes.[39] Repeatedly in the interview scenes, the camera zooms in on Lecter's eyes from directly in front. Lecter stares out at the viewer (unlike in the conventional, angled shot), unequivocally involving the audience, as Anthony Heald observes in an interview for "Into the Labyrinth."[40] As Demme observed, "you always had to see what Clarice was seeing"; the "subjective positions" of the cameras were intended to bring "that heightened sense of intimacy we associate with confessionals or with the psychiatrist's couch."[41]

Meeting Lecter's stare in a way that neither *Psycho* nor *Schindler's List* ever affords, the audience finds itself in the dual position of examining and being examined by Lecter, returning his monstrous gaze along with Clarice. While Lecter's penetrating intrusion into his visitor's space visually and physically defines his monstrosity, it simultaneously implicates Clarice and the audience in the same type of activity. As in *Schindler's List* and *Psycho*, the audience participates in monstrous voyeurism. *The Silence of the Lambs*, like *Psycho*, contrasts with *Schindler's List* in the degree to which it openly acknowledges the complex dynamics of horror. The "normal," intruding on the sphere of the other, is in turn penetrated by the monstrous, who is fascinating and attractive in its monstrosity, unlike *Schindler's List*'s Goeth. Roles are repeatedly reversed, and a conclusive, unproblematic identification of monstrosity or the other is denied.

In contrast, *Schindler's List* appears to render identification of monstrosity with Goeth difficult only at one specific point (his attempted confession in the basement as he circles and stalks Helen while pacing restlessly, like Clarice, as though it were he who were entrapped), but the film elides and simplifies this problematic dynamic. As Lecter doubles as a suave version of Gumb's monstrosity, so Oskar Schindler (Liam Neeson) himself can stand as a more superficially attractive double for Goeth. Like *Psycho*, *Schindler's List* engages in doubling. Cross-cut scenes, alternating between a Jewish wedding, a nightclub performance, and Goeth's assault on Helen, engage in extensive mimicking of gestures. The sequence reveals that the Nazi monster and the "savior" enact similar performances, although the film shows that the similarity is there principally to contrast the two as archetypal figures of good and evil (fig. 4.12).

As Goeth attempts to seduce his Jewish housekeeper—both of them backlit in the darkened cellar—the camera cuts to a bar in which Schindler, backlit by stage lights, observes a female singer. The singer reaches out, caressing Schindler as part of her act, while the film match cuts to Goeth fondling Helen in an almost identical pose. Soon after, Goeth's near-kiss of Helen

Fig. 4.12. Goeth and Schindler as doubles in *Schindler's List*.
Publicity still courtesy of the Academy of Motion Picture Arts
and Sciences. Amblin/Universal, 1993.

match-cuts back to the bar, where Schindler receives the amorous attentions
of the performer. While Goeth assaults Helen, the editing begins to ac-
celerate, matching his blows with the crunching of a lightbulb at the Jewish
wedding ceremony, the kisses of the participants, and Schindler's clapping
for the performer back at the nightclub. Schindler, like Lecter, emerges from
this sequence ambivalently heroic—Lecter for supplying the information
needed to apprehend Gumb, Schindler for working within the system to
save—troublesome as that term is—his Jewish "employees."

Nevertheless, Schindler's visual mimicking of Goeth's actions do not identify him as monstrous in the film but instead underline his emergence as an angel, only against Goeth (fig. 4.13). Notorious acts, such as Schindler's indulgence in fleshly pleasures (like Goeth) or his pouncing kiss on the Jewish woman at his birthday party (echoing the Nazi's assault on Helen), seem to exonerate Schindler rather than indict him, despite the same types of actions performed by Goeth. The outcome, the film seems to rationalize, is for the good, whatever its form.[42] Precisely by demonstrating the similarity of the two characters' actions, the film shows how Goeth and Schindler are kindred spirits with similar impulses; yet it is also clear that despite these mirror-imaging analogies, Schindler is the good/sane one and Goeth is the bad/insane one. *Schindler's List* creates an unacknowledged version of Lecter's fascinatingly attractive monster—although where *The Silence of the Lambs* foregrounds his monstrosity and the irony of identifying and sympathizing with him, Spielberg's narrative renders Schindler's attractive monstrosity simply attractive, which works only in clear similarity and contrast to Goeth's evil.

Fig. 4.13. The Holocaust's Angel hovers over Helen, a gesture that mimes Goeth's predatorial gaze, in *Schindler's List*. Publicity still courtesy of the Academy of Motion Pictures Arts and Sciences. Amblin/Universal, 1993.

Schindler's role, monstrous like Goeth's, also corresponds to Clarice's in the sense that both characters perform the same kind of acts that characterize the monstrous and both indict the audience. *The Silence of the Lambs* complicates the gaze as it creates layers of voyeurism participated in by monstrous and normal alike. The penetrating gaze in *The Silence of the Lambs*, at first the apparent possession of only Gumb and Lecter, turns out to be shared by Clarice and in multiple ways by the audience as well. *The Silence of the Lambs* follows *Psycho* in removing monstrosity from surface appearances and into the realm of performance, rendering it the common property of various types of viewers.

The Silence of the Lambs suggests that the monstrous is the property not only of the physically horrific but also of the normal and the everyday, and even of the audience. *Schindler's List*, despite its claim to reality, contrasts with both of the psychological thriller–horror films in its desire to hold the monstrous apart from the sphere of the normal. Any ambivalence, instead of connecting the two realms, highlights one as particularly monstrous against the other. Analysis of the contemporary horror films we have discussed suggests that monstrosity is a problem of vision and voyeurism, implicating the audience in its dynamics. It is a problem, perhaps, of reification, of sorting and defining the areas between the safely delineated borders of other and self. Whereas *Psycho* and *The Silence of the Lambs* recognize and complicate the relationship between the self and the other, *Schindler's List* avoids the interdependency, trying to maintain the boundaries between the monstrous and the normal and denying any commonality between the two. What results from the narrative dynamics is ironic: movies like *Psycho* and *The Silence of the Lambs* that code themselves as fictional emerge as presenting more complex narratives than the particular grand historical docudrama *Schindler's List*, which comes across as a spine-chilling and entertaining fable with moral lessons writ large. Nevertheless, *Psycho*, *The Silence of the Lambs*, and *Schindler's List* converge in one area of storytelling: their harnessing of the feminine to the realm of the terrorized. Even Clarice Starling, the tough heroine-monster of *The Silence of the Lambs* must be domesticated in Demme's film version. Unlike the ending of the novel, in which she lies sleeping peacefully in a romantic interlude with entomologist Noble Pilcher, the film moves from a close-up of her large, terrified eyes to a high, overhanging shot, which pins her down.

This movement of the camera emphasizes her smallness and entrapment as the scene cuts to reveal Dr. Lecter heading off for his next meal. The lambs, like Clarice, keep on silently screaming in the film and shooting script versions, unlike the novel, where they are peacefully brought to rest. Though Clarice has advanced in the ranks of the FBI, she remains within the realm of the potentially victimizable female, which is a conventional necessity of horror and psychological thrillers, however conflicted the horror frame may be.

Having outlined key characteristics of the gaze and the politics of spectatorship in contemporary and the more conflicted frames of horror, we now turn to Bryan Singer's *Apt Pupil*, which returns predominantly to the classic model of horror while exhibiting elements of the conflicted frame.

Apt Pupil: The Hollywood Nazi-as-Monster Flick

Bryan Singer's *Apt Pupil* (1998) is certainly not the first film to tell the story of "Nazi as bogeyman" or of Nazism as evil incarnate corrupting the innocent.[1] In the wake of Singer's success at directing the mystery–crime thriller *The Usual Suspects* (1995),[2] expectations were high that he would build on the spectacular success of Spielberg's *Schindler's List* to revolutionize the retelling of the horrors of the Holocaust. Thus many of the critics' appraisals of the film tended to fall back on a comparison with his earlier film. James Greenberg remarked, "As he did in *The Usual Suspects*, Singer creates a human face for monstrous people"[3]; Eleanor Ringel less generously wrote, "As the stakes escalate, the movie doesn't know where to take us. We're left with the feeling of a psychological horror show interrupted by a generic suspense thriller."[4] Yet the narrative, visual coding, and marketing of the film as a horror film–psychological thriller rather than as a Holocaust "faction" (i.e., "fact" and "fiction") were so overt that numerous critics exploited the film's potential for quips and analogies. J. Hoberman described *Apt Pupil* as a "naturalized *Nightmare on Elm Street*" and a "Faust story with a neat-o Spielbergian resonance"[5]; Bill Brownstein claimed there were many affinities between *Apt Pupil* and *Marathon Man*, "one of the rare horror movies to dabble in heavyweight moral issues"[6]; Eleanor Ringel located *Apt Pupil* among the increasingly iconic Nazi Next Door movies, like *Marathon Man* (1976), *The Boys from Brazil* (1978), *Hotel Terminus: The Life and Times of Klaus Barbie* (1987), and *The Music Box* (1989)[7]; J. Hoberman dubbed it a "Nazi monster flick."[8] That the movie's story was derived from a short story with the same title in Stephen King's blockbuster anthology *Different Seasons* (which also inspired the films *Stand by Me* and *Shawshank Redemption*) seemed to provide critics with an even richer array of allusions. According to Stuart Klawans,

> Scheduled to open during the Halloween season—but recently screened (at the Toronto International Film Festival) as if it were as serious as it takes itself to be—*Apt Pupil* is essentially a high school horror movie about the kid who messes with the Forces of Evil. As if he were a character in any old [yarn] by Stephen King (who was, in fact, the point of origin for the movie), Todd toys with a power that might emanate from an Egyptian amulet, or a book of spells or a mad ventriloquist's dummy unearthed from an Indian burial mound by a red-eyed dog named Fausto. But such contrivances have worn thin, and so *Apt Pupil* uses the Holocaust to kick off its plot.[9]

Noma Faingold gives it a slightly more salutary cast when she writes, "*Apt Pupil*, set in the early '80s, is based on the Stephen King novella of the same name. It's not a straightforward horror flick. The monster is not some chainsaw-wielding wacko with a really bad complexion."[10] On the other hand, Ted Anthony maintains a tight and ambiguous balance between praising and damning the movie: "It is a taut, low-key thriller of blackmail and spiritual decay that is chilling in its almost documentary depiction of the bad things that men do and the violence that can be passed by osmosis through generations. . . . From its opening moment, a slow-paced montage of sundry Nazis and their atrocities, the movie latches on and never lets go."[11] Despite TriStar Pictures having sought to distance itself from King's reputation as a prodigious creator of pulp horror,[12] it is clear that even Bryan Singer himself envisaged his film "narrative" as somewhere between horror and history.

In an interview with Ruthe Stein, Singer spoke candidly: "Obviously, it is difficult to sell on the subject matter. . . . It is creepy. But it's also an intriguing premise: A boy plays with a monster and gets eaten. It is a true horror story."[13] In another interview, falling back on what is a cliché among King's devotees, Singer characterized *Apt Pupil* as a "gripping examination of the contagiousness of evil . . . 'done with the emotions, not the supernatural.'" The thirty-two-year-old director then proceeded to draw continuities between *The Usual Suspects* and *Apt Pupil* (despite his earlier protests that he wanted to do something "very different" from "another crime story"): "My line now is that *The Usual Suspects* had a twist at the end, and *Apt Pupil* has a twisted end."[14]

Singer set himself up rhetorically as Steven Spielberg did in linking his direction of *Schindler's List* to the rediscovery of his Jewishness and his attempts to work through the Holocaust. Singer reframes his fascination with King's short story in terms of his own biography—how, when he was eight years old, he had done a "very stupid thing" by creating a crayon facsimile of a Nazi armband, which he rushed off to show his mother proudly, only to be profoundly moved by her distress.[15] Singer also astutely welcomed the endorsements that came from Jewish political and spiritual leaders and performed an interesting rhetorical dance between describing the film as a Holocaust memorial and as an entertaining film. "Any time you refer to the Shoah in any form, whether in popular entertainment such as a horror movie like *The Keep*, or *Schindler's List*, which is more of a docudrama, or *Apt Pupil*, which is somewhere in the middle, it is a good thing, because it reminds you that the event happened and it should always be remembered."[16] In addition, the ambitious and much touted youthful director attempted a tightrope act between a universal or metaphysical way of talking about the depiction of evil and a historically grounded analysis of both the repulsion and fascination Nazism exerts as a contemporary monstrosity. Thus, in back-to-back statements, he declared, "*Apt Pupil* is not about Nazism. This character [Kurt Dussander as the Nazi] could have been any monster who committed murder and, if not enjoyed, thrived somehow on it. . . . I think anybody could be fascinated by the Holocaust and the atrocities. I was tremendously fascinated when I was young."[17] *Apt Pupil* is Singer's attempt to work through this fascination.

In this film, evil has a face—Nazism, which is configured as quintessentially innate, supernaturally crafty, and in a more subterranean way, dangerously blurring of the boundaries between homoeroticism and homosexuality. This chapter focuses on the latter characteristic, because most critics, when they have noticed it, tend to frame this interpretation as an undercurrent rather than a clear indication of what makes the relationship between Todd Bowden (Brad Renfro) and Kurt Dussander (Ian McKellan) monstrous (fig. 5.1).

Jami Bernard notes the "vague and unsettling suggestion of homosexuality,"[18] while Gary Arnold comments that the conversations between the boy

Fig. 5.1. The monstrous relationship between Todd Bowden (*top*) and Kurt
Dussander (*bottom*), Nazism and homosexuality, in *Apt Pupil*. Stills courtesy of
the Academy of Motion Picture Arts and Sciences. *Apt Pupil* Productions/Canal+
Droits Audiovisuels/Happy Ending Productions/JD Productions/Paramount
Pictures/Phoenix Pictures/TriStar Pictures, 1998.

and the geriatric man "acquire an outrageously kinky dimension."[19] As another example, Hoberman wittily strings together the following set of double entendres, drawing out the erotic and sadomasochistic themes of a pivotal scene in the movie in which the boy commands his captive Nazi criminal to dress up in a Nazi costume: "To complicate things, Singer imbues their [Todd and Dussander's] relationship with an undercurrent of homosexual attraction while Renfro's cloddish character, who seems to be reinventing the s/m dress-up of *The Night Porter*, slyly encourages audience empathy for McKellan's foxy grampa."[20]

Sexual "abnormality" is the means by which both King and Singer structure a specific monstrosity. In other words, the historical malevolence of the Nazi atrocity as a social and ethical problem is conveyed and constructed as a sexual problem.[21] And this construction is achieved through the erection of a series of binary dichotomies: normal versus monstrous, heterosexual versus homosexual, healthy versus sick. Yet this attempt to create easy dichotomies unveils hidden tensions, because the line between victim (feminized) and victimizer (masculinized) is a thin one, as revealed in the reversals of power that bind Todd to Dussander and vice versa.

This focus on monstrous sexuality, which may reflect Singer's attempt to work through the Holocaust, displaces an ethic of response by favoring the ritualistic and scopophilic thrills and chills that the Hollywood horror tradition allows. Like Spielberg, Singer ultimately acts out, rather than works through, a representation of the Holocaust by reducing it to yet another backdrop for the unfolding of a set of perversions (misogynistic in the novella and ambivalently homoerotic and homophobic in the film) that render Nazism monstrous. Thus the bulk of this chapter deals with LaCapra's rigorous adaptation of Nietzschean *Schwergewicht* to critique the failure of imagination and the triumph of fantasy in the face of the increasing commercialization of the Holocaust.

Homophobia, Misogyny, Monstrosity

Critics of Stephen King's horror fiction have often focused on its homophobic and misogynistic representations.[22] Noël Carroll notes that abnormality in general functions in horror fiction as one characteristic for the "othering" of an evil or monstrosity that finally is always socially constructed.[23] In addition, Harry Benshoff draws attention to the classic horror movie construction of homosexuality as one of "gender deviance" rather than of "sexual-object choice."[24] Hence, King replicates and engages in psychological transference as an ideological strategy in which "normal" forms of sexuality are threatened by homoerotic monsters and feminine-as-monstrous victims. The solution to this "problem" is all about the obliteration of qualities defined as feminine and the reaffirmation of traditional, heterosexual masculinity. Michael R. Collings has accused King of not only depicting vicious sexual stereotypes in his writing but also having a personal share in the sexuality of his central characters.[25]

Douglas Keesey, on the other hand, interprets King's depiction of sexuality as both exploitive and satirical[26]; he sides with King, who has claimed that homophobia in his work is a reflection of the prejudiced "real world" of popular culture, which King in turn exposes with satirical horror fiction.[27] However, such a distinct and binary opposition between King's fiction and popular culture is counterintuitive at best. In many senses, King is popular culture[28] and his prose depends on a "short-circuit thought, plugging directly into prefabricated images" of popular culture.[29] Indeed, King has proclaimed himself "the literary equivalent of a Big Mac and Fries" (which is not unlike Hitchcock's rhetorical posing as simply a maker of popular mystery movies.)[30] Thomas Gifford has equated Stephen King with no other arbiter of popular culture than Steven Spielberg.[31] Thus for King to attribute his portrayals of sexuality to an external "real world" utterly belies his vital contribution in propagating a specific sex-gender system.

Unlike the overtly social-structural and ideological meaning often inherent in terms such as *racism* and *classism*, *homophobia* and *misogyny* (often translated as "the fear of women") seem to have an individual psychological connotation. Such locating of homophobia and misogyny as individual psychological phenomena, which is itself a misleading social construct, is one crucial reason why *homophobia* and *misogyny* as social keywords should be reevaluated.[32] For instance, to assert that the "real world" is homophobic, while King is not, or likewise, to posit that King is a homophobe, although other authors are homophiles, reverts from the social-structural and ideological explanations of sexual oppression and places the onus on individual psychology.

For the critical evaluation of King's horror fiction, homophobia and misogyny must be viewed as ideology, that is, a system that has no "outside" in theoretical practice. In effect, popular fiction (along with Hollywood cinema) is an ideological constituent of social structuring. It presents and controls the only categories through which popular culture itself can navigate ideologies of sexuality, separating "normal" sexuality from "monstrous" sexuality. Positing homophobia and misogyny as ideology implicates heterocentrism, or compulsory heterosexuality, as a type of ideological hegemony[33] without the derogatory and stereotypical consequence of singling out individuals such as King. Like the other films we have studied, *Apt Pupil* was derived from a novella, which is deserving of close study.

The Novella

In the novella *Apt Pupil*, homophobia is a sexual "problem" associated with the monstrosity of Nazism. Todd's expectation that Dussander be the hypermasculine "fiend of Patin" is initially dashed by the decrepit old man's appearance at the door in a squalid bathrobe (112; fig. 5.2).[34]

Todd feels a desire for Dussander that is associated with his longing to make the old man look the part of his infamous name, to make him sexually attractive again: "He was really going to have to do something about the way Dussander dressed when he was at home. It spoiled some of the fun" (133). Thus Todd decides to buy Dussander an SS uniform, which Dussander is loath to wear (141), but Todd insists firmly. "Dussander let [his] robe fall to

Fig. 5.2. Dussander, the Nazi monster next door in *Apt Pupil*, appearing in his bathrobe. Still courtesy of the Academy of Motion Picture Arts and Sciences. *Apt Pupil* Productions/Canal+ Droits Audiovisuels/Happy Ending Productions/JD Productions/Paramount Pictures/Phoenix Pictures/TriStar Pictures, 1998.

the floor and stood naked except for his slippers and boxer shorts . . . but the uniform, Todd thought. The uniform will make a difference" (142). When Dussander appears in the outfit, Todd is "pleased . . . for the first time Dussander looked to Todd as Todd believed he should look" (142). Although it initially appears that Todd's demands to remake Dussander in the image of his fantasies about the perfect Nazi killing machine are nonsexual, the sexual dimensions of the narrative become more overt as the momentum of the narrative picks up.

As the novella progresses, Dussander increasingly appears as a homo-erotic object in Todd's nightmares; yet the proximity of homoeroticism to homophobia within a heterosexual universe is immediately signaled. In one dream, Todd is in a selection line of camp deportees and Dussander chooses him, "Take this one to the laboratories." In blackmailing Dussander, Todd secures the control that allows him to assault the man whenever he chooses, but in the process of "remaking" Dussander, he has the pleasurable sensation of controlling the gaze on the old man's body. Thus, for Todd, Dussander is a homoerotic object, a monstrous variation of "normal" heterosexual desire. Although Dussander first exhibits animosity to wearing the uniform, he later wears the SS uniform to bed at night (150, 155, 206).

After the dream in which Dussander selects Todd for laboratory experi-mentation, this laboratory ends up being the same one in which the young Jewish woman is bound to a table—and Dussander is also present. "Dussander was assisting him. Dussander wore a white butcher's apron and nothing else. When he pivoted to turn on the monitoring equipment, Todd could see Dussander's scrawny buttocks grinding at each other like misshapen white stones" (189). Nevertheless, in the novella, Todd's monstrous sexual drives ap-pear to fluctuate between the paradigms of heterosexuality and homosexuality. Despite the grotesque eroticization of Dussander's buttocks, it is clear that at this point, Todd's conscious "object-choice" is a sixteen-year-old Jewish virgin, whom he rapes with a metal-tipped dildo under Dussander's "scientific" men-torship. "Dimly, far off, he could hear Dussander reciting: 'Test run eighty-four. Electricity, sexual stimulus, metabolism . . .' She cried out when the tip of the dildo touched her. Todd found the cry pleasant, as he did her fruitless struggles to free herself, or, lacking that, to at least bring her legs together."[35] In the film, this nightmare sequence is replaced by three shower–gas chamber scenes, in which it is now the male body that emerges as simultaneously eroticized and terrorized; this is what codes these scenes as nightmarish and monstrous. We discuss these scenes in depth in the next subsection.

Repeatedly in the short story, Todd and Dussander's relationship is coded with homoerotic undertones, which recur whenever the two speak their relationship (fig. 5.3). Dussander tells Todd he is "mixed up" with him, that their "fate[s] are inextricably entwined" (163), and they "are in this together, sink or swim" (165). Todd continually wishes to break off the association and asks Dussander, "Why don't you go fuck yourself?" To which Dussander replies, "My boy . . . we are fucking each other—didn't you know that?" (197).

As their relationship evolves, Dussander gets an equal hold on Todd and he fears that those around him will detect the "abnormality" of their liaison. Todd grows angry when his father complains that he "is spending a little too much time with Mr. Denker [Dussander in the film]" (139). Todd imagines having to explain this relationship to his friends. "Guys, I got mixed up with this war criminal. I got him right by the balls, and then—ha ha, this'll killya, guys—then I found out he was holding my balls as tight as I was holding his. I started having funny dreams and the cold sweats" (178).

Similarly, both Dussander and Todd strive to reinforce their heterosexual masculine identities by feminizing and victimizing homeless men. "They both dreamed of murder. . . . Todd awoke with the now familiar stickiness of his lower belly. Dussander, too old for such things, put on the SS uniform and then lay down again, waiting for his racing heart to slow" (206). Todd first meets a wino who offers him sexual favors: "For a buck I'd do you a blowjob, you never had better. You'd come your brains out, kid, you'd—" (199). Later, he begins a killing spree against the homeless and masturbates after each murder. Dussander, in the role of a "well-to-do old faggot," similarly tempts winos back to his house with the promise of money for sex, then murders and buries them in his basement (207–10).

Although Todd exhibits misogynistic tendencies from the beginning of the novella,[36] his degradation of women chiefly reflects an attempt to reaffirm his masculinity. Monica Bowden and Betty Trask are objects of misogyny in *Apt Pupil* but are by no means the only disparaged female characters.[37] Todd's relationship with his mother, Monica, is just one instance. Initially, her body is consigned to oedipal fetishism. "His mother wasn't a bad-looking chick for thirty-six, Todd thought; blonde hair that was streaked ash in a couple of places, tall, shapely, now dressed in dark red shorts and a sheer blouse of a warm whiskey color—the blouse was casually knotted below the breasts, putting her flat, unlined midriff on show" (135). They converse as though age-mates in affectionate idioms such as "Toddy-baby" and "Monica-baby" (135).

Fig. 5.3. Homoerotic undertones: predator and victim. Stills courtesy of the Academy of Motion Picture Arts and Sciences. *Apt Pupil* Productions/Canal+ Droits Audiovisuels/Happy Ending Productions/JD Productions/Paramount Pictures/Phoenix Pictures/TriStar Pictures, 1998.

Todd becomes increasingly hateful in his treatment of Monica. When his mother develops suspicions about the purpose of Todd's visits to Denker's house, Todd suddenly hates her, "hating the half-informed intuition he saw swimming in her eyes" (221). Shortly thereafter, Denker has a heart attack and Todd calls his parents in a panic, aiming to rush the old man to the hospital. When Monica's "soft, cultured voice" answers the phone, Todd sees himself "slamming the muzzle of the .30-.30 into her nose and pulling the trigger into the first flow of blood" (225).[38] This shift in Todd's attitude toward his mother is characterized by King as emblematic of a larger sexual "abnormality" cultivated by Todd's perpetual descent into the degenerate universe of the Nazi Dussander.[39]

Todd's girlfriend, Betty Trask, conveys yet another relationship in misogynistic terms. Initially, Todd's sexual exploits with Betty are successful, but Todd's prowess figures more as a proof of his masculinity in the eyes of his friends than as constitution of any emotional bond with her. When, at the breakfast nook, Todd's father, Dick Bowden, inquires about the progress of his dates with Betty, Todd is annoyed by the mere mention of Betty's name. Todd thinks to himself, "Oh, by the way, did you know your good friend Ray Trask's daughter is one of the biggest sluts in San Domingo? She'd kiss her own twat if she was double jointed . . . she'd fuck a dog if she couldn't get a man" (253). Betty is portrayed as a hypocrite (and oversexualized *Untermensch*), who tells her girlfriends she doesn't "put out," when in reality, "[she] was the kind of girl who fucked on the first date" (254).

As Todd is increasingly caught up with Dussander, he explicitly begins to despise Betty, and not managing to get an erection, he utilizes misogynistic fantasies to "get hard." In one episode, Todd imagines forcing a crying Betty to strip naked in front of his friends, yelling to her, "Show your tits! Let them see your snatch, you cheap slut! Spread your cheeks! That's right, bend over and SPREAD them!" (255). On yet another occasion, Todd invokes the fantasy of raping the young Jewish woman. Finally, Todd begins to wonder if he can't just dump Betty and tell his friends that he "fucked 'er out" (256). In addition, Todd's misogynistic view of Betty is mingled with racism, perhaps prompted by his commerce with Nazism. He begins to wonder whether she is a "sheeny" and if the Trasks are "passing for white" (257). "One look at her nose and that olive complexion—her old man's was even worse—and you knew. That was probably why he hadn't been able to get it up. It was simple: his cock had known the difference before his brain" (257).

Todd also defends his masculinity through rape.[40] For instance, in an incident briefly characterized earlier, Todd's first wet dream takes place after a continual series of nightmares instigated by Dussander's vivid storytelling: In a concentration camp laboratory, a young and attractive Jewish woman is bound to a table with clamps. As a "reward" for bringing up his grades at high school, Todd is permitted sexually to assault her with a hollow metal dildo, which is fitted with an electrical cord and then placed over Todd's penis. "The lubricated interior of the dildo pulled and slid against Todd's engorgement. Delightful. Heavenly" (190).

The vocabulary of this narrative clearly seats the reader in the position of Todd, who is aroused by the encounter and attains pleasure as he violently penetrates the Jewish woman, but it does not identify with her torment at being violently assaulted. Thus King's telling of this incident is all the more misogynistic, because it is constructed from the perpetrator's position, in which the presupposed masculine reader engages with Todd in guilty pleasure.[41] This spectatorial dynamic, as we have shown in chapter 3, is remarkably similar to that encouraged by Goeth's gaze on Helen in the basement, as he hovers predatorily around her.

Novella into Film

Brandon Boyce's script for and Bryan Singer's film adaptation of *Apt Pupil* (Phoenix/TriStar Pictures, 1998) predominantly effaces the misogynistic threads in the novella. In particular, the most virulent and graphic misogyny toward Monica, Betty (Becky in the film), and the young Jewish woman are excised.[42] Instead, the film leaves the homophobia of the novella intact to signify monstrosity. The primary source of homoeroticism in the novella, the relationships Todd has with Dussander and the homosexual derelict, Archie (Elias Koteas), remain prominent in the film. In addition, the movie intensifies the connection between homophobia and the portrayal of male Holocaust victims. Lastly, a further instance of homoeroticism surfaces in the depiction of Ed French (David Schwimmer).

One factor that accentuates homoeroticism in the film adaptation is the proximity between male bodies within both the diegesis and spectatorship. Todd and Dussander are the only central characters in the novella, so it is not astonishing that they would remain prominent in the film adaptation. In fact, Singer saw this limitation to two main characters as a particular challenge with *Apt Pupil*: "The most difficult part of making this film is basically that unlike *Usual Suspects*, you're given only two characters. . . . So there aren't many places to go with the camera and storytelling."[43] Despite its wide-screen format, the film restricts most of the development of Todd and Dussander's relationship—framed mostly in close-ups[44]—within a crepuscular, dimly lit and claustrophobic bungalow, in which the hidden Nazi lives in obscurity, with the exception of the bus ride, dinner at the Bowdens', and the hospital scene.[45] This close proximity, framed in close-ups every time Dussander touches Todd,[46] intensifies a homoerotic intimacy, punctuated by dread of contact with the monstrous, that cannot be attained visually in the novella. Paul Emmons notes the intimidating effect of Dussander's proximity to Todd: "Kurt slowly approaches Todd as though to embrace him, only at the last second turning the gesture into a reach for an object behind the boy."[47]

Homoeroticism in the film is further created by the camera's gaze on Todd's body, a factor that is conveyed in the novella (e.g., the focus on the "moistness" of Todd's genitals and lower abdominal region; 189, 206) but explored to a greater degree in the film. Jake Wilson draws attention to a memorable "pin-up shot," in which, "teenage hunk Brad Renfro [is] sprawled on his bed in his underwear, gazing up at the hovering camera."[48] Yet the knife cuts both ways: the "pin-up hunk" is thinly separated from the *eronemos* (beloved)—the "beautiful" boy-man who apprentices under the tutelage of the *erastes* (lover), whose mentorship includes the realm of sexual initiation. This relationship, within the contemporary characterization of male-male homoerotic relationships, is construed often as dangerously homosexual.

The film is quite different from the original script. In the script, Boyce describes a rumbling in Todd's room similar to an earthquake; Todd rises from his bed and begins to walk, suddenly finding himself in a much larger space.[49] In the film, however, an arcing god's-eye-view long shot of Todd lying on his side in bed moves in slowly, in a manner just the opposite of Hitchcock's receding arcing shot of Marion's eye in *Psycho*.[50] We note the series of shots in what becomes the first of the shower–gas chamber sequences: (1) His body fills the center of the frame horizontally. He is side lit from the top of the frame with night-light blues; shadows cling to his back. (2) We cut into a tighter God's-eye view (medium long shot). He now lies on his back, and his body still fills the center of the frame horizontally, suggesting the twisting and turning of insomnia. Blue side lighting pours in from the top of the frame. (3) Jump cut into an even tighter shot of Todd's face (close-up). Now in a vertical position, his face, turned to the side (but still frontal), fills the left portion of the frame and his eyes gaze off to the right. Blue side lighting comes from the right of the frame, with clinging shadows on his left side. In the middle of the shot, the image is solarized, blending both negative and positive images, causing a halo effect. This effect is analogous to briefly exposing a print to light when one is developing a photograph and is used to suggest the dream-state unconscious.

The ever-encroaching camera and the lighting fetishize Todd's youthful body in a manner customarily applied to the female body, particularly in the shower or peeping-tom scenes in *Psycho*, *The Silence of the Lambs*, and *Schindler's List*. This insight may be applied to a broader number of scenes throughout the film, when Todd's white face, with its mild complexion and his white youthful body are fetishistically captured by the close-up and he is given to wandering about without a shirt on.[51] Wilson does not miss the implication of this structuring: "At times it's hard to say whether deviant sexuality is meant as a metaphor for evil or vice versa, given the film's fixation on Renfro's muscular body, pale fine skin, and rosebud lips (held vacuously open, like an actress playing a bimbo)."[52] Neither does Stuart Klawans of *The Nation*: "*Apt Pupil* devotes a lot of time to hinting that its clear-eyed hero, with his sensitive lips and lithe, hairless torso, might desire something other than the standard-issue girlfriend."[53]

We understand the homoerotic fetishism of Todd's body as one instance in a trend that is imposed on an assumed white masculine spectator and is complicit with a looming homophobia, which in turn is conflated with the evil of Nazism. Through this depiction, however, Todd enters the space of Mary Russo's "monstrous feminine."[54] That is, far from being the haughty, unimperiled predator, he is now simultaneously dangerous and endangered. This dualism is evidenced in the same sequence, which may be detailed in the following way: (1) At close-up range, the bars of the portal window mark the film frame in horizontal and vertical grids. In the center grid, a prisoner's face, shot in close-up, approaches from the other side. Fog rolls up, somewhat distorting clarity. (2) A match cut occurs: we see Todd's face framed in a similar fashion with rolling fog (i.e., from within the chamber, the camera's point of view looking out at Todd, now from the other side of the door, placing him in the space of the prisoner, rather than as the voyeuristic outsider who peers in. (3) We see Dussander in heavy backlighting in the center of the frame (medium shot), standing in a hallway with the window in the left background of the frame. Dussander swiftly unsheathes a dagger and holds it in the air. The weapon is a holdover from the script and is one of the few surviving mementos of Dussander's past and his power to determine who lived and who died; for the most part, this theme is obscured or lost in the film.

Whereas the novella describes Dussander's transformation from a decrepit old man to a powerful SS officer, the film furnishes an image all too familiar from imposed-makeover scenes in such films as Hitchcock's *Vertigo* (1958) and Buñuel's *Viridiana* (1961).[55] Though the changes between the novella and the film are minimal, it is evident that in the film, Todd's demands are more dominant and voyeuristic. In the novella, Todd solicits Dussander to put on the uniform and when Dussander resists, Todd remarks that he has saved all summer to be able to afford it and shakes his head at Dussander's pleas. By contrast, in the film, Todd threatens to betray Dussander to the Israelis and declares, "I tried to do this the nice way, but you don't want it. So fine, we'll do this the hard way. You will put this on, because I want to see you in it. Now move!" A detailed analysis of the formal elements of this scene provides the following details:

(1) Todd is seated, facing away from the camera in frame right foreground (medium close-up). In left frame background, viewed via a long shot, Dussander, now dressed in an SS uniform, walks down the hallway toward Todd. The camera dollies forward. Dussander stops halfway there. (2) In a medium close-up reaction shot of the side-lit Todd (from an assumed window source) in left frame, Todd's eyes ascend, "checking out" Dussander from his toes to his head. (3) A medium long shot shows Dussander continuing toward the camera (or Todd's point of view) and then pausing at medium shot. (4) A reaction shot of Todd obviously experiencing visual pleasure occurs. The camera tilts on Todd, as he rises from his seat, and then shifts to a low-angle, directed up at Todd. The camera dollies back as Todd moves forward. (5) Dussander is shown in frontality, with a low-angle medium shot. The camera dollies forward, suggesting Todd's approach. Dussander is expressionistically lit from the right with light blue side lighting. He is side-lit on the left with lighter amber tones. Todd enters from the left side of the frame and stops on the right side, examining the uniform. (6) The camera setup shifts 60 degrees to the right and is now behind Dussander, who, from shoulder to elbow, fills the foreground of the right side of the frame. Amber light accentuates the contour of the uniform. In frame right, Todd, mid-ground, looks and comments on the perfect fit of the uniform.

The editing style constructs juxtaposition in frames, in which we view Dussander in the SS uniform and then anticipate Todd's reaction. The mobile camera is employed to show Todd's emotional response to Dussander's arousing appearance. Whereas Todd as a subject is lit with an apparently natural light source, Dussander, as the object of the gaze, is side-lit with an expressionistic blue lighting. Finally, a comparison of camera angles between shots reveals that Todd's reaction shots are predominantly from a low angle. The selection of these formal elements exemplifies sexual difference between the characters as one often expects in the heterosexual, institutional cinematic construction of sexual difference, with Todd being masculinized as the bearer of the gaze and Dussander being feminized as the object of the gaze. In addition, the content of the frames (Todd as looker, Dussander as fetishistic object) and the relation of camera angles renders the scene as sadomasochistically homoerotic, despite Singer's claim that "for some strange reason, some weird reason, shooting him from the lower angle, where normally you would think the character would be empowered, up on high, made Brad weaker."[56] This formal structuring becomes more evident when we look at the following montage sequence:

(1) A close-up of Todd's fascinated reaction as he orders, "Face right!" (2) A close-up of Dussander's boots as he rapidly turns from profile to frontality. (3) Another close-up of Todd as he barks out, "March!" (4) A low-angle medium close-up of Dussander; he begins to march more fervently. (4) A frontal medium close-up of Dussander's waist. His belt comes across the center of the frame; his Nazi buckle is captured in center frame. (5) A close-up of Todd. (6) The setup shifts 180 degrees, to behind Todd. Dussander halts and raises his right arm in a "sieg heil" salute. (7) The setup shifts 180 degrees, to behind Dussander. We see Dussander's arm cut diagonally into the left top of the frame (out of focus). Todd is in frame right (visualized with a medium shot in focus). (8) A medium shot of Dussander's waist; he slaps his hand on his belt and then lowers his hand to his side. He begins to turn, which motivates the cut to (9) a close-up on Dussander's hat with the Nazi eagle symbol. (10) A continuity cut as Dussander turns, with the camera veering in for a close-up on the collar of his uniform with Nazi SS patches and stars.

In this accelerated montage, Todd continues to appear in low-angle close-ups, but Dussander's body becomes increasingly fragmented. Thus, Todd actively controls the gaze on Dussander as a fragmented and fetishized object of the gaze; it is a gaze, much like Goeth's gaze at Helen, that we share. This domination is clearly stipulated in Boyce's script: "Dussander does what he is told," and "[Todd] enjoys the domination."[57] It should now be clear that our reading of the camera's framing of the narrative does not concur with such neutral assessments that claim, "Renfro's character may also be deflecting latent homosexual tendencies, but Boyce's script pulls back from that early intimation."[58] Quite the opposite: the cinematic construction of Dussander and Todd for the first half of *Apt Pupil* does anything but pull back; rather, it clearly corroborates a homoerotic arrangement of images. However, we think that Singer's filmic construction is merely visualizing the homoeroticism of the makeover that is already manifest in King's novella.

This is also the scene in which Todd begins to lose control of his sadistic power over Dussander. An examination of formal elements shows this shift: (1) A close-up of Todd. His reaction now shows discomfort as he tries to regain control with the words, "That's enough!" (2) A close-up of Dussander's waist in profile as he continues to march; his arm moves in and out of the frame. (3) Dussander's arm is shown in frame left, out of focus, with Todd in right frame in the background, shot in a medium close-up, as he cries out, "Stop!" (4) Dussander marches more fervently, as if possessed or goaded by an innate force. What follows is a rapid series of shot–reverse shots between Todd and Dussander (nearly two shots per second), in which both characters are shot in close-up, thus radically rupturing the structure of power. By the end of this scene, Dussander in a close-up shot warns Todd, "Boy, be careful; you play with fire!" Todd is finally rendered powerless, as the scene ends with his baffled and apprehensive face in a close-up reaction shot.

This inversion of the power structure has an effect on Todd's sexual and academic life, effectively ending his days of normality. As Todd McCarthy explains, "For his part, Todd is now so preoccupied with Nazi evil that he can no longer perform sexually and shortly sees his outstanding grades decline to a level that threatens his chances for college."[59]

However, between the novella and film there is a significant difference in what constitutes Todd's "abnormal" sexuality. In the novella, Todd begins to have misogynistic dreams, one of which includes the rape of a restrained and tortured Jewess, which we described in detail earlier. The film replaces the rape scene with a homophobic shower scene, in which Todd witnesses the transformation of his peers into homoerotically coded Holocaust victims. One victim rubs his chest and gazes licentiously at Todd, while another victim, emaciated and octogenarian, stares ruefully through "night and fog."

This second shower–gas chamber scene, which is rife with references to both the gas chambers of the Holocaust and Marion's lethal shower in *Psycho* (staples in Holocaust and horror films), is described in the following way in Boyce's script:

> Todd gets under the nozzle and allows the warm water to blast
> the top of his head. He closes his eyes. Against the high tile walls

the boys' voices echo loudly. A dozen running shower heads con-
tribute to the din. Todd opens his eyes. . . .

Writhing bodies, thin, malnourished. These are bodies he
has seen before. The room is darker, concrete. The steam rises.
Or is it steam? Smoke, thick smoke, surrounds him. The voices
of the boys are more like screams.

One by one the boys file out of the shower. Through the heavy
steam we see Todd virtually motionless under the raging steam
of water. His eyes are clamped shut.

Finally, Todd opens his eyes, realizing, suddenly, that he is
alone. He turns the shower off. His skin is red and steaming
from the prolonged exposure to the hot water. . . .[60]

No overtly naked old men are described in the passage cited above—only
thin and malnourished ones.

Yet the film visualizes the grotesque geriatric body and lustful gaze prominently. A closer look at the mechanics of this scene reveals the following
details: (1) With a long take, the camera pans right on Todd as he approaches
the shower, revealing two boys on each side of him. The camera then moves in
on Todd while arcing to the left 80 degrees until he appears in frame left and
the boy next to him is at the right side of the frame. The camera rests. Then
the camera arcs in the opposite direction, to the left, framing out the other
boy and leaving Todd in center frame. As the camera turns 45 degrees to the
left, the color hue is manipulated from orange and tan tones to gray and blue
tones, an effect possibly created by either digital editing[61] or, less probable,
dark lensing[62] to signal the blurring from waking life to nightmare.

According to John Ottman, the editor of *Apt Pupil*, the effect started as a
computer-generated manipulation using AVID and is nonlinear; later, color
timing, the process of selecting printing lights to allow for the proper rendition of exposure and color when making a print, was used.[63] As Ottman
recounts, "I remember first treating the entire scene with the color effect in
the Avid to be blue—much to the dismay of the cinematographer, who had
shot it all in a muted brownish color. Then it was simply a matter of eventually color timing the footage optically to get it close to the same blue."[64]

The arc then continues another 45 degrees left until it reveals an old man
in the left frame background and Todd in a right-frame-foreground medium
close-up. The camera again rests. Then it pulls back, revealing another man,
this one middle-aged, in frame right, at the foreground, who faces away from
the camera toward Todd (in close-up). Todd is now in the middle of the

frame at mid ground, shown with a medium shot, and the old man is in frame left, shown in the background with a medium long shot. Once again, the camera rests. Todd, continuing to wash his face, has not noticed these men but then lowers his hands from his face to see the aged man, in the right frame foreground, who washes his chest and returns Todd's gaze.

As Todd holds his hand over his mouth and begins to tremble in fear, the camera slowly moves toward him. A cut occurs. (2) A medium close-up of a middle-aged man in the center of the frame is top-lit from the right of the frame, creating an eerie look. As the man continues to wash his chest and stare frame left (implicitly at Todd), the camera slowly zooms in and an eerie Phrygian motif with a sharpened, leading tone begins. The musical sequence E C# E F D F—F tone motivates a cut. (3) What follows is a close-up of Todd. The side of Todd's face takes up the left side of the frame. Todd turns his head right to look at the middle-aged man. Todd turns away quickly to the left and faces the camera, looking over it at the old man. As he stares, fog fills the foreground until he is no longer visible. During this shot, the motif is repeated—E C# E F D F—F tone, which again motivates a lap dissolve. Eventually, fog fills the frame but dissipates to reveal the turning, lacerated, and cadaverous frame of the old man. The musical motif of E C# E F D F resounds with the sudden crescendo of screeching strings and a choir of moaning and dissonant voices and with the faint noise of a barking voice (possibly Dussander's) over a loudspeaker, perhaps replicating the sounds of a concentration camp. In a close-up in center frame, Todd's face appears stupefied and horrified. The camera moves into an extreme close-up of Todd's eyes as fog rolls through the frame. Then, from Todd's point of view, it moves from a medium close-up of the disfigured old man to an extreme close-up. The old man's face is scarred and disfigured, his eyes blank and fatigued. The image begins to fade to gray, matching the hue of the fog. A fade-out and fade-in from gray reveal Todd in mid frame (in a close-up), with his hands covering his face. As the fade continues, the colorization returns from grays and blues back to bright tans, signifying the return to normal consciousness and the present. Once again, as in the earlier shower scene, the camera shots, musical motif, and background sounds link Todd to the old man—as monstrous gazers and victims of the voyeuristic gaze.

The production of this scene erupted into a lawsuit, which alleged that Singer and his crew forced the teenage actors who play Todd's classmates to perform in the nude.[65] Though the case was eventually dismissed because of insufficient evidence, the charge of pedophilic exploitation haunted the film's release when the Women's Coalition, an organization that represented some of the teenage actors involved in the case, staged a press conference to exert public pressure on the Screen Actors Guild to arbitrate the case.[66] Christian Leopold Shea comments, "This [i.e., the shower scene] coupled with a statement by Dussander, in which he hisses that he and Todd 'are fucking each other' . . . has led some, including the attorneys for the plaintiffs in a lawsuit against director Singer and the production company, to allege that Singer deliberately turned the story into one with a strong homosexual subtext.[67]

The last of the gas chamber–shower sequences envisaged in the film is a subtle but significant departure from the novella and the script. The novella describes Todd's murderous anger at having been blackmailed by Dussander, who posed as his grandfather at school, into slaving over books in an attempt to save his plummeting grades. As he bikes home, Todd is described as "washed out, hot-eyed, drained, impotently angry."[68] In its stead, the script envisages a scene in which the obsessively angry Todd slips from his bike and flails wildly at thorny, whiplike vines that threaten to consume him.

> Todd is freaking out. The music builds. Voices we have heard before come in. . . . The thorns cut into him. The more he flails, the more the briars slap against him.
>
> Finally, he tears free of the briars. He climbs back up the treacherous hill and retrieves his bike. Exhausted and bloodied, Todd rides away.[69]

Though the film stays true to the emotional temperament and many of the details of the script, it adds one significant detail: as Todd looks up, from his point of view, the overhanging arc of the tunnel he has crashed into appears mist-filled, like a gas chamber, and an extreme close-up reveals the Nazi swastika; he scrambles off with his bike in a frenzied manner. In this scene, Todd moves unambiguously into the victim position, unlike the earlier shower–gas chamber scenes, in which there is a fluctuation across the roles of victimizer and victim. But the dynamics of the narrative soon move him out of that feminized position.

Another crucial emendation from novella to film adaptation involves Todd's continual rendezvous with Betty Trask being reduced to a single encounter with Becky (Heather McComb) in which he cannot perform sexually.[70] In King's novella, the reader can actively recognize a cause-effect relationship between Todd and Dussander's homoerotic liaison and Todd's progressively impotent interactions with Betty. However, in the film adaptation, there can be no mistaking this connection, because of the patent crosscutting between Todd and Becky in the car and Dussander at home. In the novella, Todd aggressively counteracts this impotence by imagining that Betty is a Jewess, a concentration camp inmate, whom he can rape and torture. In the film, Todd merely claims he is not in the mood and lets Becky assume he "doesn't like girls." Again, these modifications are in accordance with the progressive homoeroticism of an initially misogynistic structure in the novella.

It seems, when Todd and Dussander have a drink to the "beginning and the end of their relationship," that everything might return to "normal" heterosexuality for Todd. Now follows a "Hollywood montage" time-lapse sequence, which reveals the following details: (1) Todd is successful in pitching a shutout baseball game, in which the editorial intercutting presents Becky encouraging him with applause. (2) Todd competes like a professional at basketball practice and meets with the admiration of his coach. (3) Todd enjoys himself thoroughly on a date at the movie theatre with Becky, as they express amusement in each other's company and share a box of popcorn. However, this indulgence of normality is greatly destabilized by the presence of a man, seated a few rows in front of them, who resembles—and cackles like—Dussander. Moreover, the unavoidability of Dussander's curse lingers for the duration of this montage sequence as a result of the background score, "Das ist Berlin."

Dussander in the meantime has begun to recapture a sense of identity that he had lost long ago. Whereas in the novella it is clear that Dussander is a tad too old for sex (206), the film directly shows a correlation between his wearing the SS uniform and his boasting of a homosexual identity. In a nighttime scene, Dussander stands before the mirror in the SS uniform, fingering the buttons. In a close-up, he puts on his hat and begins caressing his face, then his neck; the camera pans on his hand as it progresses down the jacket and his other hand moves down below his waist. In a medium shot, Dussander stands narcissistically in front of the mirror, grasping at his crotch. This moment is disturbed when he hears a derelict, Archie, outside, rummaging through a trash can.

As Dussander watches Archie through the window, the homeless man catches a glimpse of Dussander in uniform before the ex-Nazi steps out of view. Next in a close-up, Dussander's eyes close tightly as he possibly continues to rub his crotch. During this shot, we hear a prelap sound from a television show, which seems to be the release of a coiled spring, arguably conflating the slapstick effect of the sound of a spring with Dussander's erection. The original script is unquestionably subtler and more ambiguous in its homo-eroticism: Dussander awakes to "a clanking sound" and looks like "he could have been having a wonderful sex dream." He watches Archie, and then they "stare at each other for a long moment." The script then elapses five minutes. "The bedroom is nearly dark except for the glowing tip of a cigarette. Dussander is in bed, wide awake."[71]

If the succession of murdered derelicts presented in the novella is meant to reaffirm Todd and Dussander's heterosexuality, the one derelict in the film, Archie, serves a similar purpose. (Archie may appear in the second, or extended, shower sequence; the person in the shower resembles him but may be a different character, as the point may hinge on the interchangeability of Holocaust victims to their victimizers rather than Archie's literal representation in the scene.) However, the visual structuring of eye-line matching by which the film evokes homoeroticism in the aforementioned scene is unattainable in the novella. Another scene that lays bare the technique of eye-line matching is one in which Dussander is returning by bus from the liquor store and again notices Archie, who is seductively gazing at him. Curiously, the bus scene is not in Boyce's original script. In scene 62, "Dussander emerges from a liquor store carrying two bags"; then in scene 63, "Dussander steps off the bus and plods down the sidewalk with his sacks of groceries."[72] Thus the bus scene seems to have been fashioned in keeping with the homoeroticism of an omitted scene in the original script, in which Archie sits uncomfortably near Dussander on a bus stop bench.[73]

An analysis of the formal properties of the bus scene can be detailed in the following way: (1) There is a profile medium close-up shot of Dussander on the bus. He fills the left side of the frame, while Archie is in the background, obscured by the use of selective focus. As Dussander turns his head to look to the back of the bus, the camera lens rack-focuses to Archie. (2) Then comes a cut closer to a medium shot of Archie, who smiles and nods at Dussander. (3) There is a cut back to the medium close-up of Dussander, and the camera rack-focuses back to him as his face shows irritation. (4) There is a cut back to a medium shot of Archie, who is looking out the bus window but turns back to gaze again at Dussander. (5) Once again, there occurs a cut back to a close-up of Dussander, still looking away. As Dussander looks to the back of the bus again, the focus racks again on Archie. (6) Archie looks at Dussander and begins to smile and wave to him. Archie nods and a wide grin spreads across his face. (7) Then follows a cut back to a close-up of Dussander as he turns away again and the focus racks back to Dussander. Dussander looks back again, and the camera rack-focuses back to the wino. (8) The wino now smiles even more and giggles, nodding his head, as if he has made some discovery about Dussander. The structure of this shot–reverse-shot montage implicates Dussander and Archie in a homoerotic division of glances, in which a presumed male heterosexual spectator might identify with Dussander's homophobic discomfort. Singer recognizes this as a potential,[74] but we believe that he underplays the extent to which Archie is meticulously coded as gay (and therefore, aberrant) in his remarks in a footnote to an interview.

Indeed, the scenes in which Archie approaches Dussander in the street and they drink in Dussander's bungalow are manipulative. In the street, Archie assures Dussander, "You don't . . . There's no reason to be rude. I know something about you. I know you're a nice guy. I'm nice too. Just like the boy." He then invites himself for a drink and offers, "Maybe you'll let me use your shower, but first a drink. And then I'll do anything you say." As Dussander shifts his eyes and motions toward his bungalow, Wagner's *Liebestod* sounds in the background, signaling the diegetic music for the next scene. The use of Wagner, of course, alludes not only to Nazism but also to the *Liebestod* (love-death motif) and emphasizes more strongly the implication of a sadistic homoeroticism between Dussander and Archie than does the "soft music" that is suggested in Boyce's script.[75]

The auditory introduction of *Liebestod* motivates the cut to the interior of Dussander's bungalow, where the two share a drink of bourbon. Soon, Dussander begins to stroke Archie's face and hair with his hand and asks, "Do you mind?" "No, not at all," replies Archie. Archie solicits, "You know maybe in the morning, after everything goes o.k., you can let me have ten dollars . . . Maybe even twenty . . . You can relax you know, I've done this before." Now, Dussander moves behind the wino and rubs his head with the knife in his hand, responding, "That's alright, so have I." Richard Scheib correctly observes, "The sensual pleasure with which McKellan caresses and then slits Koteas's throat [*sic*], [is] something that Koteas takes to be a homosexual caress."[76]

Thus Archie is viciously circumscribed as sexually promiscuous and "abnormal" and therefore designated as a justified victim of Dussander, who plunges the knife into his back. First, as a homoerotic object, wearing what appears to be a woman's sweater and scarf and offering sexual favors,[77] Archie serves as a scapegoat for Dussander's gender anxiety, a victim through whom the old Nazi can rearticulate his masculinity. Second, his status as a transient renders him an *Untermensch*, which makes his death insignificant.

When Todd arrives and Dussander manipulates him into finishing off Archie with a shovel, not only are the two joined vis-à-vis the homophobic obligation of traditional masculinity in exterminating homosexuality[78] but also Todd has a share with Dussander in being an *Übermensch.*[79]

Another arguable facet of homoeroticism in the film, which has not been missed by critics, is the portrayal of Todd's high school guidance counselor, Ed French (David Schwimmer). An awkward consultation takes place, in which Dussander poses as Todd's grandfather and claims that Todd's parents are battling at home. French proposes to manipulate Todd's grades: "I offered to go a step further. That means you and I gotta make a deal," French negotiates. Then he asks Dussander to let him be alone with Todd. French commiserates with the boy: "I understand what you're going through. My ex-wife and I went through the nastiest divorce since Henry the Eighth." Then he offers, "I don't want you to feel that you have no one to talk to . . . your parents, girl problems, anything at all . . . here's my home phone. Anything at all . . . anything. You call me, Todd. Call me." As Todd and he shake hands, there is a pointed close-up of the handshake and French squeezes intensely. This close-up, framed in a manner similar to Dussander's making contact with Todd, heightens the homoerotic tension. J. M. Clark appropriately detects that "Singer plants doubts in us as to whether French is gay and whether his concern carries with it a hidden agenda."[80] This is a much subtler subtext in the novella, in which French's actions could be read either paternalistically or homoerotically (fig. 5.4).

The homoerotic subtext would be more evident had one scene in the script, in which French meets Todd in the principal's office, been incorporated into the released film. In Boyce's script, Todd enters the office and as his eyes search the floor, he notices a pair of yellow high-tops. He looks up to see Ed French leaning against the wall. Morgan, the principal, orders Todd to have a seat and pores over Todd's files. The principal commends Todd's improvement and compares his progress to that of another student, Sally Chang, whom Todd has surpassed in advanced-placement biology because she refused to dissect a fetal pig. Besides the obvious racial stereotyping in this scene and the implicit bliss of the principal that white Todd has surpassed an Asian female student,[81] the principal is proud of Todd's "masculinity" in his managing to dissect the pig. So is French. As the principal finishes lavishing praise on Todd, Ed French beams and moves to shake Todd's hand.

The script's direction element reads, "French shakes Todd's hand, an uneasy moment passes between the two of them." After Todd exits the office,

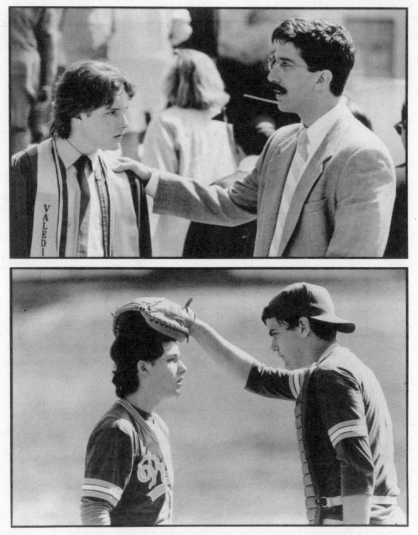

Fig. 5.4. A choice between (potential) homosexual and heterosexual liaisons: Todd and Ed French, his guidance counselor *(top)*, and Todd and Joey (Joshua Jackson), his school chum *(bottom)*. Stills courtesy of the Academy of Motion Picture Arts and Sciences. *Apt Pupil* Productions/Canal+ Droits Audiovisuels/Happy Ending Productions/JD Productions/Paramount Pictures/Phoenix Pictures/TriStar Pictures, 1998.

"French bounds after him." French detains Todd in the hallway, exclaiming, "It's just that I'm really proud of you." Todd tries to escape, and French sympathizes, "This is supposed to be a great time in your life and you don't seem to be enjoying it. . . . Is there anything else I can do?" Todd declines and walks away. The script's direction element reads, "French is left standing a little stunned, a little hurt." The dialogue element states, "Okay, Todd. . . . You let me know if you need anything." Todd does not turn around. French stares after Todd, as he is swallowed into a stream of students.

However, the elision of this sequence does not necessarily weaken the sense that French's fondness for Todd may extend beyond mere professionalism. In fact, both Boyce's script and Singer's conclusion to the film hinge on at least the high probability of French's homoeroticism, as Todd blackmails him when the guidance counselor intends to inform Todd's parents that he knows Dussander has played the impostor and Todd has lied. Todd yells to French, "Does it ever work? I really want to know, does it ever work, or am I the first one? Cause if I'm the first, I'm flattered really, but somehow I can't believe that . . . not after fixing my grades, and then giving me your home phone number, and then you come out here when my parents aren't home."[82]

French grasps for meaning: "What are you talking about?" Todd continues, "I mean you've got some balls! Is this why your wife left you? You really must have wanted to shake my hand . . . or something else." French asks, "Now wait a minute what are you . . . You're gonna tell people I . . . I did something to you, Todd?" French then attempts to reason with him, but Todd continues to make threats, now echoing the words of Dussander: "The things I'm going to say, they'll never go away, not for you. Think of your job," and then bursting out in laughter, "Think of your son." Thus Todd blackmails French into silence with the accusation that he is a pedophile and that he has intended to molest Todd. And the threat is effective not only because French has deceived and manipulated the system like Todd but also because a vicious stigma is attached to homosexuality throughout the film.

Nazism and Monstrous Sexuality

In all of the above cases, one observes the recurring representation of sexual "abnormality," which is baffling to some critics[83] but which we read as a series of codes meant to signal Todd's descent into Nazism, as well as a recurring pattern of acting out the Holocaust. Indeed, not only does Todd spiral downward into the insanity of Nazism that Dussander represents, he also becomes sexually "abnormal." Throughout the novella, King establishes Dussander as a homoerotic surrogate and as a monster because he threatens heterosexual masculinity. However, we argue that this sexual abnormality is not by any means a result of Nazism, despite the insightful comments of some critics concerning the movement's suppressed homoeroticism.[84]

King and Singer employ landscapes of misogyny and homophobia, respectively, to increase the stakes of evil in their monsters. The ideological and social-structural implications of this formation are essentially problematic, for they apparently rely on the same heterocentric assumptions that give rise to fascist values, that is, the criminalization and extermination of individuals on the basis of sexuality. This equation of othered sexuality with evil is not surprising in the wake of a tradition of Holocaust historiography that has silenced the atrocities perpetrated against thousands of homosexual men, lesbians, and bisexuals in the process of the Final Solution. As Robin Wood writes,

> The fact that the Nazis attempted to exterminate gays as well as Jews points to certain fundamental traits of Fascism that our culture generally prefers to gloss over for its own comfort. Alongside the demand for racial purity went the insistence on extreme sexual division: 'masculinity' and 'femininity' must [be] strictly differentiated, women relegated to the subordinate position of the mothers who produce future generations of 'pure' Arians. The reason why patriarchal capitalist society is so reluctant to confront this aspect of Nazism is clearly that it has its own stake in the same assumptions.[85]

The spectatorial relation in *Apt Pupil*, in view of a LaCapran reminder that the victims' voices must not be silenced, seems markedly even less appropriate than *Schindler's List*. Yet unlike its famous docudrama predecessor, *Apt Pupil* makes little claim to authenticity or "historicality" in its commercial packaging. The only documentary footage is shown in the beginning, when credits roll, as we peep over Todd's shoulder and gaze through his eyes at the faded photographs of Nazis and camp inmates in which doctored images of McKellan are seamlessly inserted. Thus, unlike *Schindler's List*, which ends up being a false witness in its exacting pursuit of the look of "the real," *Apt Pupil* ends up honest in its unabashed display of its simulated ontology, steeped in the expectations and conventions of the horror–psychological thriller film. Like *Psycho* and *The Silence of the Lambs*, *Apt Pupil*'s ending may be read as filtered through a conflicted lens, where evil (and vulnerability) are not simply out there but are part of us in our uncritical and voyeuristic consumption of these images.

The film's final scenes crosscut between Dussander's escape from his captors by suicide and Todd's escape from French by blackmail, in which he repeats some of the lines Dussander himself had used to counter-blackmail Todd into submission earlier: "[A scandal like] this will never go away, not for you." The film ends with a dimly lit close-up of the dead Dussander's steely-eyed gaze. Yet it is clear that Dussander's spirit lives on through Todd. In other words, while the novella ends like a classic horror film, in which the monster has been successfully vanquished (the now deranged Todd being gunned down by a SWAT team), the film ends like a contemporary or "postmodern" Gothic narrative, in which the monster lives and is unveiled as part of ourselves rather than as an alien force out there. Thus, whereas the more overtly fictional rendition of the Nazi-as-monster thematic ends up problematizing the boundaries that separate the normal from the monstrous, *Schindler's List*, which attempts a more realistic story, ends up unrealistically preserving them.

The arc from *Schindler's List* to *Apt Pupil* connects the two films as attempts, by two Jewish directors, to work through the Holocaust. Yet, both films act out the meaning of the Holocaust with a Gothic vocabulary, framing the mass murder of the Jews as a horror film. Unlike *Schindler's List*, *Apt Pupil* features so-called sexual abnormality as a distinguishing characteristic of monstrosity, supporting several key binaries, including the normal-monstrous and the heterosexual-homosexual. Nevertheless, despite their differences, both *Schindler's List* and *Apt Pupil* end up drawing from the Nazi-as-monster motif and ultimately reify stereotypic links between horror and the Holocaust. Thus, like so many popular entertainments, *Schindler's List*, *Apt Pupil*, and other films "get to have it both ways," using the Holocaust to depict victims yet at the same time associating the spectacle of their demise with latent reactionary attitudes toward the identity politics of these "victims." Our final chapter works through possible meanings of the Holocaust through film and offers an ethics of spectatorship, which we believe may assist a critical audience in identifying and resisting the temptations of voyeurism, demonization, and the creation of rigid binaries.

6

Framing Evil: Toward an Ethics of Response

The monster remains with us, as Ingebretsen has recently demonstrated in his careful study, as the primary site for explaining social discord and evil.[1] "The ubiquity of the monster in the last two decades is astonishing and practically unnoticed."[2] As much as Arendt's controversial book called into question Eichmann's abnormal monstrosity and that of the Nazi regime, the social commitment to the creation and embellishment of abnormal monsters remains in place as the dominant public explanation of the Holocaust.[3] The tension between Arendt's thesis of the banality of evil and the dominant public framework that sets forth the abnormal monster as the source of the Holocaust's horror is at the heart of our study. In this concluding chapter, we develop the implications of our study and suggest how audiences might better work through the consequences of the Holocaust's horror.

In working through the horror of the Holocaust, we identified, using structural and formal analyses of key films, the role played by frames in the representation of the Holocaust in film. Our contribution to the discussion of frames and framing has been to identify how those involved in the construction and reception of cinematic renditions of the Holocaust are influenced by preexisting traditions of Gothic and horror—a visual vocabulary they inherit in the representation and interpretation of the perpetuators and the victims. David J. Skal, along a parallel track, conducts a genealogy of how the wolf-man story, among other universal monster stories, provided a rich metaphorical depiction of the bestialities of war and examines how Nazi culture was infused with mythical wolf imagery.[4] We have outlined crucial characteristics of the classic horror frame, such as the nature of the gaze and the "shower scene" dynamic; how cinematic renditions of the Holocaust, most notably Spielberg's *Schindler's List*, have appropriated the horror film template; and how other films, like *The Silence of the Lambs*, using a more conflicted frame, acknowledge the Holocaust (even if only through a visual footnote) while interrogating the binaries (e.g., normality-abnormality, active monster–passive victim) at the base of traditional conceptualizations of evil and mass murder.

The relationship between Holocaust studies and horror films is one of critical importance. Until Arendt's *Eichmann in Jerusalem*, traditional representations and explanations of the Holocaust assumed the gratuitous evil of the Nazis, bracketing them as the monsters responsible for the Holocaust.[5] Until the advent of Hitchcock's *Psycho*, horror films were distinguished by their monsters that made "ontological breaks" with the norm. As Carroll writes, "In works of horror, the humans regard the monsters they meet as abnormal, as disturbances of the natural order."[6] In contrast, *Eichmann in Jerusalem* and *Psycho* offered a different frame of evil by collapsing the abnormal into the natural order. This alternative frame has questioned but not sufficiently challenged the culturally dominant mode of explaining horror, one that centers on the abnormal monster.

The classic horror frame of the Holocaust is dominant because the monsters of classic horror films and the Third Reich have been visually conflated through still photographs and the cinema. We have also identified the reciprocal relationship between Holocaust films that use the classic horror frame and post-Holocaust horror films. Holocaust films have appropriated the classic horror frame, and post-Holocaust horror films often deploy Nazis and Holocaust imagery. This relationship may be among the most important implications of our study as both the classic frame of horror and the agents of the Holocaust become archetypal. They become the default ideological explanations of evil in our contemporary real and reel worlds, which intersect in complex ways.

This explanation invites us to reconsider Steffen Hantke's observation that "horrors on the screen and horrors in history occur on different ontological levels, a difference that translates into *profound ethical differences*" (emphasis added).[7] This remark leads us to consider the difference between reel and real horror and the functions played by frames and tropes in Holocaust representation. When Hantke asks whether there is something "frivolous" about "imagining the tropes of horror film and memories of the Third Reich operating side by side," if there "are horrors far worse than those imagined by special effects experts, script writers, and directors," and if the "use of the Holocaust as a source of cinematic horror [is] frivolous and tasteless at best, morally reprehensible at worst?" he poses questions at the heart of our study.[8] Our identification of the classic horror frame in Holocaust movies and subsequent analysis illuminate how directors have represented horror on the screen and how this mode of narration converges with but also diverges from various historical accounts.

The classic horror frame imposed by Steven Spielberg on *Schindler's List* and the fifty thousand survivor testimonies asserts an authentic representation of the Holocaust's horror and promises redemption in the form of Israel or the restoration of a life of health. This dominant "reel" horror frame of the Holocaust, however, is incommensurate with its historical reality. Indeed, some real-life survivors never shed the experience of the concentration camp. As one survivor observed, "I didn't survive the German camps. I am still there. I live at Auschwitz."[9] Still other survivors, such as Peter Szondi, Bruno Bettelheim, Tadeus Borowski, and Primo Levi, committed suicide. Elie Wiesel notes that Levi "died at Auschwitz forty years later."[10] Finally, the classic horror frame of the reel Holocaust excludes the possibility of the "third shadow," that fluid, blended agent of mixed motives that could create both the context and motive for a simultaneously endangered and dangerous agent to act.

As we first explained in chapter 1, the notion of the third shadow builds from the theoretical vocabulary set up by Janice Rushing and Thomas Frentz.[11] Borrowing from Jung, Rushing and Frentz lay the groundwork for an approach that attempts to speak of a "cultural shadow" born in response to the limitations of the conscious perspective of an era and often appearing in the guise of archetypal symbols.[12] Although Rushing and Frentz are aware of the difficulties of attempting to speak about a "collective psyche" as opposed to an individual one, it appears that one of their aims is to resurrect the notion of myth as a useful concept within rhetorical criticism. As they write, "Some myths (what we are now calling 'shadow myths') are revelatory insofar as they visualize the repressed as a precursor to social change. Seen in this way, such myths are rhetorical, not in that they advance the interests of a particular social group but that they narratively advocate a view that simultaneously subverts the dominant cultural ideology and affirms a new image."[13]

In other words, Rushing and Frentz adopt Jung's term for that which is hated, feared, and disowned yet is responded to with intense attraction and repulsion, particularly as projected onto a scapegoat. That term is *shadow*. For as long as the illusion of projection holds, we are saved from the realization that that shadow, whether personal, cultural, or archetypal, is part of us. Rushing and Frentz differentiate between two types of shadows, or two ways through which the psyche excises what it wishes to repress or disown. These two shadows are the "inferior," or first, shadow and the "overdeveloped," or second, shadow. In the first case, the ego sharply sets itself against the other, or "not-I"—the realms of the feminine, body, people of color, and anything else that deviates from rational ego-consciousness.

The overdeveloped, or second, shadow results when the ego sets for itself the mission of absolute control of the other. To accomplish this task, the ego extends itself, first to create tools and later to (d)evolve into a tool itself. However, this (d)evolution results in a radical splintering of the psyche, wherein the inflated ego acts like a God and its split-off alter-ego possesses the same devilish power as the inferior, or first, shadow. For Rushing and Frentz, "the primary form of the overdeveloped shadow . . . is Frankenstein's monster—the ultimate tool, the replication of our bodies and our intelligence through scientific technology."[14]

Thus the technological, or Frankensteinian, myth unveils two primary reactions to the machine: humans approach it either as the monstrous other they must harness or as a part of themselves they must acknowledge. The first reaction continues the deadly projection and splintering; the second begins to recognize that the other is a part of the self—and points out a possible solution to the crisis presented in the myth. The process of splintering and projecting can be halted through recognizing the other as a part of the self. Integration with the technological, overdeveloped shadow is possible only if the hero of a narrative contacts elements in his inferior shadow (such as the feminine or the beast) through either dreams or wakeful experiences.

The first and second shadow figures are easily recognizable in both *Schindler's List* and *Apt Pupil*. *Schindler's List*'s Helen Hirsch, the innumerable naked female bodies in the first shower scene, and even the vulnerably aging and emaciated male bodies reduced to pure flesh on display during medical "inspections" in the concentration camp scenes are all instances of the first shadow. Similarly, Goeth, with his hypermasculinized, bloated body and his pathological appetites for violence and sex, signified in his boastful and careless deployment of his gun and penis, marks him as a second shadow; Dussander, despite his aging-next-door-neighbor look, and Todd, despite his perfect all-American-boy-next-door appearance, share the same appetites and the obsessive defense of their masculinities. The narrative is slightly more complex in *Apt Pupil* than in *Schindler's List* because evil or the monstrous is not simply "out there" to be unproblematically staked or exorcised but is lurking within the very heart of contemporary America and lives on in disguise.

A third type of shadow, a natural offshoot of Rushing and Frentz's framework, is the "feminine-as-monstrous," or the female monster. We use the term *feminine-as-monstrous* to refer to women whose beauty, intelligence, and ambition render them dangerous; female monsters, even more so than male creatures, occupy the hybrid locus of being both powerful and vulnerable, compelling and repulsive, attractive and grotesque. Neither dangerous females nor female monsters survive for long in Frankensteinian films. They are either murdered (justifiably, according to the narrative logic) or given no narrative alternative to death. It is interesting that no third shadow figures exist in either *Schindler's List* or *Apt Pupil*. Monica, Todd's mother, is a potential third shadow figure in King's novella because of the "half-informed intuition" that Todd imagines he sees in his mother's eyes regarding his relationship with Dussander; in the film, she is not only unsuspecting and utterly domesticated but also devoid of the dangerous physical attractiveness that characterizes her portraiture in the novella. One could argue that Hirsch is a potential third shadow by virtue of her sexual desirability, which moves Goeth to want to rape, marry, or torture her and Schindler to comfort or rescue her. Yet insofar as the narrative always depicts her as an object acted upon rather than an agent of action, even if ambivalently so, she remains safely within the first shadow categorization. A minor character, a female architect who tries to warn the Nazis that the foundations of a structure should be rebuilt because of faulty construction, is a third shadow because of her knowledge, audacity, and even idealism in trying to issue the warning. That she is summarily shot in the head before her advice is, ironically, followed is not surprising.

One of the key insights of *The Cinematic Rebirths of Frankenstein* is that, using Rushing and Frentz's framework, one could argue that the degree of hyperbole required to maintain the myth of parthenogenesis—masculine self-birthing—at the heart of the Frankensteinian "cinemyth" is so great that it critically undercuts the repressive movement. In other words, the extreme denial of the ego's shadows results in their confrontation; the most crucial figure to track in this development is the third shadow, the female monster or the feminine-as-monstrous. Unlike *The Silence of the Lambs*, in which Clarice moves fluidly across the realms of (potential) first shadow and third shadow (as when she penetrates Gumb's basement), or *Psycho*, in which Lila Crane occupies a similar position of being both potentially endangered and dangerous as she descends into the basement of the Bates motel, no such third shadow emerges from either *Schindler's List* or *Apt Pupil*. The upshot is that Holocaust-as-horror films actually end up being less progressive or at least less nuanced in their depictions of gender and power than even classic horror films.

A more detailed look at female monsters in Holocaust and horror films would significantly add to what we have contributed here. An example could be Shirley Stoler's performance in *Seven Beauties*, coupled with her casting in *Honeymoon Killers*.[15] But few women occupy such roles in movies that move across both the Holocaust narrative and the horror genre—an observation very much in keeping with the main theses of this book. Third shadows do not typically abound in Holocaust-as-horror narratives. Even *Seven Beauties* itself fits more into a horror comedic or comedic melodramatic format than a strict horror classification.

There are hints that the reach and the influence of the Holocaust-as-horror film are now global. In *Red Cherry* (1995), a Chinese film that won the Golden Goblet award for best actress at the Shanghai International Film Festival, a Chinese woman finds her way to Nazi Germany, where she is captured and then tortured by a Nazi general, who ties her down and tattoos her back. *Red Cherry*'s Nazi fetishism is clear, as is the same pattern of voyeurism on display in *Schindler's List*. The woman is naked in the scene in which she is tattooed, making *Red Cherry* one of the first such Chinese films to pass the scrutiny of Chinese censors (fig. 6.1). That justification seems grounded in the "naturalness" of this spectacle against the milieu of female victimization and Nazi torture.

In addition, several popular Japanese anime films exploit the same narrative motif. *The Adventures of Kekkou Kamen: Naked Justice* (1995), a comedy, sets up a scene in which sadistic schoolteachers make jokes while a young girl is hung up, whipped, and then tortured by a sadistic Nazi. Though the scene could be justified as a satirical critique of the Japanese educational system, the sexualization of violence (and its use of Nazism as a prop) is clear: an eroticized view of the girl's breasts, reinforced by a change in music, introduces "an element of arousal and titillation."[16] An even more exploitive

Fig. 6.1. Exportation of the Nazi motif in *Red Cherry*. Still courtesy of the Academy of Motion Pictures Arts and Sciences. Ye Daying, 1995.

adult Japanese anime, the video game *UltraVixen*, features a large-eyed college student, Ariel, who is trapped in various torture chambers, in spaceships, or in Nazi Germany; the goal of the game is to use a variety of sex toys to induce the trapped woman into "super-orgasms," which enable her to "time warp" out of these torture chambers.[17] Another anime, called *Wizards*, features "drugs, sex, Nazis, pixies, fairies, and Hitler . . . World War 2 . . . set in a fantasy land with lots of sex, drugs, and Nazi propaganda that ends with an assassination during a major anticlimax with the world destroyed and everyone killed in concentration camps."[18] The tie between Nazi Germany and sexual violence in Japanese anime is justified, tongue in cheek (though with a cutting candidness), by the following response: "In the last AnimEssence, the question was raised: why do Japanese anime and manga use Germanic trappings to invoke militaristic imagery? The facile answer is: why should they not? The symbols and regalia of Nazi Germany are certainly what we Americans would use to represent militarism run amok. To paraphrase Indiana Jones, we hate these guys."[19]

Thus the tie between eroticized violence, the fetishism of Nazi symbols, and the perpetuation of Nazi-as-sexualized-monster has come to function as an international visual narrative currency (fig. 6.2). The need to understand frames of evil becomes an international imperative.

Frames of Evil

Because the mass media and cinema act as the primary conveyances for the ideology of the Holocaust as horror and horror as the Holocaust, it is essential that viewers of the mediated image understand the role played by frames in the representation of evil. The framing and representation of the "monster" is deeply inflected by ideology, and the means by which monsters are constructed and depicted "go willfully unnoticed, and this might be said to constitute the ideological burden carried by the genre."[20] Ingebretsen critiques the rhetorical shaping of narratives through which prejudice masks

Fig. 6.2. Nazi-as-sexualized-monster becoming international visual narrative currency. Still from *Schindler's List* courtesy of the Academy of Motion Pictures Arts and Sciences. Amblin/Universal, 1993.

itself as fear—a simulation and stimulation of public feelings similar to the pornographic mode, which also entails an erotic striptease of the body of the monster. Monster-talk, like Freud's mythic patricide and rape of the primal mother and sister, justifies and cements violent commonality as it simultaneously relieves individuals from responsibility for these "uncivilized" emotions, much like Freud's notion of the ritualized and communal slaughter of the totem animal. As we noted in chapter 1, this is particularly true in framing Germany as a unique or demarcated space and then staking the Nazis as abnormal monsters, outside the pale of the German culture, and treating Nazism as an aberration in German history; all these absolve modern-day Germans of responsibility for the Nazi era.[21]

We have identified a pattern in the representation of monsters and victims in Holocaust and horror films. To discover the common ways in which the Holocaust is represented and horror films are constructed, we analyzed the formal characteristics of both. In so doing, we revealed the unnoticed ideological burden carried by the two genres, in both their separate and their joined expressions. American Holocaust films draw from a preexisting Gothic and horror frame for their renditions of the Shoah. This template posits the repulsive monster, separate from normal society, as the explanation for social trauma.

Ingebretsen notes "the telling of the monster, caught up in ideology, can only be spoken in formulas that preexist it."[22] The frame for the "telling of the monster," invented in Gothic laboratories, lives on in media constructions of monstrosity.[23] Despite the power of Ingebretsen's critique, his frame of horror joins classic horror (such as Whale's *Frankenstein*), in which the monster is portrayed as radically abnormal and is destroyed by angry mobs, with more contemporary hybrid versions of horror. In the latter, the divide between normality and the monstrous is less clear. Witness, for example, Demme's *The Silence of the Lambs*, in which all the characters, even Clarice Starling, share the monstrous or penetrative gaze; the gender deviancies of Jame Gumb (Buffalo Bill; fig. 6.3) are hinted to be outgrowths of a monstrous childhood and the Vietnam war; and Hannibal Lecter becomes a dark angel with whom we identify. This conflation of horror frames fails to acknowledge the clear patterns of framing in the horror genre.

The dynamic of monster-talk in American Holocaust film narratives is more akin to classic than to contemporary horror. This seems a natural move, given that images of Gothic monstrosity provide a natural archetype or template that moviemakers, attempting to work through the trauma

Fig. 6.3. Jame Gumb from *The Silence of the Lambs*. His gender deviancies are hinted as outgrowths of a monstrous childhood and the Vietnam war. Still courtesy of the Academy of Motion Picture Arts and Sciences. Orion Pictures Corporation, 1991.

of the Holocaust, use to frame the agents they represent in their films. In turn, post-Holocaust horror films have appropriated the Nazi monster as an archetypal monster. Both film genres invisibly serve as "formal emotional shorthand of civic possibility,"[24] teaching us what boundaries we must not breach if we are to remain within the realm of the "civilized" and "normal." Both dynamics are evident in Spielberg's *Schindler's List* and Singer's *Apt Pupil*, among other films.

The monster in the Holocaust film and in the classic horror film is beyond the pale of normality; indeed, it represents the inhuman. As Carroll observes,

"In examples of horror, it would appear that the monster is an extraordinary character in our ordinary world."[25] Ingebretsen traces this frame to a deep societal need to project its evil.[26] The monster becomes the literal other onto which society can pin all of its anxieties, fears, and guilt. The monster is the recurring and repetitive source of social trauma: "[m]onsters announce, work through, and negotiate social trauma in the very formulaic terms of which they are thought to be unique."[27] When this formula is translated into cinematic frames, then historical events like the Holocaust are rendered as Gothic horror stories.

Frankenstein, Dracula, and other classical monsters, before they became overused and domesticated, evoked fear and nausea on the part of their audiences. Schindler's List's Amon Goeth is a repugnant character, his bloated and sweaty body swaggering from one cruel action to another. What Frankenstein (especially the Hammer studio versions), Dracula, and Goeth share is their repellant nature; they are framed as the embodiment of evil. As such, the repetitive acting out of social trauma can be traced to the culturally embedded and valorized role played by the monster.

Monsters also represent deviance, most notably in gender and sex. In Apt Pupil, the relationship between homosexuality and Nazism is framed as essential. Ingebretsen points to the iconic popularity of Hitchcock's Psycho (1960) and Castle's Homicidal (1961) as pivotal in establishing the link between homicide and gender deviancy. He points to the media construction of the serial killer Andrew Cunanan as "homicidal homosexual" to illustrate how the modern frame of evil draws a necessary relationship between gender "deviancy" and murder. The visualization of Cunanan's body in the media was rife with his ambiguous status as a "man": "Cunanan was dressed like a woman; he was seen in a peach dress, shopping for cereal; he shaved his body hair like a woman; he was found with the gun by his groin; he shopped and spent extravagantly and was loose sexually."[28] Ingebretsen points out discrepancies between firsthand accounts that draw a portrait of Cunanan as inept and barely surviving and the fluctuations of the media across images of Cunanan as spendthrift boy toy (who showed up at his high school dance in a red jumpsuit, draped in the arms of an older man) and as a national threat, the capture of whom requires "machine-guns, helicopters, boats, dogs and a SWAT team in black armour [sic] bearing shields."[29] He also shows how Cunanan's story fails as a criminal portrait (as he did not fit the standard narrative of the serial or spree killer) but succeeds as a Gothic one focused on Cunanan's "killing queerness."

That sadomasochism and homoeroticism are framed as central to Nazism in the Holocaust film has long been recognized and is frequently observed. Ilan Avisar, in *Screening the Holocaust*, traces what he calls the connection of Nazism and sexual deviance to Rossellini's *Open City*.[30] Gerd Gemünden suggests that in 1943, "the association of male homosexuality with sadism and perversion [as in the effeminate portrayal of Heydrich in *Hangmen Also Die*] . . . anticipates postwar films such as *The Damned* (Visconti, 1969) and *Night Porter* (Cavani, 1974)."[31] However, Richard Plant, in *The Pink Triangle*, indicates that the Soviet film *The Fighters* (Wangenheim, 1936) depicted Nazis as effeminate perverts.[32] Indeed, this mythic pairing between gender deviance and violence has become so commonplace in contemporary American films that in *American Beauty* (1999), which was produced by Spielberg's Dreamworks movie factory, Colonel Frank Fitts (Chris Cooper) possesses Nazi artifacts and expresses homophobic attitudes, yet makes a sexual pass at the protagonist Lester Burnham (Kevin Spacey). The tie between homosexuality and Nazism is a recurring theme in many contemporary films and is a prominent expression of LaCapra's notion of acting out that echoes through contemporary cinema.

In addition, there is dominant frame of the victim in horror and Holocaust films. If the monster's body is the locus of abnormal behavior, the female body is the site of the monster's destructive behavior. This is true in both genres. Scherr's analysis of sexuality in Holocaust fiction brings this thesis home, as she detects a pattern we identified in *Schindler's List*.[33] The female body becomes the site of the viewer's voyeuristic pleasure (fig. 6.4), as the camera places the spectator within the shoes of the tormentor in such movies as Liliana Cavani's *The Night Porter* (1974). Once again, a key scene involves a shower; the scene is coded as a resurgence of memory through its wordlessness and its being set up as a flashback.

> In one flashback, a very thin and naked Lucia stands alone, cowering against a wall of showers. Max is shooting at her, purposefully missing, but marking his absolute power over her fate. Her body is extremely skinny, an obvious signifier of the "real" starvation actual prisoners suffered. But here Lucia's emaciated body becomes an erotic site, because we are also aware of Max's interest in Lucia, so that "shooting one's gun" is evident also as a sexual metaphor.[34]

A furious debate rages over whether *The Night Porter* is a film shot from a "woman's point of view," because the director, Liliana Cavani, is a woman (and

Fig. 6.4. The beautiful masochistic victim redux in *The Night Porter*. Still courtesy of the Academy of Motion Picture Arts and Sciences. Italonegglio Cinematografico/ Lotar Film Productions, 1974.

therefore represents deeper and unsettling existential truths concerning the female human condition) or whether the film is still about Max's (the Nazi officer turned night porter, played by Dirk Bogarde) fantasy-nightmare with which Lucia (Max's former "little girl" at the camp now turned bourgeois wife to a famous conductor, played by Charlotte Rampling) is problematically constructed to be complicit.[35] Nevertheless, despite the construction of Max as also a victim (he and Lucia eventually being killed by his fellow Nazis, in a manner that mimes his own torture and murder of prisoners), it is clear that it is his point of view the audience is invited to share, while Lucia's is more vague and indeterminate. Throughout the film, the only aspects of Lucia's character that are developed are her passion for Max and her reactiveness to his presence. The result thus remains within LaCapra's characterization of acting out: Holocaust memory becomes "sexy memory," in which the spectacle of the vulnerable, eroticized female body elicits a reaction of pleasure (fig. 6.5), inevitably "warping the historical facts of the Holocaust."[36] The use of soft-porn techniques creates a sentimental idyll between victimized victimizer and utter victim against the backdrop of Nazi brutality.

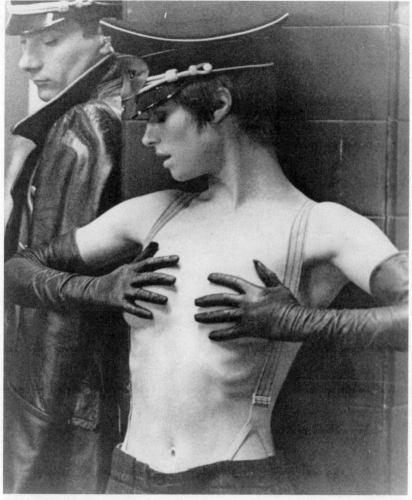

Fig. 6.5. The Holocaust as "sexy memory" in *The Night Porter*. Still courtesy of the Academy of Motion Picture Arts and Sciences. Italonegglio Cinematografico/Lotar Film Productions, 1974.

In the classic horror genre and the American Holocaust film, monsters and their victims are spatially, chronologically, and psychologically framed in the domain of the other. The horror genre established the space inhabited by monsters as separate and distinct from common society. Similarly, the Holocaust is framed in many films about it as occurring in a particular place, Germany.[37]

Our formal analysis reveals that the audience's gaze is framed to demarcate a space of murder and genocide. The peephole, vivid in *Psycho*, *Schindler's List*,

The Silence of the Lambs, and *Apt Pupil*, is the cinematic wedge placed between the spaces of murder and normality. In *Schindler's List* and *Apt Pupil*, as we illustrated in the previous chapters, the peephole is the entrance for the audience into a domain of evil from which one can leave or view in an apparently neutral or merely documentary fashion; in *Schindler's List* the women discover the shower streams are not toxic, and in *Apt Pupil* Todd awakens from his dream of the Holocaust showers. Though Todd becomes increasingly haunted by these visions, we also become increasingly alienated from him, thus reestablishing our boundaries between the monstrous (which can never escape evil) and the normal (which may glimpse evil but escape from it, unscathed).

In addition, the time frame occupied by the traditional monster is the past; so, too, is the event of the Holocaust. If the monsters responsible for victimization can be left in the past, then those who follow in time can jettison any connection with them. This pattern, according to Brenner, is particularly true in postwar Germany, as many Germans use *Schindler's List* and Goldhagen's *Hitler's Willing Executioners* as the visual and intellectual means of shedding their connection to and responsibility for the "sins of the father."[38] Finally, the horror genre and the Holocaust film separate the viewer psychologically from monsters. Monsters, in their bodies and sexuality, prompt revulsion, allowing the viewer to disavow any sentient or psychological identification. At the same time, the audience is often allowed the guilty pleasure of viewing their acts on the female body while absolving them of responsibility.

In summary, the classic horror frame and the historical school of ideological intentionalism overlap in identifying the Nazi monster as the dominant cause of the Holocaust. As a narrative structure, the story of the Holocaust, with the abnormal monster in the limelight, is instantly recognizable by audiences raised in the Gothic and classic horror tradition. We are not alone in suggesting historians, like Goldhagen, use the classic horror frame when they construct historical explanations of the Holocaust. Regardless, in working through the trauma of horror and the Holocaust, one must unveil the cultural assumptions regarding monstrosity, victims, and the other, illuminating the willfully unnoticed and unconscious sources and explanations of horror and the Holocaust. Once unveiled, they can be worked through.

Working Through the Horror of the Holocaust

One benefit of our attempt to bridge LaCapra's psychoanalytic framework with film criticism is that we can highlight the patterns displayed in and the relationship between horror and Holocaust films, doing so within the

constraints of historical inquiry. We have established the link between the
cinematic frames of the Holocaust and the creation of not only the written
history but also the popular memory of the event. LaCapra's work acknowledges the aesthetic realities and forces in the representation of social trauma,
as well as the brute realities that may not readily yield to nuance or an ac-
curate accounting.[39] Rather than bracket and then privilege the aesthetic or
its purported opposite, reality, LaCapra sets forth a mode of inquiry based
on the notion of the Nietzschean *Schwergewicht* that interrogates, seeks, and
resists simplistic definitive answers and a complete blurring of boundaries,
which constitute a form of nihilism.[40]

LaCapra offers a system of reason and judgment that allows for the possibility of limited understanding and rectification. He is careful not to transform "acting out" and "working through" into a pair of antonyms or binaries;
both are part of the psychological process engaged by trauma. The notions
of "acting out" and "working through" help to illuminate the dimly understood cultural ingredients that foster repetitious narratives for the negotiation of social trauma. For us and for those who come to the history of the
Holocaust through film, LaCapra's framework demands a deep immersion
into cinematic texts, not to search for immaculate or objective truths but
to derive insights into human behavior that cannot be reduced to one ideological package or set of explanatory principles. The framework he offers
arms the film critic with a theoretical apparatus that places cinema in its
psychohistoric context.

There are good answers, if not definitive or closed, about such traumas as
the Holocaust. In working through the Holocaust, LaCapra acknowledges
some of the partial truths in Goldhagen's arguments about the monstrosity of the Nazis and the German people but points to the better historical
scholarship that provides more refined and textured accounts of Germany, the
Jews, and genocide. Consistent with LaCapra's framework, we have offered
the results of historical inquiry as the measure of the cinematic representations of the Holocaust. The judgments offered about the horror depicted
in Holocaust films should be informed by the research of Browning and the
detailed research on the origins of genocide.[41] Our addition to this literature
is an analysis of cinematic frames and framing, which, given the importance
of film in the creation of historical consciousness, serves both critics of film
and those of history.

We have argued for the use of multiple and blended frames in representing the Holocaust. In working from history to film and back, we turn in

particular to the writings of Yehuda Bauer and his recent book, *Rethinking the Holocaust,* for additional support of this argument.[42] Bauer's lifelong study of the Holocaust, as well as the primary and secondary literature, helps us to assess the patterns of acting out we have highlighted in Holocaust films. First Bauer insists that the Holocaust is open to explanation and that attempts to explore, with research and reason, how and why the Holocaust took place are legitimate. Contrary to Lawrence Langer and others, Bauer does not believe the Holocaust is incomprehensible and mysterious.[43] That said, he does not settle for either the ideological intentionalists or the functional-structuralist explanation of the Holocaust. Similarly, LaCapra sees some strength in the Arendt thesis of banality but at the same time acknowledges that the Nazis activated what Bauer terms a "moderate" rather than a virulent form of anti-Semitism, particularly compared with Romania and Russia.[44] There were elite Nazis motivated by anti-Semitism, yet rank-and-file Germans were much less driven by a hatred of the Jews than by patriotism. Indeed, argues Bauer, relative to other European countries, Germany provided greater, albeit restricted, freedoms to Jews.[45] What comes out of Bauer's research is a much more complicated representation of Germany and of those responsible for the Holocaust than is found in many American Holocaust films. His history successfully restricts the degree to which German monstrosity should be held responsible for the Holocaust.

Bauer also questions the depiction of Jews as passive in the face of the Nazi monstrosity. He assembles impressive evidence that they resisted the Nazis, with and without the use of violence. Jews fought the Nazis with whatever means they had at their disposal, even turning sexuality into a weapon. Corroborating Bauer's contention, Scherr refers to the famous Jewish woman "dancer" at Auschwitz who removed her clothing in front of leering SS officers, then seized a gun and proceeded to shoot at the officers before committing suicide to deprive the Nazis of the satisfaction of revenge.[46] This story, which was recounted in several memoirs by Auschwitz survivors, has undergone several novelistic renditions, with perhaps the most famous one being Arnold Lustig's version. Lustig's *Darkness Casts No Shadow* was confiscated by the Czech Communist government and banned for twenty-one years. *A Prayer for Katarina Horovitzova,* a film version of the story, casts the protagonist as a beautiful Polish singer, who is forced to strip in front of the SS and then rips the pistol from an SS officer's holster and shoots him before she and her companions are killed. Bauer's work, like *Darkness Casts No Shadow* and *A Prayer for Katarina Horovitzova,* demonstrates that while

Jews were certainly victims, they were not all completely passive; nor did they accept their fate without resistance. In working through the horror of the Holocaust, Bauer's powerful condensation of the research confronts and problematizes many of the images of monstrosity and passive victimhood represented in the films we have studied.

Countervailing frames in both the horror genre and Holocaust scholarship locate the monstrous and evil within the structures of society and the norm. While Halberstam may have overstated her case that "the [classic] monster is dead," she is certainly to the point when she identifies *Silence of the Lambs* as a postmodern horror film, visualizing Hannah Arendt's thesis of the commonness of evil developed in *Eichmann in Jerusalem*. However, this frame still yields to an overriding ideology promoted by the classic horror genre and a historical narrative that features the Nazi monster and the passive Jewish victim. We believe audiences working through the horror of the Holocaust will benefit from the habits of reasoning we have used in this book, as they help to identify the patterns of acting out that prevent many from coming to terms with the social trauma of the Holocaust. We are also hopeful that our study will assist in the development of LaCapra's vision of an "ethic of response."

This issue of an ethics of spectatorship is particularly pressing, given one incident that has not been discussed much, in relation to the reception of *Schindler's List*. In Oakland, California, a group of between sixty-eight and seventy Castlemont High School students (mostly African Americans and Hispanics) undergoing a crash course in "sensitivity," "racial and ethnic tolerance," and the effects of the deprivation of human rights, were ejected from a movie viewing of *Schindler's List* when they giggled through a pivotal and poignant scene: the sudden and dispassionate shooting in the head of a Jewish female architect by a Nazi officer.[47] When Spielberg later visited the school and asked some black students in Oakland, California, why they laughed during that particular scene, he was told it was because they thought the violence was "not realistic enough." Spielberg reported that one sixteen-year-old student claimed to have seen three people killed in real life, and as such, the film rendition of the killing did not seem convincing.[48] The incident thus underlines the significance of the issues we grapple with in this book: how the "look of the real" sets up, to some extent, the conditions of possibility of an ethic of response. Finally, the event provoked an array of countercharges of Jewish racism and black anti-Semitism, thus revealing "a morality tale on the dangers of the current hair-trigger mind-set toward anything that might qualify as cultural insensitivity."[49] It also reflects how this project is not interested in simplistic moralistic formulations regarding what criteria should be fulfilled in creating artistic representations of violence, trauma, and in particular, the Holocaust.[50]

Toward an Ethic of Response and Spectatorship

Beyond the relationship between historical inquiry and the veracity of cinematic texts, we seek to develop the outlines of what LaCapra has called an "ethic of response" to the trauma of those who suffered during and since the Holocaust.[51] In setting forth an ethic of response, we are not claiming that film theorists and critics have failed to consider the moral implications of film. Rather, we believe that the work of historians like LaCapra can assist scholars of film to make more explicit the ethical touchstones that they and audiences might use in making judgments of film that claim to represent history. While LaCapra's position on ethics is integral to his theory of working through trauma, he does not develop it as an ethic for audiences of Holocaust film as such. Our concern is with the audience and its reception of cinematic renditions of the Holocaust.

We attempt in this book to develop LaCapra's ethic of response in several directions. Our approach shifts the focus from those responsible for the creation of the film (although such a focus can be appropriate, among many other possible points of examination) to the critical practices of viewership and an audience's sense of responsibility in consuming films that intersect with the Holocaust, particularly when, as in the case of *Schindler's List*, there is a premium placed on historical "truth telling." Thus, in bringing historical inquiry to bear on representations of horror in Holocaust films, we examine a crucial factor in our search for a possible ethics of spectatorship.

As LaCapra has pointed out, some practitioners of critical studies detach aesthetics from other concerns, thereby severing ethical responsibilities borne by the artist. LaCapra argues that an ethical challenge to aesthetics helps account for the historicity and the political implications of representation, in particular for those cinematic texts that, like *Schindler's List*, perform pedagogical, historical, and legal functions, even serving as the punishment for the crime of anti-Semitic action in some states. One can link aesthetics to history with an ethic of response but still not know what is meant, in this context, by the notion of ethics.

As spectators of Holocaust films, audiences make judgments about mediated representations of Nazis, Jews, and the attending events. These judgments become ethical when they move beyond pure aesthetics into history, memory, and politics, affecting policy and the lives of others. *Schindler's List*'s coda, which highlights Israel as the site of Jewish redemption, illustrates how contemporary politics are reinforced by renditions of the Holocaust. At another level, the Gothic mode and classical horror frame affect the manner in which many explain monsters and victims, influencing accounts of the Holocaust.

An ethic of response and spectatorship calls for the use of blended and multiple frames in representing and understanding the Holocaust. The use of such frames actively resists definitive answers and allows the issues raised by the Holocaust to remain open to further interrogation. In his *Imagining the Holocaust*, Daniel Schwarz notes that "as [Holocaust] survivors pass away . . . the written and oral records that they leave behind become necessarily the basis for future imaginative reconstructions."[52] Echoing LaCapra, Schwarz concludes, "The intelligibility of history, even the place of evil in history, depends on reconfiguring its imaginative and aesthetic terms."[53] Unfortunately, Schwarz does not develop in his book just how that ethical impulse would affect the reconfiguration of an imagined history. In this book, we have attempted to show how frames are used to create dominant representations of the Holocaust and how blended and alternative frames cultivate a more robust interplay of memory and imagination. Historical explanations of the Holocaust, particularly of perpetrators and victims, are vastly more complicated than the clean depictions of monsters and their prey seen in the cinematic representations of the Holocaust.

LaCapra, in his *Yad Vashem* interview, provides another entrance to an ethic of response when he observes, "Moreover, especially in an ethical sense, working through does not mean avoidance, harmonization, simply forgetting the past or submerging oneself in the present. It means coming to terms with trauma, including its details, and critically engaging the tendency to act out the past."[54] In extending the ethical impulse described by LaCapra, we believe knowledge of framing and history can lead to a better sense of evil, trauma, and horror.

For example, we detailed how the Hirsch character was transformed from one who deserved sympathy from an audience into an object of the audience's sexual gaze. In resisting the guilty pleasure invited by such representations, the audience can become part of a larger movement that could challenge such cinematic constructions. This resistance would be predicated on a LaCapra-inspired concern for history and for other human beings as they are imagined and then represented on the screen.

Our hope is that audiences, working through the social trauma of horror and the Holocaust, will come to recognize their participation in much larger narrative formulae that place a premium on monstrosity and elide the role of modernity in depriving millions of their lives and dignity. These narratives often frame the suffering of others in a manner that allows for merely "documentary" enjoyment. Our ethical response to the suffering and murder of others, both real and imagined through film, is a measure of our humanity. One of our goals has thus been, as Elana Gomel elegantly phrases it, "not to castigate narrative representations for supposedly inciting violence. Rather, it is to look at the diverse ways in which narrative representation makes us into subjects capable of both violence and of resistance to it."[55]

NOTES
BIBLIOGRAPHY
INDEX

Notes

Foreword

1. A "'limit event' is an event or practice of such magnitude and profound violence that its effects rupture the otherwise normative foundations of legitimacy and so-called civilising tendencies that underlie the constitution of political and moral community." Simone Gigliotti, "Unspeakable Pasts as Limit Events," 164.

Introduction

1. Ellis, *Contested Castle*, 7.

2. Schwarz, *Imagining the Holocaust*, 1.

3. Schwarz, *Imagining the Holocaust*, 5, 6.

4. Cynthia Ozick, "Who Owns Anne Frank?," *New Yorker*, Oct. 6, 1997, 76, quoted in Schwarz, *Imagining the Holocaust*, 20.

5. Schwarz, *Imagining the Holocaust*, 14.

6. Langer, *Holocaust Testimonies*, quoted in Schwarz, *Imagining the Holocaust*, 13.

7. Michael Andre Bernstein, "Lasting Injury: Competing Interpretations of the Nazi Genocide and the Passionate Insistence on Its Uniqueness," *TLS*, Mar. 7, 1997, no. 4901, 3, quoted in Schwarz, *Imagining the Holocaust*, 8.

8. Schwarz, *Imagining the Holocaust*, 12.

9. Irving Howe, "Writing and the Holocaust," *New Republic*, Oct. 27, 1986, 28, quoted in Schwarz, *Imagining the Holocaust*, 22.

10. Wiesel, *Night*, 32.

11. Schwarz, *Imagining the Holocaust*, 6.

12. Wiesel, *Night*, 31.

13. Langer, "Alarmed Vision."

14. Adorno, "Essay on Cultural Criticism," 34.

15. Steiner, Preface to *Language and Silence*.

1. The Horror Frame and the Holocaust Film

1. Doneson, *Holocaust in American Film*, 7. For a comprehensive survey of Holocaust films, see Picart, *Holocaust Film Sourcebook*.

2. Rosenfeld, "Rush of Remembrance."

3. See Doneson, *Holocaust in American Film*; Insdorf, *Indelible Shadows*; and Avisar, *Screening the Holocaust*.

4. See Lentin, *Re-Presenting the Shoah*; and Hoffman, *After Such Knowledge*.

5. See Loshitzky, *Spielberg's Holocaust*.

6. Blum, "Race, Community and Moral Education"; and Scapperotti, "Stephen King's *Apt Pupil*." For recent scholarship on *Schindler's List*, see Norris, *Writing War*; Schwarz, *Imagining the Holocaust*, 209–38; and Modleski, "Context of Violence."

7. Schwarz, *Imagining the Holocaust*, 7.

8. Hirsch, *Afterimage*, 41.

9. Nichols, *Introduction to Documentary*; and Renov, *Subject of Documentary*.

10. Staiger, *Media Reception Studies*; and Staiger, *Interpreting Films*.

11. Staiger, *Interpreting Films*, 4.

12. Staiger, *Interpreting Films*, 93.

13. Staiger's sample of readers for an analysis of Hitchcock's *Rear Window* is the same as ours: "I have not tried," she writes, "to find marginal readings in nondominant media sources. The reading public studied is film reviewers . . . [and] academic scholars" (*Interpreting Films*, 89).

14. Hirsch, *Afterimage*, 147–48. To corroborate this observation, Hirsch cites Horowitz, "But Is It Good for the Jews?" and Hoberman, "Myth, Movie, Memory."

15. Irwin-Zarecka, *Frames of Remembrance*.

16. LaCapra, *Writing History, Writing Trauma*; LaCapra, *History and Memory after Auschwitz*; and LaCapra, *Representing the Holocaust*.

17. LaCapra, *Representing the Holocaust*, 210.

18. Rothberg, *Traumatic Realism*.

19. Stier, *Committed to Memory*, 71.

20. Pinedo, "Postmodern Elements," 85–117.

21. Pinedo, "Postmodern Elements," 90.

22. For a consideration of how monsters were depicted in classic horror films and, in particular, how Frankenstein movies have evolved, see Picart, Smoot, and Blodgett, *Frankenstein Film Sourcebook*; and Picart, *Cinematic Rebirths of Frankenstein*.

23. Hantke, "Horror Film and the Historical Uncanny," 121.

24. Hantke, "Horror Film and the Historical Uncanny," 121.

25. Deren, *Legend of Maya Deren*, 37.

26. Carroll, *Philosophy of Horror*, 4.

27. Ingebretsen, *At Stake*, 25.

28. Ingebretsen, *At Stake*, 25, 28.

29. Carroll, *Philosophy of Horror*, 16.

30. Prince, "Dread, Taboo and The Thing."

31. Berenstein, *Attack of the Leading Ladies*, 10.

32. See, for example, Benshoff, *Monsters in the Closet*.

33. Jackson, *Fantasy*, 179.

34. Korner, "Arrogance of Youth."

35. Weinraub, "For Spielberg."

36. Bob Keeler, "The Holocaust Remembered; An Ambitious Project Is Videotaping 350–400 Survivors Each Week," *Newsday*, Feb. 24, 1997, B4.

37. Stier, *Committed to Memory*, 76.

38. These criticisms have been rebutted by Michael Berenbaum, former chief of the U.S. Holocaust Memorial Museum's research institute, hired by Spielberg to be the foundation's president to offset the charge that the Survivors of the Shoah Visual History Foundation was too "Hollywood-ized" to be credible. To track the controversy, refer to the following: Fisher, "Fragments of Memory," D1; Marc Fisher, "Respecting to Facts Vs. the Desire to 'Glitz It Up,'" *Washington Post*, Apr. 7, 1998, features section, 11–12; Michael Berenbaum, "Shoah Foundation," *Jerusalem Post*, May 6, 1998, opinion section, 10; "Remembering the Holocaust: Whose Place?" Free for All, *Washington Post*, Apr. 18, 1998, op-ed section, A17.

39. Arendt, *Eichmann in Jerusalem*; and Halberstam, *Skin Shows*, 161.

40. Halberstam, *Skin Shows*, 161.

41. Halberstam, *Skin Shows*, 161.

42. Hantke, "'Kingdom of the Unimaginable.'"

43. Hantke, "'Kingdom of the Unimaginable.'"

44. Elsaesser, *Weimar Cinema and After*, 20–21.

45. Eisner, *Haunted Screen*.

46. Budd, "Cabinet of Dr. Caligari."

47. Kracauer, *From Caligari to Hitler*, 68–69.

48. Eisner, *Haunted Screen*, 21.

49. Budd, "Cabinet of Dr. Caligari."

50. See Picart, Smoot, and Blodgett, *Frankenstein Film Sourcebook*; Picart, "Re-Birthing the Monstrous"; Picart, "Visualizing the Monstrous"; and Picart, *Cinematic Rebirths of Frankenstein*.

51. See Caroline Joan (Kay) Picart, *Remaking the Frankenstein Myth on Film: Between Laughter and Horror* (Albany: State University of New York Press, 2003); Caroline Joan (Kay) Picart, "Humor and Horror in Science Fiction and Comedic Frankenstein Films," *Scope*, May 2004, http://www.nottingham.ac.uk/film/journal/articles/humour-and-horror.htm; and Caroline Joan (Kay) Picart, "The Third Shadow and Hybrid Genres: Horror, Humor, Gender and Race in Alien Resurrection," *Communication and Critical/Cultural Studies* 1 (2004): 335–54.

52. Janice Rushing and Thomas Frentz created work on "shadows"—points of extreme psychic ambivalence, revelatory of fears regarding technology and gender. In brief, they identify two types of shadows: the first, or "inferior," shadow is represented by the feminine, women, the body, minorities, and anything that deviates from rational ego consciousness. The second, or "technologized," shadow is represented best by Frankenstein's monster. There is a third type of shadow, which is a combination of the two—either a female monster or the feminine configured as monstrous, which is the crucial shadow to track in resolving the tensions of the Frankenstein myth within

straight horror film renditions. It is this third shadow that often serves as the scapegoat, whose sacrifice is necessary for conventional closure. For Rushing and Frentz's work, refer to Rushing and Frentz, *Projecting the Shadow*; see also "The Frankenstein Myth in Contemporary Cinema," *Critical Studies in Mass Communication* 6 (1989): 61–80.

53. Deborah Wilson, "Technologies of Misogyny: The Transparent Maternal Body and Alternate Reproductions in Frankenstein, Dracula, and Some Selected Media Discourses," Bodily Discursions: Genders, Representations, Technologies (Albany: State University of New York Press, 1997), 109.

54. Rushing and Frentz, *Projecting the Shadow*, 67.

55. Berenstein, *Attack of the Leading Ladies*, 10.

56. For a more in-depth discussion, refer to Picart, *Remaking the Frankensteinian Myth on Film*, 1–11.

57. Laura Mulvey, "Visual Pleasure and Narrative Cinema."

58. See Browning, "Beyond 'Intentionalism' and 'Functionalism'"; Browning, *Collected Memories*; Browning, *Nazi Policy*; Browning, *Ordinary Men*; Browning, *Origins of the Final Solution*; Saul Friedlander "History, Memory, and the Historian"; and Moses, "Structure and Agency in the Holocaust."

59. Primo Levi, The Drowned and the Saved (New York: Summit Books, 1988), 37.

60. LaCapra, *History and Memory after Auschwitz*, 113.

61. Schwarz, *Imagining the Holocaust*.

62. LaCapra, *History and Memory after Auschwitz*, 199–210.

63. Rothman, "Filmmaker as Hunter," 25.

64. LaCapra, *History and Memory after Auschwitz*, 210.

65. LaCapra, *History and Memory after Auschwitz*, 199–210.

66. LaCapra, *History and Memory after Auschwitz*, 149.

67. LaCapra, *Writing History, Writing Trauma*, 105. In Nietzsche, *Schwergewicht*, which Walter Kaufmann translates as "the greatest weight" (*The Gay Science*, trans. Walter Kaufmann [New York: Vintage, 1974], 12), is the only possible positive response to the "weightlessness" of nihilism and its utter dissolution of boundaries. The threat of nihilism, envisaged in the nightmare of eternal recurrence, may be overcome only through a joyful and rebellious embrace of this nightmarish vision—which is the ultimate measure of the nobility of one's soul. As Kaufmann describes it, "to understand Nietzsche it is important to realize how frightful he himself found the doctrine and how difficult it was for him to accept it. Evidently, he could endure it only by accepting it joyously, almost ecstatically. That is what he said more indirectly when he finally presented the idea as 'the greatest weight.'" *Schwergewicht* is therefore Nietzsche's search for a moral imperative in the face of the potential meaninglessness that nihilism portends.

68. *Gay Science*, trans. Walter Kaufmann, 12.

69. Eley and Grossman, "Watching *Schindler's List*," 41.

70. See Moses, "Structure and Agency," 194–230, for an elaboration of the characteristics of the two schools. See, as well, Friedlander, "From Anti-Semitism to Extermination," and Marrus, "Reflections."

71. Moses, "Structure and Agency," 198.

72. Moses, "Structure and Agency," 204. See Arendt, *Eichmann in Jerusalem*.

73. Moses, "Structure and Agency," 200. See Browning, "Beyond 'Intentionalism.'"

74. Friedlander, "History, Memory."

75. Pinedo, "Postmodern Elements," 90.

2. Horror in Holocaust Films and the Holocaust in Horror Films

1. Baron, "Rebels with an Aryan Cause."

2. Our anonymous second reviewer is responsible for this insight and several others we include in this chapter.

3. Carr, *Hollywood and Anti-Semitism*, 283.

4. Douglas, *Memory of Judgment*, 12.

5. Quoted in Douglas, *Memory of Judgment*, 23. Dominick LaCapra pointed out this reference to us.

6. Flanner and Drutman, *Janet Flanner's World*, 100.

7. Barbie Zelizer, *Remembering to Forget: Holocaust Memory Through the Camera's Eye* (Chicago: University of Chicago Press, 1998), 94.

8. Zelizer, *Remembering to Forget*, 112–13.

9. Culler, *Pursuit of Signs*, 13.

10. Staiger, *Perverse Spectators*, 1.

11. Our second reviewer provided this insight.

12. Atrocity films constitute a subgenre of the "fact film." See Crowther, "Atrocity Films"; "Screen News Here"; "Atrocity Films Released"; "Germans Are Unmoved"; "More Atrocity Films"; and Weiler, "By Way of Report." For a detailed look at the historical circumstances surrounding this film, see Picart and McKahan, "Visualizing the Holocaust."

13. Douglas, *Memory of Judgment*, 26.

14. Our second reviewer provided this insight.

15. Leventhal, "Information and Technology."

16. Quoted in Jones, *Clive Barker's A–Z of Horror*, 28.

17. Jones, *Clive Barker's A–Z of Horror*, 32.

18. For an in-depth description of the evolution of serial killer-as-vampire themes in slasher films, refer to Picart and Greek, "Compulsions of Serial Killers."

19. An earlier and more extended version of this section appears in Picart and Greek, "Compulsions of Serial Killers."

20. Atkinson, "Ed Gein."

21. Cortez, "Ed Gein."

22. "Ed Gein," *E!Online*, April 2004, http://www.eonline.com/Reviews/Facts/Movies/Reviews/0,1052,82655,00.html.

23. Dennis Schwartz, "Vampires Are Compared to Junkies."

24. Addiego, "Life Bites for Grad Student."

25. Hinson, "Addiction."

26. Ebert, "American History X."

27. Maslin, "'American History X.'"

28. On the difference between American and European depictions of the Holocaust, see Jarausch and Geyer, "'Great Men' and Postmodern Ruptures."

29. Avisar, *Screening the Holocaust*, 129.

30. Rothberg, *Traumatic Realism*, 221–23.

31. Farrow, "How Hitler Conquered Hollywood." Among the examples he enumerates are *Life Is Beautiful*, *American History X*, and *Apt Pupil*.

32. Gourevitch, "Between the Holocaust Museum."

3. Classic Horror in *Schindler's List*

1. Byrge, "Schindler's List."

2. Koplin, "Why Is This Film." From the Academy of Motion Picture Arts and Sciences clipping section.

3. Denby, "Unlikely Hero."

4. Wieseltier, "Close Encounters of the Nazi Kind."

5. Jenkins, "Stories That Get in the Way." From the Academy of Motion Picture Arts and Sciences clipping section.

6. Rothberg, *Traumatic Realism*, 223. See also Brenner, "Working Through the Holocaust."

7. Brenner, "Working Through the Holocaust."

8. Brenner, "Working Through the Holocaust."

9. Schiff, "Seriously Spielberg," 170.

10. Friedman and Notbohm, "Introduction," vii.

11. Brode, *Films of Steven Spielberg*, 16.

12. Rubin, *Steven Spielberg*, 10.

13. Schiff, "Seriously Spielberg," 172.

14. Brode, *Films of Steven Spielberg*, 240.

15. Carroll, *Philosophy of Horror*, 3.

16. Reed and Cunneff, "Steven Spielberg." See also Freer, *Complete Spielberg*, 5–8.

17. See footnote 6 for some proponents of converging views concerning the conventions of horror-psychological thriller spectatorship.

18. For an expanded exposition of this notion of monstrosity, refer to Picart, *Cinematic Rebirths of Frankenstein*; and Picart, Smoot, and Blodgett, *Frankenstein Film Sourcebook*.

19. Franciszek Palowski, *The Making of* Schindler's List, trans. Anna and Robert G. Ware (Secaucus, NJ: Birch Lane, 1998), 101.

20. Palowski, *Making of* Schindler's List, 101.

21. Palowski, *Making of* Schindler's List, 108.

22. Palowski, *Making of* Schindler's List, 118.

23. Palowski, *Making of* Schindler's List, 118–119.

24. Zaillian, *Schindler's List* screenplay.

25. See as illustrations the focus on these two scenes by the contributors to *Spielberg's Holocaust*.

26. Rajeev Syal and Cherry Norton claim a direct "influence" by *Psycho* on Stephen King and Steven Spielberg. See Syal and Norton, "Cut!," Academy of Motion Picture Arts and Sciences clipping.

27. Carroll, *Philosophy of Horror*, 16.

28. Schickel, "Heart of Darkness," 75.

29. Richardson, "Steven's Choice," 168.

30. Richardson, "Steven's Choice."

31. Grunwald, "Steven Spielberg Gets Real."

32. Grunwald, "Steven Spielberg Gets Real."

33. Grunwald, "Steven Spielberg Gets Real," 54, 58.

34. Richardson, "Steven's Choice," 166.

35. Sterritt, *Films of Alfred Hitchcock*, 103.

36. Gough-Yates, "Private Madness and Public Lunacy," 27.

37. Robin Wood, "Hitchcock's Films," 133.

38. Rebello, "Behind the Curtain." Adapted from Stephen Rebello, *Alfred Hitchcock and the Making of Psycho* (New York: Dembner Books, 1990; distributed by Norton), 78. From the Academy of Motion Pictures Arts and Sciences clippings collection.

39. Rebello, "Behind the Curtain," 78.

40. Lehmann-Haupt, "Norman Bates, His Mom," C13.

41. Schickel, "Heart of Darkness," 76.

42. Weinraub, "'Psycho' in Janet Leigh's Psyche."

43. Gough-Yates, "Private Madness and Public Lunacy," 30.

44. Robin Wood, "Hitchcock's Films," 133.

45. See Elizabeth Sussex, "The Fate of 3080," *Sight and Sound* 53 (1984): 92–97.

46. For more information, see Picart, *Holocaust Film Sourcebook*, vol. 2. *Documentary and Propaganda*.

47. F3080 is more a precursor to *A Painful Reminder*, also known as *Memory of the Camps*, than it is to *Nazi Concentration Camps*. For detailed notes, refer to Picart and McKahan, "Visualizing the Holocaust in Gothic Terms," 2:508–15.

48. Rebello, "Behind the Curtain," 79.

49. Rebello, "Behind the Curtain," 78.

50. Horowitz, "But Is It Good for the Jews?," 129.

51. Weissman, *Fantasies of Witnessing*, 178.

52. Freer, *Complete Spielberg*, 225.

53. Freer, *Complete Spielberg*, 226.

54. Brode, *Films of Steven Spielberg*, 240.

55. Bartov, "Spielberg's Oskar," 49.

56. Pizzello, "Craft Series."

57. Pizzello, "Craft Series."

58. Jason Grant McKahan provided the initial description of the formal properties of chosen scenes in both *Schindler's List* and *Psycho*.

59. Similarly, Carol Clover argues that in *The Accused*, Ken's masculine and "neutral" gaze establishes that the gang rape occurred, as opposed to Sarah Tobias's (the rape victim's) impassioned testimony. See Carol J. Clover, *Men, Women and Chainsaws: Gender in the Modern Horror Film* (Princeton, NJ: Princeton University Press, 1992), 150.

60. Our second reader provided this observation.

61. Mamet, "Why Schindler Is Emotional Pornography."

62. Kleinman and Kleinman, "Cultural Appropriations," 8.

63. Rushing and Frentz, *Projecting the Shadow*, 39–40.

64. Zaillian, *Schindler's List*.

65. Rushing and Frentz, *Projecting the Shadow*, 40, 67–68.

66. Curtis, "Lest We Forget."

67. Horowitz, "But Is It Good for the Jews?," 130.

68. Hoberman, "Spielberg's Oskar," Voice, 21 December 1993.

69. Richardson, "Steven's Choice," 163.

70. Hoberman, "Myth, Movie, and Memory."

71. Koplin, "Why Is This Film." From the Academy of Motion Picture Arts and Sciences clipping section.

72. Thomson, "Watching Them Watching Us."

73. Lehmann-Haupt, "Norman Bates," 24.

74. Zaillian, *Schindler's List*, sec. 7, 8.

75. Koch in Hoberman, "Myth, Movie, and Memory," 24.

76. Hoberman, "Myth, Movie, and Memory," 24.

77. Horowitz, "But Is It Good for the Jews?," 127–28.

78. Weissman, *Fantasies of Witnessing*, 157.

79. Weissman, *Fantasies of Witnessing*, 157.

80. Jason Grant McKahan provided this insight.

81. Rothman, *Hitchcock*, 251.

82. Wood, "Whatever Happened to *Apt Pupil?*,"129.

83. Thomson, "Watching Them Watching Us."

84. Douglas, *Memory of Judgment*, 62.

85. Douglas, *Memory of Judgment*, 63.

86. Insdorf, *Indelible Shadows*, 6.

87. Ronald Steel, "Kramer's Nuremberg," *Christian Century*, March 14, 1962, 32.

88. Alan Mintz, *Popular Culture and the Shaping of Holocaust Memory in America* (Seattle: University of Washington Press, 2001), 100.

89. Sterritt, *Films of Alfred Hitchcock*, 116.

90. Lauretis and Rajchman theorized the concept of "atrocity footage" and its effect on film ideology. See Lauretis, "Cavani's 'Night Porter'; and Rajchman, "Foucault's Art of Seeing."

91. German atrocity films were indeed shown earlier than 1948, but the complete film *Death Mills* was indeed not viewed until 1948. The earlier screenings of footage were distributed by newsreel companies, who had been given Signal Corps footage by Office of War Information. Imagery of Ohrdruf and Nordhausen was shown. In 1946 the French *Camps of Death* was shown, which was basically reedited Signal Corps footage of Dachau, Buchenwald, and Belsen. See "Reporters Detail City"; Waggoner, "Army Shows Films"; "Atrocity Films Released"; "Nazi Prison Cruelty Film."

92. For an extended discussion, refer to Picart and McKahan, "Visualizing the Holocaust."

93. Loshitzky, "Introduction," in *Spielberg's Holocaust*, 12.

94. Lang, *Act and Idea*; Friedlander, "From Anti-Semitism to Extermination." Also see the lucid discussion in Marrus, "Reflections."

4. The Monstrous Gaze: *The Silence of the Lambs* as the New *Psycho*

1. Halberstam, "Skinflick."

2. Halberstam, "Skinflick," 37.

3. Steiner, *Portage to San Cristobal of A.H.* See for example, Steiner's characterization of Hitler's gaze as "cold ash" in which "a minute, sharp crystal of light blazed" (29); of his hypnotic rhetorical power as embodied in his mouth, which is like a "furnace" and whose tongue is like a "sword laying waste" (45); and of his ability to "brush the fever from his skin" while his captors wither from it (133). Dominick LaCapra pointed out the reference.

4. Hantke, "'Kingdom of the Unimaginable,'" 179. Peter Reed helped with the preliminary research and initial concepts for this chapter.

5. Hantke, "'Kingdom of the Unimaginable,'" 180.

6. Hantke, "'Kingdom of the Unimaginable,'" 180.

7. A fuller exposition of this reaction to monstrosity in classic horror Frankenstein films as simultaneous fascination and repulsion, rather than simple rejection, may be found in Picart, *Cinematic Rebirths of Frankenstein*; see also Picart, "Re-Birthing the Monstrous; and Picart, "Visualizing the Monstrous."

8. Smith, "Identity Check," 29.

9. Smith, "Identity Check," 29.

10. The gendered implications of the horror heroine are discussed in Stewart's "Feminine Hero" and Mizejewski's "Picturing the Female Dick." In addition, popular responses to the film have noticed the gender dynamics of Foster's character; see, for example, Maslin's "Heroines Need Guts, Not Glamour," 2: 11.

11. Harris, *Silence of the Lambs*, 1.

12. Ted Tally, "The Silence of the Lambs," screenplay based on the novel by Thomas Harris, fourth draft, shooting script, October 6, 1989, revised November 28, 1989, A1. From the Academy of Motion Pictures Arts and Sciences scripts collection.

13. Smith, "Identity Check," 29.

14. Smith, "Identity Check," 33.

15. Harris, *Silence of the Lambs*, 319.

16. Tally, "Silence of the Lambs," 114 (Academy of Motion Picture Arts and Sciences script).

17. Demme in Smith, "Identity Check," 33.

18. Negra, "Coveting the Feminine."

19. Craig McKay, the film's editor, called the scene "editorially, a leap"; he recounts that "they shot some second unit material and Jon said, do something with it." Bliss and Banks, "Cutting It Right," 152.

20. Harris, *Silence of the Lambs*, 123.

21. Tally, "Silence of the Lambs," 60 (Academy of Motion Picture Arts and Sciences script).

22. In addition to the other works cited, Buffalo Bill's depiction is discussed in depth by Julie Tharp, "The Transvestite as Monster: Gender Horror in *The Silence*

of the Lambs and *Psycho,*" *Journal of Popular Film and Television* 19 (1991): 106–13; Joseph Grixti, "Consuming Cannibals: Psychopathic Killers as Archetypes and Cultural Icons," *Journal of American Culture* 18 (Spring 1995): 87–96; K. E. Sullivan, "Ed Gein and the Figure of the Transgendered Serial Killer," *Jump Cut* 43 (July 2000): 38–47; and Kendall R. Phillips, "Unmasking Buffalo Bill: Interpretive Controversy and *The Silence of the Lambs,*" *Rhetoric Society Quarterly* 28, no. 3 (1998): 33–47.

23. One of Gumb's tattoos, the simulation of an open wound over his ribs, evokes the piercing of Christ's side, picturing him as a monstrous version not only of the hyperfemininity but also of Christ's sinlessness.

24. Ted Tally, "The Silence of the Lambs," screenplay based on the novel by Thomas Harris, second draft, July 28, 1989, http://www.godamongdirectors.com/scripts/lambs.shtml, 1–2 (accessed Apr. 15, 2006).

25. Bliss and Banks, "Cutting It Right," 152. McKay, Bliss and Banks report, has experience in the horror genre, having developed his skills as an assistant editor on *The Exorcist.*

26. Harris, *Silence of the Lambs,* 14.

27. Tally, "Silence of the Lambs," 8 (Academy of Motion Picture Arts and Sciences script).

28. See, for example, *Interview with the Vampire* and *Queen of the Damned,* both of which have been made into movies.

29. Smith, "Identity Check," 30, 33.

30. Demme, "Into the Labyrinth."

31. Demme, "Into the Labyrinth."

32. Kennedy, "He Knows about Crazy."

33. Seidenberg, "*Silence of the Lambs.*"

34. Sundelson, "Demon Therapist."

35. Grobel, "Playboy Interview," *Playboy,* March 1994, 10.

36. Harris, *Silence of the Lambs,* 231.

37. This depiction of Lecter contrasts sharply with one discarded in the editing process, a scene in which he harangues Clarice, the doctor shot from below in a hellish red light and sporting the shadowy suggestions of satanic horns ("Deleted Scenes," *The Silence of the Lambs,* special ed. DVD, 2001).

38. Tally, "Collaborations."

39. Demme, "Into the Labyrinth."

40. Demme, "Into the Labyrinth."

41. Smith, "Identity Check," 33.

42. One could also argue that the film presupposes a distinction between humanity as conflicted and monstrosity as monomaniacal.

5. *Apt Pupil:* The Hollywood Nazi-as-Monster Flick

1. Jason Grant McKahan helped us with an earlier version of this chapter. A more aesthetically oriented reading of *Apt Pupil,* with a critical analysis of the psychodynamics set up by films that focus on the ritualistic spectacle of sexualized torture, was cowritten by Picart with McKahan and has been published with *Jump Cut.* See Caroline J. S.

Picart and Jason G. McKahan, "Sadomasochism, Sexual Torture, and the Holocaust Film: From Misogyny to Homoeroticism and Homophobia in *Apt Pupil*," *Jump Cut* 45 (Sept. 2002): 23, http://www.ejumpcut.org/archive/jc45.2002/picart/index.html.

2. *The Usual Suspects* won Oscars: Christopher McQuarrie for screenwriting and Kevin Spacey for best supporting actor. Sterngold, "War and Peace"; Weinraub "Usual Suspects."

3. Greenberg, "Apt Pupil." From the Academy of Motion Picture Arts and Sciences clipping section.

4. Eleanor Ringel, "Probing the Nature of Evil," *Atlanta Journal and Constitution*, Oct. 23, 1998, 11.

5. Hoberman, "Nazi Business."

6. Bill Brownstein, "Nazi Horror a La King." From the Academy of Motion Pictures Arts and Sciences.

7. Ringel, "Some True Heavies."

8. Hoberman, "Nazi Business."

9. Klawans, "*Scream 4*: The Holocaust?"

10. Faingold, "Jewish Director of 'Apt Pupil.'" From the Academy of Motion Picture Arts and Sciences.

11. Anthony, "At the Movies: *Apt Pupil*." From the Academy of Motion Picture Arts and Sciences clipping section.

12. Sparks, "Evil Lurks in Thriller, *Apt Pupil*."

13. Stein, "Apt Pupil's Unusual Suspect."

14. Singer in Sterngold, "War and Peace," 10. From the Academy of Motion Picture Arts and Sciences.

15. Singer in Faingold, "Jewish Director of 'Apt Pupil.'" From the Academy of Motion Picture Arts and Sciences.

16. Singer in Farrow, "How Hitler Conquered Hollywood."

17. Singer in Farrow, "How Hitler Conquered Hollywood."

18. Bernard, "*Apt Pupil's* Curiosity."

19. Arnold, "Pupil Is a Lesson."

20. Hoberman, "Nazi Business."

21. A perfect example of this conventional substituting of sexual problems for ethical and social problems is the vague remark of King when asked in an interview why he included the episode of Todd brutally raping the young Jewish woman: "That was consistent with the kid's twisted character." See Norden, "Playboy Interview."

22. Collings, *Stephen King Phenomenon*; Keesey, "Face of Mr. Flip"; and Schopp, "From Misogyny to Homophobia."

23. Carroll, *Philosophy of Horror*, 199. See also Magistrale, *Stephen King*, 22.

24. Benshoff, *Monsters in the Closet*, 31.

25. Collings, *Stephen King Phenomenon*, 23.

26. Keesey, "Face of Mr. Flip," 191.

27. King, "Stephen King Comments on It."

28. Gifford, "Stephen King's Quartet"; and Atchity, "Stephen King."

29. Gray, "Master of Postliterate Prose."

30. Norden, "Playboy Interview." See also King, *Different Seasons*, 506.

31. Gifford, "Stephen King's Quartet," 1.

32. Wickberg, "Homophobia."

33. See for instance, Bentley, "Homosexual Question," 307–8; Rich, "Compulsory Heterosexuality"; Kitzinger, "Heteropatriarchal Language"; Card, "Why Homophobia?"; and Logan, "Homophobia? No, Homoprejudice."

34. King, *Different Seasons*, 89–190.

35. King, *Different Seasons*.

36. Todd, during his first visit with Dussander, is particular interested in hearing about scenes of German soldiers torturing and "raping all the women they wanted" (130); he asks the old man, "Did you spank any of them? The women? Did you take their clothes off and—" (117).

37. Dick Bowden denigrates Monica's mother and grandmother as "Polack[s]" (183); Morris Heisel's wife, Lydia, is depicted as a "nag" (230) who cooks "wretched suppers" (232) and speaks in "bays" and "trills" (249); Morris also "loathes" Lydia's mother (232); Todd refers to his girlfriends' mothers as "cunty" (254); and Edward French's wife, Sondra, is described as an "irritating woman!" (260).

38. Todd's hatred no doubt extends to the "nuclear family" in general, as he envisions perpetrating violence on his father: "I'm going to stick my knife up your fucking nose" (253). Perhaps the parents are implicated in the negative influence of adults. See Magistrale, "Inherited Haunts"; and Newhouse, "Blind Date with Disaster."

39. Magistrale, *Landscape of Fear*, 87.

40. Keesey, "Face of Mr. Flip," 199.

41. Rothman, *Hitchcock*, 251.

42. There is a minor skirmish between Dick and Monica about her accumulation of bills, but Todd's hatred for his mother is no longer perceptible. In addition, Monica's mother and grandmother, Morris Heisel's wife, Lydia, Lydia's mother, and Edward French's wife, Sondra, are not referenced.

43. Scapperotti, "Stephen King's *Apt Pupil*."

44. Wilson, "Apt Pupil."

45. Had the earlier film adaptation been released, which was slated for 1988 but fell through after ten weeks production, we would have seen Todd and Dussander congregate in exterior scenes such as a puppet show and a café! See Gary Wood, "Whatever Happened to *Apt Pupil*?"

46. Scheib, "Apt Pupil."

47. Emmons, "Apt Pupil."

48. Wilson, "Apt Pupil."

49. Boyce, *Apt Pupil: Screenplay*, 18. The dream sequences also differ radically.

50. In *Psycho*, there is a match dissolve from the shower drain to Marion's eye (extreme close-up). The camera pulls away, arcing slowly. The rotation stops as the camera continues to pull out, revealing Marion's face on the floor (close-up).

51. McDonald, "Apt Pupil."

52. Wilson, "Apt Pupil." From the Academy of Motion Picture Arts and Sciences.

53. Klawans, "*Scream 4*: The Holocaust?," 35.

54. Russo, *Female Grotesque*, 1–2, 6, 10, 12, 29, 37, 40, 53, 56, 63, 65, 93, 106, 120, 159, 164–65, 168, 176.

55. In *Vertigo* (1958), John makes Judy dress up to resemble Madelein, while in *Viridiana* (1961), Viridiana's uncle makes her dress in his late wife's wedding gown. Compare a similar Pygmalion replication in Steve Cohen's *Devil in the Flesh* (1998), in which Debbie's grandmother makes her wear her mother's old clothes to school. Such scenarios are most common in pornographic films, such as *The Fever of Laure*, in which a client makes the prostitute Laure dress up as Alice in Wonderland.

56. Cockrell, "One Good Hard Step."

57. Boyce, *Apt Pupil: Screenplay*, A33.

58. Stuart, "Yes, Sir."

59. McCarthy, "Apt Pupil."

60. Brandon Boyce, "'Apt Pupil,' Based on the Novel by Stephen King," shooting script, February 3–March 14, 1997, 61. From the Academy of Motion Picture Arts and Sciences script section.

61. Silberg, "Future of Digital Filmmaking."

62. Howell, "Apt Pupil."

63. Related materials, not only those that define what timing is but also theories encompassing techniques such as timing and how they have affected the genealogy and development of film include Schlemowitz, "Glossory of Film Terms"; Wasko, "Work of Theory," 221–33; O'Regan, "Shooting Back," 262–94; Bordwell and Thompson, *Film Art*.

64. John Ottman, email message to author, September 9, 2005. Jason Grant McKahan helped to set this up.

65. For details, see Ascher-Walsh, "Clothes Call"; Ascher-Walsh, "Parents Sue"; Ascher-Walsh, "Second Suit Filed"; and Ascher-Walsh, "Third Suit."

66. Olson, "Org Renews Protest over 'Pupil.'"

67. Shea, "Apt Pupil." See Cheevers and Ebner, "Naked Shakedown": "In interviews with journalists, Rub and Gordon like to milk the 'irony' of a group of innocents herded into showers and forced to strip during the making of a movie related to Nazi death camps—even if it's a bit of a stretch to compare Eliot Middle School with Dachau." From the Academy of Motion Picture Arts and Sciences clipping section.

68. King, *Different Seasons*, 177.

69. Boyce, *Apt Pupil: Screenplay*, 58.

70. Shea, "Apt Pupil."

71. Boyce, *Apt Pupil: Screenplay*, 47, 51.

72. Boyce, *Apt Pupil: Screenplay*, 62–63.

73. Boyce, *Apt Pupil: Screenplay*, 56–57.

74. Cockrell, "One Good Hard Step": "I never intended any [erotic tension] between the two characters [i.e., Todd and Dussander], but there is a smattering of that with the guidance counselor and with the homeless guy, which can be kind of interesting."

75. Boyce, *Apt Pupil: Screenplay*, 66.

76. Scheib, "Apt Pupil."

77. Verniere, "Master Class."

78. Verniere, "Master Class."

79. Hunter, "Shaking Hands with the Devil."

80. Clark, "Apt Pupil," 18.

81. If Singer removed this scene on account of its racial and gender stereotyping, it nevertheless remains elsewhere in both the script and final film version. At scene 37 in Boyce's script, Todd is looking at an official school letter clipped to a series of flunk cards and sweating over his bad grades. The direction element reads, "TWO STU-DENTS catch his eye. They are both Asian." See Boyce, *Apt Pupil: Screenplay*, 37; In the film, Todd receives a failing mark on his test and looks distressed over his grades; a rack focus reveals an Asian girl behind him, who is obviously in high spirits about her grades. This patently insidious scenario, which plays up on white fears of academic comparison to racial "others," is appallingly collusive with Nazi ideology.

82. King's novella ends with Todd shooting Ed French and then heading out to the freeway to carry out a mass sniping of commuters. "It was five hours later and almost dark before they took him down" (King, *Different Seasons*, 290). The Todd of the film is no longer the sniper of the novella; Singer argues that he left instead Todd's "potential to become one." Naturally, King was not pleased. See Scapperotti, "Stephen King's *Apt Pupil*," 21.

83. See Scheib, "Apt Pupil": "What it all serves is a complete mystery." See also, Klawans, "*Scream* 4: The Holocaust?": "And so I ask, Why does Bryan Singer do what he does? Why turn the Holocaust into a cross between Cujo and gay S&M?"

84. Shea, "Apt Pupil." "There was a strong element of homoeroticism in the Nazi cult of the Aryan male body to begin with (see Leni Riefenstahl's *Olympia* for ample evidence of that!)."

85. Wood, "Nuit et Brouillard," 332.

6. Framing Evil: Toward an Ethics of Response

1. Ingebretsen, *At Stake*.

2. Ingebretsen, *At Stake*, xv.

3. Ingebretsen, *At Stake*, xv.

4. Skal, "Horrors of War."

5. See Arendt, *Eichmann in Jerusalem*.

6. Carroll, *Philosophy of Horror*, 16.

7. Hantke, "Horror Film," 121.

8. Hantke, "Horror Film," 121.

9. Quoted in William Galberson, "Judge Is Assailed in Holocaust Fund," *New York Times*, Apr. 30, 2004, A22.

10. Diego Gambetta, "Primo Levi's Last Moments," *Boston Review* 24 (1999): 23.

11. Rushing and Frentz, *Projecting the Shadow*.

12. Janice Hocker Rushing and Thomas S. Frentz, "The Frankenstein Myth in Contemporary Cinema," *Critical Studies in Mass Communication* 6 (1989): 63.

13. Rushing and Frentz, "Frankenstein Myth," 76–77.

14. Rushing and Frentz, *Projecting the Shadow*, 40–41.

15. Our second reviewer pointed this out.

16. BBFC examiner, description of cuts from *Adventures of Kekkou Kamen, Part I: Naked Justice*, Japanese anime by Go Nagai (East 2 West Films, 1995), http://www. melonfarmers.co.uk/hitsa.htm (accessed Apr. 15, 2006). Jason Grant McKahan assisted us in finding information on selected Japanese anime that feature the motif of sexualized violence and Nazism.

17. Mike Tanner, "Beyond the (Silicon) Valley of the Ultra Vixen," *Wired News*, April 2004, http://www.wired.com/news/culture/0,1284,8397,00.html.

18. Tanner, "Beyond."

19. McGee, "Response to German Militarism."

20. McGee, "Response to German Militarism," 27.

21. Brenner, "Working Through the Holocaust."

22. Ingebretsen, *At Stake*, 41.

23. Carroll, *Philosophy of Horror*, 4.

24. Ingebretsen, *At Stake*, xvi.

25. Carroll, *Philosophy of Horror*, 17.

26. Ingebretsen, *At Stake*, 27.

27. Ingebretsen, *At Stake*, 27.

28. Ingebretsen, *At Stake*, 72.

29. Ingebretsen, *At Stake*, 95.

30. Avisar, *Screening the Holocaust*, 134–48.

31. Gemünden, "Brecht in Hollywood." The earliest book in English to conflate Nazism with sexual perversion was Samuel Igra's *Germany's National Vice* (London: Quality, 1945).

32. Plant, *Pink Triangle*, 16.

33. Scherr, "Uses of Memory."

34. Scherr, "Uses of Memory."

35. See, for example, Waller, "Signifying the Holocaust"; Bassi, "Fathers and Daughters"; and Stone, "Feminist Critic and Salome."

36. Scherr, "Uses of Memory."

37. See Brenner, "Working Through the Holocaust," on this point.

38. Brenner, "Working Through the Holocaust."

39. LaCapra, *Writing History, Writing Trauma*, 150.

40. LaCapra, *Writing History, Writing Trauma*, 150.

41. Lang, *Act and Idea*; Hilberg, *Perpetrators, Victims, Bystanders*; and Browning, *Nazi Policy, Jewish Workers, German Killers*.

42. Bauer, *Rethinking the Holocaust*.

43. Lawrence L. Langer, *Preempting the Holocaust* (New Haven, CT: Yale University Press, 1998).

44. Bauer, *Rethinking the Holocaust*, 5.

45. Bauer, *Rethinking the Holocaust*, 5–6.

46. Scherr, "Uses of Memory," 9–10.

47. Citizen News Services, "Students in Trouble"; Citizen News Services, "Spielberg Teaching Holocaust History"; Mengel, "Film Bid to Cut Racism"; "Suffering May Be Far Away."

48. "Spielberg Urges Teaching of Tolerance."

49. Schwartz, "Laughter in the Movie House."

50. For a detailed discussion of the Oakland High School incident, see Jeffrey Shandler, "Schindler's Discourse: America Discusses the Holocaust and Its Mediation, from NBC's Miniseries to Spielberg's Film," in Loshitzky, *Spielberg's Holocaust*, 163.

51. LaCapra, *Writing History, Writing Trauma*, 86–112.

52. Schwarz, *Imagining the Holocaust*, 23.

53. Schwarz, *Imagining the Holocaust*, 37.

54. LaCapra, *Writing History, Writing Trauma*, 244.

55. Gomel, *Bloodscripts*, xiv.

Bibliography

Addiego, Walter. "Life Bites for Grad Student." *San Francisco Examiner*, Nov. 10, 1995, 29. http://www.sfgate.com/cgi-bin/article.cgi?f=/e/a/1995/11/10/WEEKEND482. dtl (accessed Aug. 29, 2003).

Adorno, Theodore W. "An Essay on Cultural Criticism and Society." In *Prisms*, trans. Samuel and Shierry Weber, 17–34. Cambridge, MA: MIT Press, 1967.

Anthony, Ted. "At the Movies: *Apt Pupil*." *Entertainment News*, Oct. 21, 1998.

Arendt, Hannah. *Eichmann in Jerusalem: A Report on the Banality of Evil*. New York: Penguin Books, 1994.

Arnold, Gary. "*Pupil* Is a Lesson in Evil and Bigotry." *Washington Times*, Oct. 23, 1998, C17.

Ascher-Walsh, Rebecca. "A Clothes Call: An Indecent Proposal Made on the *Apt Pupil* Set?" *Entertainment Weekly*, May 2, 1997, 21.

———. "Parents Sue over Alleged 'Pupil' Nudity." *Daily Variety*, Apr. 18, 1997, 50.

———. "Second Suit Filed over 'Pupil' Lensing." *Daily Variety*, April 22, 1997, 22.

———. "Third Suit Against 'Pupil' Principals." *Daily Variety*, May 16, 1997, 52.

Aschheim, Steven E. "Reconceiving the Holocaust?" *Tikkun*, July-August 1996, 62–65.

Atchity, Kenneth. "Stephen King: Making Burgers with the Best." *Los Angeles Times Book Review*, Aug. 29 1982, 7.

Atkinson, John. "Ed Gein." *Kamera*. 2001. kamera.co.uk (accessed Sept. 1, 2003).

"Atrocity Films Released; Movies of German Prison Camps to Be Shown Next Week." *New York Times*, Apr. 27, 1945, 3.

Avisar, Ilan. *Screening the Holocaust: Cinema's Images of the Unimaginable*. Jewish Literature and Culture. Bloomington: Indiana University Press, 1988.

Baron, Lawrence. "Rebels with an Aryan Cause: Neo-Nazis in American Feature Films since 1945." *Clio's Eye*, Fall 2002. http://clioseye.sfasu.edu/NEWCLIO/ Main%20Articles/rebelschron.htm.

Bartov, Omer. "Ordinary Monsters." *New Republic*, Apr. 29, 1996, 32–38.

———. "Spielberg's Oskar: Hollywood Tries Evil." In Loshitzky, *Spielberg's Holocaust*, 1997.

Bassi, Chiara. "Fathers and Daughters in the Camp: *The Night Porter* by Liliana Cavani." In *Gendered Contexts: New Perspectives in Italian Cultural Studies*, edited by Laura Benedetti, Julia L. Hairston, and Silvia M Ross, 165–75. New York: Lang, 1996.

Bauer, Yehuda. *Rethinking the Holocaust*. New Haven, CT: Yale University Press, 2001.

Benshoff, Harry. *Monsters in the Closet: Homosexuality and the Horror Film*. New York: Manchester University Press, 1997.

Bentley, Eric. "The Homosexual Question." In *Hidden Heritage: History and the Gay Imagination: An Anthology*, edited by Byrne R. S. Fone. New York: Avocation, 1980.

Berenstein, Rhona J. *Attack of the Leading Ladies: Gender, Sexuality, and Spectatorship in Classic Horror Cinema*. New York: Columbia University Press, 1996.

Bernard, Jami. "*Apt Pupil's* Curiosity about Teacher's Nazi Past Leads to an Education in Reich and Wrong." *New York Daily News*, Oct. 23, 1998, 63.

Bliss, Michael, and Christina Banks. "Cutting It Right: An Interview with Craig McKay." In *What Goes Around Comes Around: The Films of Jonathan Demme*. Carbondale: Southern Illinois University Press, 1996.

Blum, Lawrence. "Race, Community and Moral Education: Kohlberg and Spielberg as Civic Educators." *Journal of Moral Education* 28 (1999): 125–44.

Bordwell, David, and Kristin Thompson, eds. *Film Art: An Introduction*. 2nd ed. New York: Knopf, 1986.

Boyce, Brandon. *Apt Pupil: Screenplay*. Burbank, CA: Hollywood Collectables, 1997.

Brenner, David. "Working Through the Holocaust Blockbuster: 'Schindler's List' and 'Hitler's Willing Executioners,' Globally and Locally." *Germanic Review* 75 (2000): 296–316.

Brode, Douglas. *The Films of Steven Spielberg*. New York: Citadel, 2000.

Browning, Christopher R. "Beyond 'Intentionalism' and 'Functionalism': A Reassessment of Nazi Jewish Policy from 1939–1941." In *Reevaluating the Third Reich*, edited by Thomas Childers and Jane Caplan, 211–33. New York: Holmes and Meier, 1993.

———. *Collected Memories: Holocaust History and Postwar Testimony*. George L. Mosse Series in Modern European Cultural and Intellectual History. Madison: University of Wisconsin Press, 2003.

———. *Nazi Policy, Jewish Workers, German Killers*. Cambridge, UK: Cambridge University Press, 2000.

———. *Ordinary Men: Reserve Police Battalion 101 and the Final Solution in Poland*. New York: HarperPerennial, 1998.

———. *The Origins of the Final Solution: The Evolution of Nazi Jewish Policy, September 1939–March 1942*. Lincoln: University of Nebraska Press, 2004.

Brownstein, Bill. "Nazi Horror a La King: Master Fright Writer's Novella *Apt Pupil* a Chilling Success on the Screen." *Montreal Gazette*, Oct. 23, 1998.

Budd, Mike. "The Cabinet of Dr. Caligari." In *The Cabinet of Dr. Caligari*, special collector's ed. DVD. Sun Valley, CA: Film Preservation Associates; Chatsworth, CA: Image Home Entertainment, 1996.

Byrge, Duane. "Schindler's List." *Hollywood Reporter*, Dec. 6, 1993, 6.

Card, Claudia. "Why Homophobia?" *Hypatia* 5 (1990): 110–17.

Carr, Steven Alan. *Hollywood and Anti-Semitism: A Cultural History up to World War II*. New York: Cambridge University Press, 2001.

Carroll, Noël. *The Philosophy of Horror, or Paradoxes of the Heart*. New York: Routledge, 1990.

Carver, Benedict. "Schindler's List." *Screen International*, June 24, 1994.

Cheevers, Jack, and Mark Ebner. "Naked Shakedown." *New Times Los Angeles*, July 2, 1998.

Citizen News Services. "Spielberg Teaching Holocaust History." *Ottawa Citizen*, Jan. 28, 1994, E1.

———. "Students in Trouble for Giggling in Movie." *Ottawa Citizen*, Jan. 21, 1994, E1.

Clark, J. M. "Apt Pupil." *Magill's Cinema Annual*. Englewood Cliffs, NJ: Salem, 1989.

Clover, Carol J. *Men, Women and Chainsaws: Gender in the Modern Horror Film*. Princeton, NJ: Princeton University Press, 1992.

Cockrell, Eddie. "One Good Hard Step Beyond Innocence: A Few Moments with Bryan Singer." *Nitrate Online*, Nov. 9, 2001. http://www.nitrateonline.com/faptpupil.html].

Collings, Michael. *The Stephen King Phenomenon*. Mercer Island, WA: Starmont, 1987.

Cortez, Carl. "Ed Gein." *If Magazine* 27, no. 1 (2001). http://www.ifmagazine.com/reviews.asp?reviewID=816 (accessed May 11, 2006).

Crowther, Bosley. "Atrocity Films; The 'Hate Pictures' of This War Raise a Question as to Basic Intent." *New York Times*, Oct. 24, 1943, X3.

Culler, Jonathan D. *The Pursuit of Signs—Semiotics, Literature, Deconstruction*. Ithaca, NY: Cornell University Press, 1981.

Curtis, Quentin. "Lest We Forget." *Independent on Sunday* (London), Feb. 13, 1994, 18.

Das, Veena, Arthur Kleinman, and Margaret Lock, eds. *Social Suffering*. Berkeley: University of California Press, 1997.

Demme, Jonathan. "Into the Labyrinth." In *The Silence of the Lambs*, special ed. DVD. 2001.

Denby, David. "Unlikely Hero." *New Yorker*, Dec. 13, 1993, 82.

Deren, Maya. *The Legend of Maya Deren: A Documentary Biography and Collected Works*, edited by Millicent Hodson, Catrina Neiman, and Hollis Melton. New York: Anthology Film Archives/Film Culture, 1988.

Doneson, Judith E. *The Holocaust in American Film*. 2nd ed. Syracuse, NY: Syracuse University Press, 2002.

Douglas, Lawrence. *The Memory of Judgment: Making Law and History in the Trials of the Holocaust*. New Haven, CT: Yale University Press, 2001.

Ebert, Roger. "American History X." *Chicago Sun-Times*, Oct. 20, 1998. http://rogerebert.suntimes.com/apps/pbcs.dll/article?AID=/19981030/REVIEWS/810300301/1023 (accessed Oct. 26, 2005).

Eisner, Lotte H. *The Haunted Screen: Expressionism in German Cinema and the Influence of Max Reinhardt*. Berkeley: University of California Press, 1965.

Eley, Geoff, and Atina Grossman. "Watching *Schindler's List*: Not the Last Word." *New German Critique* 71 (2000): 41–63.

Ellis, Kate Ferguson. *The Contested Castle: Gothic Novels and the Subversion of Domestic Ideology*. Urbana: University of Illinois Press, 1989.

Elsaesser, Thomas. *Weimar Cinema and After: Germany's Historical Imaginary*. New York: Routledge, 2000.

Emmons, Paul. "Apt Pupil." *BigScreen Cinema Guide*, 1998. http://www.bigscreen.com/ReaderReview?movie=AptPupil].

E!Online. "Ed Gein." 2001. eonline.com (accessed Sept. 1, 2003).

Faingold, Noma. "Jewish Director of 'Apt Pupil' Gives Skinheads a Lesson in Loathing." *Jewish Bulletin of Northern California*, Oct. 23, 1998.

Farrow, Boyd. "How Hitler Conquered Hollywood; Why Are Today's Film-Makers So Desperate to Confront Nazism?" *Guardian*, Feb. 5, 1999, 8.

Fisher, Marc. "Fragments of Memory; as Steven Spielberg's Holocaust Survivor Project Proceeds, Scholars Question Its Methods." *Washington Post*, Apr. 7, 1998, style section, D1.

Flanner, Janet, and Irving Drutman. *Janet Flanner's World: Uncollected Writings, 1932–1975*. New York: Harcourt Brace Jovanovich, 1979.

Freer, Ian. *The Complete Spielberg*. London: Virgin, 2001.

Friedlander, Saul. "From Anti-Semitism to Extermination: A Historiographical Study of Nazi Policies Toward the Jews and an Essay in Interpretation." *Yad Vashem Studies* 16 (1984): 1–50.

———. "Nazi Germany and the Jews, 1933–1939." *The Years of Persecution*. New York: Harper Collins, 1997.

———. "History, Memory, and the Historian: Dilemmas and Responsibilities." *New German Critique* 80 (2000): 3–16.

Friedman, Lester D., and Brent Notbohm. Introduction. In Friedman and Notbohm, *Steven Spielberg: Interviews*.

———, eds. *Steven Spielberg: Interviews*. Conversations with Filmmakers Series. Jackson: University of Mississippi Press, 2000.

Gemünden, Gerd. "Brecht in Hollywood: *Hangmen Also Die* and the Anti-Nazi Film." *TDR* 43, no. 4 (Winter 1999): 65–67.

"Germans Are Unmoved by Atrocity Film; Prisoners Lay War Crimes to 'Higher-Ups'; Some Were and Some Were Not Interested." *New York Times*, June 27, 1945, 5.

Geuens, Jean-Pierre. "Pornography and the Holocaust: The Last Transgression." *Film Criticism* 20, nos. 1–2 (1995–96): 114–30.

Gifford, Thomas. "Stephen King's Quartet." *Washington Post Book World*, Aug. 22, 1982, 1.

Gigliotti, Simone. "Unspeakable Pasts as Limit Events: The Holocaust, Genocide, and the Stolen Generations." *Australian Journal of Politics & History* 49, no. 2 (2003): 164–81. http://www.blackwell-synergy.com/doi/abs/10.1111/1467-8497.00302?cookieSet=1, p. 1 of 2.

Goldhagen, Daniel. *Hitler's Willing Executioners: Ordinary Germans and the Holocaust*. New York: Knopf, 1996.

————. "A Reply to My Critics: Motives, Causes, and Alibis." *New Republic*, December 23, 1996, 41.

Gomel, Elana. *Bloodscripts: Writing the Violent Subject*. The Theory and Interpretation of Narrative Series. Columbus: Ohio State University Press, 2003.

Gough-Yates, Kevin. "Private Madness and Public Lunacy." *Films and Filming* 18 (Feb. 1972): 26–30.

Gourevitch, Philip. "Between the Holocaust Museum and 'Schindler's List,' the Spectacle of Mass Murder Has Permeated Mass Culture." *Washington Post*, Jan. 16, 1994, G1.

Gray, Paul. "Master of Postliterate Prose." *Time*, April 30, 1982, 87.

Greenberg, James. "Apt Pupil." *Los Angeles Magazine*, Nov. 1998.

Grobel, Lawrence. "The Playboy Interview: Anthony Hopkins." *Playboy Magazine*, Mar. 1994, 10.

Grunwald, Lisa. "Steven Spielberg Gets Real." *Life*, Dec. 1993, 54.

Halberstam, Judith. "Skinflick: Posthuman Gender in Jonathan Demme's *The Silence of the Lambs*." *Camera Obscura*, Fall 1992, 37–54.

————. *Skin Shows: Gothic Horror and the Technology of Monsters*. Durham, NC: Duke University Press, 1995.

Handelman, Susan A. *The Slayers of Moses: The Emergence of Rabbinic Interpretation in Modern Literary Theory*. Albany, NY: State University of New York Press, 1982.

Hantke, Steffen. "Horror Film and the Historical Uncanny: The New Germany in Stefan Ruzowitzky's Anatomie." *College Literature* 31 (2004): 117–43.

————. "The Kingdom of the Unimaginable: The Construction of Social Space and the Fantasy of Privacy in Serial Killers Narratives." *Literature/Film Quarterly* 26 (1998): 179–95.

Harris, Thomas. *The Silence of the Lambs*. New York: St. Martin's, 1988.

Hilberg, Raul. *Perpetrators, Victims, Bystanders: The Jewish Catastrophe, 1933–1945*. New York: Asher Books, 1992.

Hinson, Hal. "The Addiction." Washingtonpost.com, Oct. 27, 1995. http://www.washingtonpost.com/wp-srv/style/longterm/movies/videos/theaddictionrhinson_c03419.html (accessed Aug. 29, 2003).

Hirsch, Joshua Francis. *Afterimage: Film, Trauma, and the Holocaust*. Emerging Media. Philadelphia: Temple University Press, 2004.

"History Lesson." *Hollywood Reporter*, Apr. 8, 1994.

Hoberman, J. "Myth, Movie, Memory." *Village Voice*, Mar. 29, 1994, 24–31.

————. "Nazi Business." *Village Voice*, October 27, 1998, 135.

————. "Spielberg's Oskar." *Village Voice*, Dec. 21, 1993.

Hoffman, Eva. *After Such Knowledge: Memory, History, and the Legacy of the Holocaust*. New York: Public Affairs, 2004.

Horowitz, Sara. "But Is It Good for the Jews? Spielberg's Schindler and the Aesthetics of Atrocity." In *Spielberg's Holocaust: Critical Perspectives on Schindler's List*, edited by Yosefa Loshitzky. Bloomington: Indiana University Press, 1997.

Howell, Peter. "Apt Pupil." *Toronto Star*, Oct. 23, 1998, D3.

Hunter, Stephen. "Shaking Hands with the Devil." *Washington Post*, Oct. 23, 1998, style section, B1.

Iaccino, James F. *Psychological Reflections on Cinematic Terror: Jungian Archetypes in Horror Films*. Westport, CT: Praeger, 1994.

Igra, Samuel. *Germany's National Vice*. London: Quality, 1945.

Ingebretsen, Ed. *At Stake: Monsters and the Rhetoric of Fear in Public Culture*. Chicago: University of Chicago Press, 2001.

Insdorf, Annette. *Indelible Shadows: Film and the Holocaust*. 3rd ed. Cambridge, UK: Cambridge University Press, 2003.

Irwin-Zarecka, Iwona. *Frames of Remembrance: The Dynamics of Collective Memory*. New Brunswick, NJ: Transaction, 1994.

Jackson, Rosemary. *Fantasy: The Literature of Subversion*. London: Methuen, 1981.

Jarausch, Konrad, and Michael Geyer. "'Great Men' and Postmodern Ruptures: Overcoming the Belatedness of German Historiography." *German Studies Review* 18 (1995): 253–73.

Jenkins, Simon. "Stories That Get in the Way of Facts." *Times* (London), Mar. 12, 1994.

Jones, Stephen, comp. *Clive Barker's A—Z of Horror: Official Companion and Guide to the Critically Acclaimed BBC Television Series*. New York: HarperEntertainment, 1998.

Keesey, Douglas. "The Face of Mr. Flip: Homophobia in the Horror of Stephen King." In *The Dark Descent: Essays Defining Stephen King's Horrorscape*, edited by Tony Magistrale, 187–201. New York: Greenwood, 1992.

Kennedy, A. L. "He Knows About Crazy." *Sight and Sound* 5, no. 6 (1995): 34.

King, Stephen. *Different Seasons*. New York: Signet, 1982.

———. "Stephen King Comments on It." *Castle Rock*, July 1986, 1–5.

Kitzinger, Celia. "Heteropatriarchal Language: The Case Against 'Homophobia.'" *Gossip* 5 (1990): 16–17.

Klawans, Stuart. "*Scream 4*: The Holocaust?" *Nation* 267, no. 14 (Nov. 2, 1998): 34–35.

Kleinman, Arthur, and Joan Kleinman. "Cultural Appropriations of Suffering in Our Times." In Das, Kleinman, and Lock, *Social Suffering*.

Koplin, Philip. "Why Is This Film (No) Different from Any Other Film?" *Santa Barbara Independent*, Mar. 24, 1994.

Korner, Axel. "'The Arrogance of Youth'—a Metaphor for Social Change? The Goldhagen Debate in Germany as Generational Conflict." *New German Critique* 80 (2000): 59–77.

Kracauer, Siegfried. *From Caligari to Hitler: A Psychological History of the German Film*. Princeton, NJ: Princeton University Press, 1947.

LaCapra, Dominick. *History and Memory after Auschwitz*. Ithaca, NY: Cornell University Press, 1998.

———. *Representing the Holocaust: History, Theory, Trauma*. Ithaca, NY: Cornell University Press, 1994.

———. *Writing History, Writing Trauma*. Parallax. Baltimore: Johns Hopkins University Press, 2001.

Lang, Berel. *Act and Idea in the Nazi Genocide*. Chicago: University of Chicago, 1990.

Langer, Lawrence. "The Alarmed Vision: Social Suffering and Holocaust Atrocity." In Das, Kleinman, and Lock, *Social Suffering*.

Langer, Lawrence L. *Holocaust Testimonies: The Ruins of Memory*. New Haven, CT: Yale University Press, 1991.

Lanzmann, Claude. *Shoah*. VHS (5 videocassettes). Hollywood, CA: Paramount Home Video; New York: New Yorker Films, 1985.

Lauretis, Teresa de. "Cavani's 'Night Porter': A Woman's Film?" *Film Quarterly* 30 (1976): 35–38.

Lehmann-Haupt, Christopher. "Norman Bates, His Mom and That Fatal Shower." *New York Times*, July 6, 1995.

Lentin, Ronit. *Re-Presenting the Shoah for the Twenty-First Century*. New York: Berghahn Books, 2004.

Leventhal, Robert S. "Information and Technology in the Holocaust." In *Responses to the Holocaust: A Hypermedia Sourcebook for the Humanities*. Charlottesville, VA: Institute for Advanced Technologies in the Humanities, 1995. http://www.iath.virginia.edu/holocaust/infotech.html (accessed Sept. 1, 2003).

Levi, Primo. *Survival in Auschwitz: The Nazi Assault on Humanity*. New York: Collier, 1993.

Lévinas, Emmanuel. *Alterity and Transcendence*. New York: Columbia University Press, 1999.

———. *Otherwise Than Being: Or, Beyond Essence*. Boston, Kluwer, 1981.

Logan, Colleen R. "Homophobia? No, Homoprejudice." *Journal of Homosexuality* 31, no. 3 (1996): 31–53.

Loshitzky, Yosefa, ed. *Spielberg's Holocaust: Critical Perspectives on* Schindler's List. Bloomington: Indiana University Press, 1997.

Magistrale, Tony. "Inherited Haunts: Stephen King's Terrible Children." *Extrapolation* 26 no. 1 (Spring 1985): 43–49.

———. *Landscape of Fear: Stephen King's American Gothic*. Bowling Green, OH: Bowling Green State University Popular Press, 1988.

———. *Stephen King: The Second Decade, Danse Macabre to the Dark Half*. New York: Twayne, 1992.

Mamet, David. "Why Schindler Is Emotional Pornography." *Guardian*, Apr. 30, 1994, 31.

Marrus, Michael. "Reflections on the Historiography of the Holocaust." *Journal of Modern History* 66 (1994): 92–116.

Maslin, Janet. "'American History X': The Darkest Chambers of a Nation's Soul." *New York Times*, Oct. 28, 1998, E1.

———. "Heroines Need Guts, Not Glamour." *New York Times*, Feb. 17, 1991, late edition, 2: 11.

McCarthy, Todd. "Apt Pupil." *Daily Variety*, Sept. 11, 1998, 10.

McDonald, Fred. "Apt Pupil." Abingdon College and District Film Society Program Note, Nov. 2, 1998. http://homepage.ntlworld.com/holtnet/abcdfs/prognote/apt_pupil.pdf].

McGee, Randall. "A Response to German Militarism." *AnimEssence*, Apr. 2004. http://www.ocf.berkeley.edu/~animage/v4i3AEFB.html.

Medhurst, Martin J. "The Rhetorical Structure of Oliver Stone's *JFK*." *Critical Studies in Mass Communication* 10 (1993): 128–43.

Mengel, N. "Film Bid to Cut Racism." *Brisbane (Australia) Courier-Mail*, Apr. 13, 1994.

Mikhman, Dan. *Belgium and the Holocaust: Jews, Belgians, Germans.* Jerusalem: Yad Vashem, 2000.

Mizejewski, Linda. "Picturing the Female Dick: The Silence of the Lambs and Blue Steel." *Journal of Film and Video* 45 (Fall 1993): 6–23.

Modleski, Tania. "The Context of Violence in Popular Culture." *Chronicle of Higher Education*, April 27, 2001, B7.

"More Atrocity Films to Be Shown in Reich; by Wireless to the New York Times." *New York Times*, July 14, 1944, 4.

Moses, A. D. "Structure and Agency in the Holocaust: Daniel J. Goldhagen and His Critics." *History and Theory* 37 (1998): 194–220.

Mulvey, Laura. "Visual Pleasure and Narrative Cinema." In *Framing the Sexual Subject: The Politics of Gender, Sexuality, and Power*, edited by Richard G. Parker, Regina Maria Barbosa, and Peter Aggleton. Berkeley: University of California Press, 2000.

"Nazi Prison Cruelty Film to Be Shown Tomorrow." *New York Times*, Apr. 25, 1945, 3.

Negra, Diane. "Coveting the Feminine: Victor Frankenstein, Norman Bates, and Buffalo Bill." *Literature/Film Quarterly* 24, no. 2 (1996): 193.

Newhouse, Tom. "A Blind Date with Disaster: Adolescent Revolt in the Fiction of Stephen King." In *The Gothic World of Stephen King: Landscape of Nightmares*, edited by Gary Hoppenstand and Ray B. Brown, 49–55. Bowling Green, OH: Bowling Green State University Popular Press, 1987.

Nichols, Bill. *Introduction to Documentary.* Bloomington: Indiana University Press, 2001.

Nichols, Peter M. "Schindler and the Shoah in the Words of Survivors." *New York Times*, Mar. 9, 2004, B9.

Norden, Eric. "The Playboy Interview: Stephen King." *Playboy*, June 1983, 65–82.

Norris, Margot. *Writing War in the Twentieth Century.* Charlottesville: University Press of Virginia, 2000.

Novick, Peter. *The Holocaust and Collective Memory : The American Experience.* London: Bloomsbury, 2000.

Olson, Eric J. "Org Renews Protest over 'Pupil.'" *Daily Variety*, Oct. 23, 1998, 54.

O'Regan, Tom. "Shooting Back: From Ethnographic Film to Indigenous Production/ Ethnography of Media." In *The Work of Theory in the Age of Digital Transformation: A Companion to Film Theory*, edited by Toby Miller and Robert Stam, 262–94. Malden, MA: Blackwell, 1999.

Petit, Chris. "Portly Poses: Chris Petit Weighs Up the Hitchcock Legacy: The Hitchcock Murders by Peter Conrad." *Guardian*, Nov. 2000, 9.

Picart, Caroline J. S., and Jason G. McKahan. "Sadomasochism, Sexual Torture, and the Holocaust Film: From Misogyny to Homoeroticism and Homophobia in *Apt Pupil*." *Jump Cut* 45 (Sept 2002): 23. Http://www.ejumpcut.org/archive/jc45.2002/picart/index.html.

Picart, C. J. S., and Jason G. McKahan. "Visualizing the Holocaust in Gothic Terms: The Ideology of U.S. Signal Corps Cinematography." In Picart, Caroline Joan, *Holocaust Film Sourcebook*, 2:508–15.

Picart, Caroline J. S., and Cecil Greek. "The Compulsions of Serial Killers as Vampires: Toward a Gothic Criminology." *Journal of Criminal Justice and Popular Culture* 10 (2003): 39–68.

Picart, Caroline Joan. *The Cinematic Rebirths of Frankenstein: Universal, Hammer, and Beyond.* Westport, CT: Praeger, 2002.

———, ed. *The Holocaust Film Sourcebook.* 2 vols. Westport, CT: Praeger, 2004.

———. *Thomas Mann and Friedrich Nietzsche: Eroticism, Death, Music, and Laughter.* Value Inquiry Book Series 85. Amsterdam: Rodopi, 1999.

Picart, Caroline Joan, Frank Smoot, and Jayne Blodgett. *The Frankenstein Film Sourcebook.* Bibliographies and Indexes in Popular Culture 8. Westport, CT: Greenwood, 2001.

Picart, Caroline Joan (Kay) S., and David A. Frank. "Horror and the Holocaust: Genre Elements in *Schindler's List* and *Psycho.*" In Prince, *Horror Film*, 206–23.

Picart, Caroline Joan S. "Re-Birthing the Monstrous: James Whale's (Mis)Reading of Mary Shelley's Frankenstein." *Critical Studies in Mass Communication* 15 (1998): 382–404.

———. "Visualizing the Monstrous in Frankenstein Films." *Pacific Coast Philology* 35 (2000): 17–34.

Pinedo, Isabel Christina. "Postmodern Elements of the Contemporary Horror Film." In Prince, *Horror Film*, 85–117.

Pizzello, Stephen. "Craft Series: Cinematography and Lighting." *Hollywood Reporter*, Feb. 17, 1994, S24.

Plant, Richard. *The Pink Triangle: The Nazi War Against Homosexuals.* New York: Holt, 1986.

Prince, Steven. "Dread, Taboo and the Thing: Toward a Social Theory of the Horror Film." In Prince, *Horror Film*, 118–30.

———, ed. *The Horror Film.* New Brunswick, NJ: Rutgers University Press, 2004.

Pulzer, Peter. "Psychopaths and Conformists, Adventurers and Moral Cowards." *London Review of Books*, Jan. 23, 1997, 20.

Rajchman, John. "Foucault's Art of Seeing." *October* 44 (1988): 88–117.

Rebello, Stephen. "Behind the Curtain." In *Alfred Hitchcock and the Making of* Psycho. New York: Dembner Books, 1990.

Reed, J. D., and Tom Cunneff. "Steven Spielberg." *People*, Mar. 15, 1999, 138–41.

Renov, Michael. *The Subject of Documentary.* Minneapolis: University of Minnesota Press, 2004.

"Reporters Detail City, Albany Beat." *New York Times*, Mar. 27, 1946, 34. *ProQuest Historical Newspapers* (1851–2001). http://www.proquestK12.com/productinfo/pq_historical_newspapers.shtml

Rich, Adrienne. "Compulsory Heterosexuality and Lesbian Existence." *Signs* 5 (1980): 631–60.

Richardson, John H. "Steven's Choice." In Friedman and Notbohm, *Steven Spielberg Interviews.* Originally published in *Premiere*, January 1994.

Ringel, Eleanor. "Some True Heavies: Nazis as Aging Villains." *Atlanta Journal and Constitution*, Oct. 22, 1998, 4E.

Rosenfeld, Megan. "A Rush of Remembrance: New Wave of Holocaust Films Races Against Time." *Washington Post*, Oct. 4, 2000, C1.

Rothberg, Michael. *Traumatic Realism: The Demands of Holocaust Representation.* Minneapolis: University of Minnesota Press, 2000.

Rothman, William. "The Filmmaker as Hunter: Robert Flaherty's *Nanook of the North.*" In *Documenting the Documentary: Close Readings of Documentary Film and Video,* edited by Barry Keith Grant and Jeannette Sloniowski. Detroit: Wayne State University Press, 1998.

———. *Hitchcock: The Murderous Gaze.* Cambridge, MA: Harvard University Press, 1982.

Rubin, Susan Goldman. *Steven Spielberg, Crazy for Movies.* New York: Abrams, 2001.

Rushing, Janice Hocker, and Thomas S. Frentz. *Projecting the Shadow: The Cyborg Hero in American Film.* Chicago: University of Chicago Press, 1995.

Russo, Mary. *The Female Grotesque.* New York: Routledge, 1995.

Scapperotti, Dan. "Stephen King's *Apt Pupil: Usual Suspects* Auteur Bryan Singer on Adapting King's Timely Shocker." *Cinefantastique* 30, no. 9 (1998): 20–21.

Scheib, Richard. "Apt Pupil." *Science Fiction, Horror and Fantasy Film Review,* 1998. http://members.fortunecity.com/roogulator/horror/aptpupil.htm].

Scherr, Rebecca. "The Uses of Memory and the Abuses of Fiction: Sexuality in Holocaust Fiction and Memoir." *Other Voices* 2, no. 1 (Feb. 2000): 42.

Schickel, Richard. "Heart of Darkness." *Time,* Dec. 13, 1993, 75–76.

Schiff, Stephen. "Seriously Spielberg." *New Yorker,* Mar. 21, 1994. Reprinted in Friedman and Notbohm, *Steven Spielberg: Interviews.*

Schlemowitz, Joel. "A Glossary of Film Terms." 1999. New School Film Production Department. http://homepage.newschool.edu/~schlemoj/film_courses/glossary_of_film_terms/glossary.html (accessed Sept. 9, 2005).

Schopp, Andrew. "From Misogyny to Homophobia and Back Again: The Play of Erotic Triangles in Stephen King's *Christine.*" *Extrapolation* 38, no. 1 (1997): 66–79.

Schwartz, Amy. "Laughter in the Movie House." *Washington Post,* Mar. 16, 1994, A19.

Schwartz, Dennis. "Vampires Are Compared to Junkies Who Need Their Fix." *Sover.net,* 2003. http://www.sover.net/~ozus/addiction.htm (accessed Aug. 29, 2003).

Schwarz, Daniel R. *Imagining the Holocaust.* New York: St. Martin's, 1999.

"Screen News Here and in Hollywood; RKO Will Produce Japanese Atrocity Film—'3 Russian Girls' to Arrive Friday." *New York Times,* Jan. 31, 1944, 13.

Seidenberg, R. "*The Silence of the Lambs*: Anthony Hopkins Creates a Monster." *American Film* 16, no. 2 (1991): 49.

Shapiro, Marc. "Hitchcock's Throwaway Masterpiece." *Los Angeles Times,* May 27, 1990. 27.

Shea, Christian Leopold. "Apt Pupil." Review. *Jaundiced Eye,* 1998. http://www.geocities.com/Hollywood/Hills/1670/aptpupil.html].

Silberg, Jon. "The Future of Digital Filmmaking." *Post Industry,* May 15, 2000. http://www.postindustry.com/article/mainv/0,2108,113667,00.html.

Skal, David J. "The Horrors of War." In Prince, *Horror Film,* 70–81.

Smith, Gavin. "Identity Check: Jonathan Demme interviewed." *Film Comment* 27, no. 1 (1991): 28–30, 33–34, 36–37.

Sparks, Louis B. "Evil Lurks in Thriller, *Apt Pupil.*" *Houston Chronicle,* Oct. 23, 1998, 6.

Spiegelman, Art. *Maus: A Survivor's Tale*. Vol. 1. Irvington, NY: Voyager, 1994.

"Spielberg Urges Teaching of Tolerance." *Glasgow Herald*, June 29, 1994, 4.

Staiger, Janet. *Interpreting Films: Studies in the Historical Reception of American Cinema*. Princeton, NJ: Princeton University Press, 1992.

———. *Media Reception Studies*. New York: New York University Press, 2005.

———. *Perverse Spectators: The Practices of Film Reception*. New York: New York University Press, 2000.

Stein, Ruthe. "*Apt Pupil's* Unusual Suspect." *San Francisco Chronicle*, Oct. 11, 1998, 48.

Steiner, George. *Language and Silence; Essays on Language, Literature, and the Inhuman*. New York: Atheneum, 1967.

———. *The Portage to San Cristóbal of A.H.* Chicago: University of Chicago Press, 1999.

Sterngold, James. "War and Peace: Inflected by a Nazi." *New York Times*, Feb. 20, 1998, 10.

Sterritt, David. *The Films of Alfred Hitchcock*. New York: Cambridge University Press, 1999.

Steru, Fritz. "The Goldhagen Controversy." *Foreign Affairs*, Nov.-Dec. 1996, 128–38.

Stewart, Jane Alexander. "The Feminine Hero of *The Silence of the Lambs*." In *The Soul of Popular Culture: Looking at Contemporary Heroes, Myths, and Monsters*, edited by Mary Lynn Kittelson. Chicago: Open Court, 1998.

Stier, Oren Baruch. *Committed to Memory: Cultural Mediations of the Holocaust*. Amherst: University of Massachusetts Press, 2003.

Stone, Mirto Golo. "The Feminist Critic and Salome: On Cavani's *The Night Porter*." In *Romance Languages Annual*, edited by Ben Lawton and Anthony Julian Tamburri, 41–44. Vol. 1. West Lafayette, IN: Purdue Research Foundation, 1990.

Stuart, Jan. "Yes, Sir." *Advocate*, Oct. 27, 1998, 75.

"Suffering May Be Far Away, but We Still Need to Do Our Part to Help, The." *Straits Times* (Singapore), July 30, 1994, Life at Large section, 14.

Sundelson, David. "The Demon Therapist and Other Dangers." *Journal of Popular Film and Television* 21, no. 1 (1993): 12–17.

Syal, Rajeev, and Cherry Norton. "Cut! How Hitchcock Took Knife to *Psycho*." *Sunday Times* (London), Oct. 6, 1998.

Tally, Ted. "Collaborations: Ted Tally on Jonathan Demme." *New Yorker* 70, no. 5 (1994): 165.

Thomson, David. "Watching Them Watching Us." *Independent on Sunday* (London), July 26, 1998, 14.

Verniere, James. "Master Class: *Apt Pupil* Studies Lure of Nazism and Other Evils." *Boston Herald*, Oct. 23, 1998, S11.

Waggoner, Walter H. "Army Shows Films on Nazi Murders." *New York Times*, Oct. 23, 1948, 4+. *ProQuest Historical Newspapers*, ProQuest Information and Learning Company. Florida State University Library. http://proquest.umi.com/pqdweb?RQT=3028&COPT=RESTPTNiMTAmSU5UPTAm&cfc=1 (accessed 2005).

Waller, Marguerite. "Signifying the Holocaust: Liliana Cavani's *Portiere Di Notte*." In *Feminisms in the Cinema*, edited by Laura Pietropaolo and Ada Testaferri, 206–19. Bloomington: Indiana University Press, 1995.

Wasko, Janet. "The Work of Theory in the Age of Digital Transformation." In *A Companion to Film Theory*, edited by Toby Miller and Robert Stam, 222–33. Malden, MA: Blackwell, 1999.

Weiler, A. H. "By Way of Report; Saturday Sessions for the Small Fry—First Nazi Trial Films—Other Items." *New York Times*, Nov. 25, 1945, 55.

Weinraub, Bernard. "For Spielberg, an Anniversary Full of Urgency." *New York Times*, Mar. 9, 2004, B2, 4.

———. "'Psycho' in Janet Leigh's Psyche." *New York Times*, May 1, 1995, 78.

———. "The Usual Suspects." *New York Times*, Oct. 18, 1998, 12.

Weissman, Gary. *Fantasies of Witnessing: Postwar Efforts to Experience the Holocaust*. Ithaca, NY: Cornell University Press, 2004.

Wickberg, Daniel. "Homophobia: On the Cultural History of an Idea." *Critical Inquiry* 27 (2000).

Wiesel, Elie. *Night*. Twenty-fifth anniversary ed. Toronto: Bantam Books, 1982.

Wieseltier, Leon. "Close Encounters of the Nazi Kind." *New Republic*, Jan. 24, 1994, 42.

Wilson, Jake. "Apt Pupil." *Urban Cinefile*, Nov. 9, 2001. http://www.urbancinefile.com/home/view.asp?a=2242&s=Video_files].

Wistrich, Robert. "Helping Hitler." *Commentary* 102 1996: 27–32.

Wood, Gary. "Whatever Happened to *Apt Pupil*?" *Cinefantastique* 21, no. 4 (Feb. 1991): 36–37.

Wood, Robin. "Hitchcock's Films." International Film Guide Series, edited by Peter Cowie. New York: Paperback Library, 1970.

———. "Nuit et Brouillard." In *International Dictionary of Films and Filmmakers*. Vol. 1. *Films*, edited by Christopher Lyon. Chicago: St. James Press, 1984.

Zaillian, Steven. *Schindler's List*. A screenplay based on the novel by Thomas Keneally (first revisions, March 1990). Academy of Motion Picture Arts and Sciences Script Collection.

Index

abnormal sexuality, 102, 114, 123, 159n. 21
acting out, 4, 137, 138, 141
Addiction, The: vampirism and Nazism in, 32–33
Addiego, Walter, 33
Adorno, Theodore, xix
Adventures of Kekkou Kamen, The: Naked Justice, 131
aesthetics, xx, 12, 15
"Alarmed Vision, The: Social Suffering and Holocaust Atrocity" (Langer), xix
Allied Signal Corps, 68
Alstoetter case, 66
alter-ego, 129
American Beauty, 137
American Gothic, 6–7, 20, 23, 28–29. *See also* Gothic
American History X, 1, 33–34
Anatomy of the Nuremberg Trials, The (Taylor), 24
Anthony, Ted, 99
anti-Semitism, 17–18
Apt Pupil (film), ix, 1, 135; abnormal sexuality in, 102, 114, 123; authenticity or historicality in, 124; classic horror frame in, 14; color timing in, 115; dominance and voyeurism in, 112, 161n. 55; dualism in, 110; editing of, 115; ending of, 162n. 82; erotic themes in, 102; fetishism in, 110–14; gaze in, 19–20, 25, 110, 112–14, 115–16, 119–20, 125;

gender stereotyping in, 121, 162n. 81; homoeroticism in, 109–14, 117–18, 118–23, 124, 161n. 74, 162n. 84; homophobia in, 124; homosexuality in, 100–2, 123, 136; misogyny in, 109, 124, 160n. 42; monstrous sexuality in, 102; music in, 116, 120; Nazism in, 34, 98–100, 123–25; pedophilic exploitation in, 116–17; peephole in, 19–20, 140; and *Psycho*, 110, 111, 124; racial stereotyping in, 121, 162n. 81; sadism in, 114, 120; and *Schindler's List*, 111, 124, 125; shadows in, 14, 129–30; shower–gas chamber scenes in, 110, 114–17, 161n. 67; shower scene in, 119; and *Silence of the Lambs*, 111, 124; spectatorial relation in, 124; spectatorship in, 19–20; victim-perpetrator dynamic in, x, 117
Apt Pupil (King), 99, 100, 114, 118–19; abnormal sexuality in, 102, 159n. 21; ending of, 162n. 82; gaze in, 105; hatred of the father in, 108, 160n. 38; homoeroticism in, 104–5, 106; homophobia in, 105, 124; misogyny in, 105, 106, 108–9, 117–18, 124, 160n. 36, 160n. 37; Nazi as monster in, 135–36; Nazism and monstrous sexuality in, 123–25; racism in, 108; third shadow in, 130
Arendt, Hannah, 8–9, 18, 126, 127, 142, 143
Arnold, Gary, 100, 102
atrocity footage, Gothic aestheticization of, 68
attraction and revulsion, 76

Caroline Joan (Kay) S. Picart, a philosopher, a former molecular embryologist, and an associate professor of English and courtesy associate professor of law at Florida State University, was educated in the Philippines; Cambridge, England; and the United States. The recipient of numerous awards and fellowships, she is an authority on German Romanticism and horror films and is the author or coauthor of eleven books.

David A. Frank is a professor of rhetoric at the University of Oregon. He has published on rhetorical theory, argumentation, and the Israeli-Palestinian conflict. He was a corecipient of the Kohrs-Campbell prize for rhetorical criticism in 2002 and received the article-of-the-year award from the Religious Communication Association in 2003.